MONS

## Here Be Monsters

A thousand years ago, vampires and shapeshifters, spirits of the ancestors and spirits that were never human at all, intelligent beings with subtle bodies or none, were as much a matter of everyday life then as electricity is now.

But we know better nowadays, of course.

Don't we?

This book is based on the uncomfortable knowledge that we don't know better—that at least some of these entities had, and still have, a reality that goes beyond the limits of human imagination and human psychology. For most people nowadays, such ideas would be terrifying if they weren't so preposterous. Plenty of modern Americans believe that UFOs are spacecraft from other worlds and psychics can bend silverware with their minds—but the existence of vampires and werewolves? To make things worse, this book explores such beings from the standpoint of an equally discredited system of thought: the traditional lore of Western ceremonial magic, which has been denounced and derided by right-thinking folk ever since the end of the Renaissance.

JOHN
MICHAEL
GREER

# MONS

# TERS

## AN INVESTIGATOR'S GUIDE
## TO MAGICAL BEINGS

2002
Llewellyn Publications
St. Paul, Minnesota 55164-0383, U.S.A.

## About the Author

John Michael Greer has been a student of monster lore and the occult since 1975. The author of numerous books, including *Circles of Power: Ritual Magic in the Western Tradition* and *Natural Magic: Potions and Powers from the Magical Garden*, he is also an initiated Druid of the Order of Bards Ovates and Druids (OBOD), a student of geomancy and sacred geometry, and an active member of two magical lodges. He lives in Seattle, where he studies the legends and monster lore of the Pacific Northwest and attends lodge meetings in a building with its own resident ghosts.

## To Write to the Author

If you wish to contact the author or would like more information about this book, please write to the author in care of Llewellyn Worldwide and we will forward your request. Both the author and publisher appreciate hearing from you and learning of your enjoyment of this book and how it has helped you. Llewellyn Worldwide cannot guarantee that every letter written to the author can be answered, but all will be forwarded. Please write to:

John Michael Greer
℅ Llewellyn Worldwide
P.O. Box 64383, Dept. 0-7387-0050-9
St. Paul, MN 55164-0383, U.S.A.

Please enclose a self-addressed stamped envelope for reply, or $1.00 to cover costs. If outside U.S.A., enclose international postal reply coupon.

Many of Llewellyn's authors have websites with additional information and resources. For more information, please visit our website at
**http://www.llewellyn.com**

## Other Books by John Michael Greer

*Circles of Power:*
*Ritual Magic in the Western Tradition*

*Earth Divination, Earth Magic:*
*A Practical Guide to Geomancy*

*Inside a Magical Lodge:*
*Group Ritual in the Western Tradition*

*Paths of Wisdom:*
*Principles and Practice of the Magical Cabala*
*in the Western Tradition*

*Natural Magic:*
*Potions and Powers from the Magical Garden*

*Sacred Geometry Oracle:*
*Become the Architect of Your Life*

FIRST EDITION
Fourth Printing, 2002

Book design and editing by Rebecca Zins
Cover and interior illustrations © 2001 by Jonathan Hunt
Cover design by Kevin R. Brown
Illustrations on pages 28, 205, 206, 224, 226, 232, 235,
236, and 238 by the Llewellyn Art Department

LIBRARY OF CONGRESS CATALOGING-IN-PUBLICATION DATA
Greer, John Michael.
Monsters: an investigator's guide to magical beings /
John Michael Greer.—1st ed.
p.   cm.
Includes bibliographical references and index.
ISBN 0-7387-0050-9
1. Magic.   2. Monsters.   I. Title.

BF1621 .G744 2001
001.944—dc21
2001032662

Llewellyn Publications
A Division of Llewellyn Worldwide, Ltd.
P.O. Box 64383, Dept. 0-7387-0050-9
St. Paul, MN  55164-0383, U.S.A.
www.llewellyn.com

Printed in the United States of America
on recycled paper

MONSTER (mŏn' stər) n. [Latin *monstrum*,
that which is shown forth or revealed]

# Contents

# FOREWORD

Every year on October 31, in those increasingly rare communities where it's safe to do so, American children don costumes and go from door to door for Halloween treats, enacting the last shreds of an ancient tradition. Even in an age of video-game heroes and trading-card characters, many of these children dress up as figures out of nearly forgotten legends: vampires, werewolves, ghosts, goblins, angels, demons, and other uncanny beings. The same entities make a yearly appearance in party decorations, store windows, greeting cards, and a hundred other products of our consumer society. It's an odd sort of tribute to the primal terrors of another age.

A thousand years ago, when people across the world believed in the stark reality of these same beings, the night of October 31 was commemorated in deadly earnest. It had other names then—Samhuinn (pronounced "sah-wain"), the Old Irish term for it, is one still remembered—and a very different character. In those days, instead of candy for children, offerings of food and drink were left out for shadowy entities that came by night—entities that might leave behind considerably worse than an uprooted picket fence if they did not find their accustomed fare. Vampires and shapeshifters, spirits of the ancestors and spirits that were never human at all, intelligent beings with subtle bodies or none, were as much a matter of everyday life then as electricity is now.

But we know better nowadays, of course.

Don't we?

This book is based on the uncomfortable knowledge that we don't know better—that at least some of these entities had, and still have, a reality that goes beyond the limits of human imagination and human psychology. For most people nowadays, such ideas would be terrifying if they weren't so preposterous. Plenty of modern Americans believe that UFOs are spacecraft from other worlds and psychics can bend silverware with their minds—but the existence of vampires and werewolves? To make things worse, this book explores such beings from the standpoint of an equally discredited system of thought: the traditional lore of Western ceremonial magic, which has been denounced and derided by right-thinking folk ever since the end of the Renaissance.

It's easy and comforting to write off monsters and magic alike as the exploded superstitions of a more ignorant time. The problem is, as the introductory essay to this book will show, that explanation simply won't wash. People still encounter many of the monstrous beings of ancient and medieval folklore, even in modern American suburbs. Equally, people in America and elsewhere still practice magic—more so with each passing year, in fact, as the occult renaissance of the last few decades continues to broaden its popularity and deepen its understanding of the traditions it follows.

Tens of thousands of people in America today have personal experience with the fact that magic works, and hundreds of thousands of Americans have encountered one or more monstrous beings over the course of their lives. Despite centuries of dismissal and condemnation, both magic and monsters are thus living realities in the modern world. Even if this were the only evidence involved, it would suggest that we're dealing with something considerably deeper than mere superstition. Nor, as we'll see, is it the only evidence.

Ideas of this sort, which challenge the foundations of our culture's map of reality, call up strange reactions in many people. One person who reviewed the original draft of this book took issue with a passage in the introductory essay where I pointed out that the Scientific Revolution's rejection of the magical side of reality was based on theoretical assumptions, not experimental evidence. Not true, the reviewer claimed; experiments had been done proving that magic didn't work. The review was anonymous, and so I didn't have the chance to ask the reviewer to back up this claim with some sort of proof from actual historical sources. It might have made for an interesting conversation, for the history of the Scientific Revolution is very well documented, and the evidence for such experiments simply doesn't exist.

This sort of mythmaking about the past is far from rare. Millions of American schoolchildren, for instance, have been taught that in 1492, when Columbus set sail, nearly everyone in Europe believed that the world was flat. Everybody knows that this is true . . . except that it isn't. It takes about fifteen minutes of research in a decently stocked library to find out that the ancient Greeks knew the actual shape of the Earth by the fourth century B.C.E., that this information was preserved in Europe through the Dark Ages in the writings of late classical encyclopedists such as Martianus Capella, and that all through the Middle Ages, the spherical nature of the Earth was a basic axiom of cosmology known to everyone with a basic education.

As for 1492, the standard textbook of astronomy studied throughout Western Europe by Columbus' contemporaries—John of Sacrobosco's *On the Sphere*—starts out with a set of sound, logical proofs showing that the Earth is a sphere, that it is infinitesimally small compared to the universe as a whole, and that the sun, moon, and planets are almost unimaginably far away in terms of earthly distances. People laughed at Columbus, not because they thought the world was flat, but because they thought the distance from Western Europe due west to the coasts of Asia was too far away to reach in a fifteenth-century sailing ship . . . *and they were right*. It's just that neither they nor Columbus nor anyone else knew that there were two undiscovered continents in the way.

"History," Henry Ford said, "is the bunk commonly believed." Every culture re-creates the past in the image of its dreams, its fears, its fantasies, and its myths. Nowadays, especially, we force history through the filter of our belief in progress, the ruling mythology of the modern age. We convince ourselves that we are smarter and better informed than our ancestors for no other reason than the fact that we live after them. It's a very comfortable sort of logic, and never more so than when we look at the ancient and often terrifying lore of monsters.

Be this as it may, this book explores the realm of monstrous beings, without apology, from the perspective of traditional magical lore. As I am a practicing ceremonial magician and an initiate of several magical orders, it would be difficult for me to approach the subject in any other way. Still, there's a point to the connection, for the teachings of Western magical tradition include a good deal of little-known information about monsters of one sort or another, and offer ways of looking at the evidence that help make sense of some of the most puzzling features of monster fact and folklore. Furthermore, since magic has its practical side as well, magical perspectives on monstrous beings also provide ways of dealing with these puzzling and potentially dangerous entities when they stray into the human world.

Those who venture into this book expecting something more in tune with the wider literature on paranormal beings and phenomena may be in for a few surprises. Some of the entities that appear in these other sources take on very different shapes when viewed through the lens of magical tradition. Still, my hope is that readers who already have a background in the literature of the unexplained will find this book useful as well.

# HOW TO USE
# THIS BOOK

*Monsters: An Investigator's Guide to Magical Beings* is divided into four parts. Part I, *An Introduction to the Field Guide*, is an introductory essay about monsters and monster lore, exploring what monsters are, how they affect the human world, and why it is that people in modern Western cultures are convinced they don't exist. It covers the basic theoretical framework we'll be using to study the realm of monstrous beings, and presents a set of questions and basic approaches that will be central throughout the rest of the book.

Part II, *A Field Guide to Monsters*, surveys nine basic classes of monstrous beings—vampires, ghosts, werewolves and other shapeshifters, creatures of faery, mermaids, dragons, spirits, angels, and demons—discussing their history, their traditional lore, their modern (and usually wildly inaccurate) images, and the uncomfortable realities that lie behind the latter. Methods for identifying each of the monsters in question, and dealing with them when they come into contact with the human world, are also given here.

Part III, *A Guide to Monster Investigation*, presents detailed methods for the fine art of investigating a reported monster sighting. Basic skills, equipment, interviewing techniques, research methods, dealing with (or avoiding) publicity, search and surveillance procedures, and actually confronting monstrous beings face to face, are all covered here. A major focus of this section is on methods of telling the difference between authentic monster sightings, on the one hand, and hoaxes, delusions, and cases of mistaken identity on the other.

Part IV, *Magical Self-Defense*, covers some basic techniques of natural and ritual magic that can be of use when dealing with monsters directly. The methods of natural magic—that branch of magic using the subtle effects of herbs, stones, and other substances—can be put to use by anyone at any time, and provide a first line of protection when monstrous activities pose a threat to human health, safety, or sanity. The methods of ritual magic, although they require a period of systematic practice before they can be used effectively, offer stronger approaches to dealing with monsters, and provide a bridge between the basic magical perspectives covered here and the wider realm of magical philosophy and practice.

All through these sections, I have had several different audiences in mind—magical practitioners who seek to study the traditional lore concerning monstrous beings; people outside the magical community who are interested in unexplained phenomena, and who may also be interested in finding out what magical tradition has to say on the subject; and those who are dealing directly with monstrous beings of one sort or another, and need practical information and guidance. Each of these audi-

ences will find it most useful to approach this book in a somewhat different way.

## Magical Practitioners

Magical practitioners will not need convincing that supernatural forces and entities exist—anyone who has done six months or more of systematic training with traditional magical disciplines knows that already, from direct personal experience—and will also be familiar with the elementary material on magical practice in Part IV of this book. The introductory essay that makes up Part I will be useful purely to give the magically literate reader some idea of this book's approach to the subject. Part II, the field guide itself, will be the most useful section for magicians, although those who intend to take their study of monster lore onto a more practical level will want to review the material in Part III as well.

## Those Interested in Unexplained Phenomena

Those interested in unexplained phenomena will find Part I a necessary introduction to this book, since the approach I have taken differs sharply from that of most modern books on the unexplained. The field guides to individual monsters in Part II may be the most entertaining part of the book, but nearly everything that's said there rests on Part I's foundations. Parts III and IV will be of interest only to those who expect or hope to deal with monstrous beings in something other than an armchair fashion, or are at least curious about how it's done.

### *Those Dealing with Monstrous Beings Themselves*

Those dealing with monstrous beings themselves will find Parts III and IV, the investigator's guide and the handbook of basic magical approaches, the most practically useful, although the profiles of individual monster types in Part II will be useful for figuring out what exactly is going on and what might best be done about it. People living in the midst of monster activity rarely need to be convinced that something uncanny is going on, and the theoretical perspectives in Part I can be left for a quiet afternoon when the poltergeist isn't acting up or the creature in the nearby lake hasn't been seen for several weeks.

# A CAUTIONARY NOTE

A little knowledge, as the proverb has it, is a dangerous thing. This is especially true when dealing with monsters and monster lore. While there's good reason to think that monstrous beings exist and interact with the human world on occasion, none of them are common, and many of the classic types are extremely rare in the present age. It's sometimes easy to forget this and imitate the character in Jerome K. Jerome's novel *Three Men in a Boat,* who spends a rainy afternoon reading a medical textbook and ends up convinced he has every disease in it except for housemaid's knee.

If you start seeing monsters under every shrub you pass, then, it's time to take a long break from monster-related studies. If matters go further than this—if thoughts and fears related to monstrous beings become obsessive, if monster research begins to take up an unhealthy share of your time and attention, or if anything connected to monsters *ever* leads you to consider violence against yourself or another person—*you need to seek professional psychological help at once.* Partly because it involves intense challenges to the accepted version of what's real, partly because it touches on archaic terrors that reach down into the most ancient levels of human consciousness, the pursuit of monsters can put a good deal of strain on one's mental health, and the student of monster lore needs to keep out a wary eye for the signs of imbalance. He or she also needs to listen when someone else says that matters are getting out of control.

It would also be best to note here that my own interest in monsters is one part, and a relatively small one, of a broader commitment to studying, practicing, and teaching the traditional magical lore of the Western world. I am not primarily a monster researcher, and my own work in the field relates to certain very specific (and very local) branches of monster lore; if you're looking for someone to investigate a monster sighting, you'll need to look somewhere else. You can also simply read Part III of this book carefully, and do the investigating yourself—that is, after all, why it was written.

If you have a monster sighting to report, whether it's one of your own or one that you've investigated, you should certainly consider contacting FATE (P.O. Box 64383, St. Paul, MN 55164), the Western hemisphere's most widely distributed magazine of the unexplained, which covers strange phenomena of all kinds and includes personal accounts of unusual experiences in every issue. Write a short letter (no more than a page) explaining what you've experienced or investigated, and asking whether they would like to hear more about it; be sure to enclose a self-addressed stamped envelope for the editors' reply.

*Part I*

# AN INTRODUCTION
# TO THE FIELD GUIDE

# ON THE REALITY
# OF THE IMPOSSIBLE

The word "monster" comes from the Latin *monstrum*, "that which is shown forth or revealed." The same root also appears in the English word "de*monstr*ate," and several less common words (such as "remonstrance") that share the same sense of revealing, disclosing, or displaying. In the original sense of the word, a monster is a revelation, something shown forth.

This may seem worlds away from the usual modern meaning of the word "monster"—a strange, frightening, and supposedly mythical creature—but here, as elsewhere in the realm of monsters, appearances deceive. Certainly, monsters are strange, at least to those raised in modern ways of approaching the world. As we'll see, too, monsters have a great deal to do with the realm of myth, although this latter word (like "monster" itself) has older and deeper meanings that evade our modern habits of thought. The association between monsters and terror, too, has practical relevance, even when the creatures we call "monsters" fear us more than we fear them.

The myth, the terror, and the strangeness all have their roots in the nature of the realm of monsters and the monstrous—a world of revelations, where the hidden and the unknown show furtive glimpses of themselves. If we pay attention to them, monsters do have something to reveal. They show us the reality of the impossible, or of those things that we label impossible; they point out that the world we think we live in, and the world we actually inhabit, may not be the same place at all.

## The Meaning of the Monstrous

For thousands of years, monstrous beings have been a source of revelations of this kind. In earlier times, in fact, monsters and what they showed forth were seen as matters of very great importance. Monsters were news, and not just for the reasons that draw crowds to monster movies and UFO-sighting areas nowadays.

To the ancient Greeks and Romans, for example, the appearance of any strange being was a message from the hidden realms of existence, and needed interpretation by skilled professionals. Like comets, meteors, the mutterings of oracles, and the behavior of birds and animals, the appearance of monsters could be read and understood by the wise, and used to cast light on future events, the unknowns of the present, and the always-mysterious purposes of the gods and goddesses. Other ancient societies had similar habits. In China, up to the time of the Nationalist takeover of 1911, for instance, the imperial government included a whole bureaucracy of omen readers, who collected reports of dragons and other monstrous creatures and recorded them as guides to the will of Heaven.

The same sort of attitude is common to most traditional cultures, and it remained standard in the West all through the Middle Ages. The monkish chroniclers of medieval times noted sightings of werewolves and mermaids in much the same spirit that leads modern newspapers to report the doings of such equally mysterious entities as the Gross National Product. The appearance of a monster was news, not just because of what the monster was, but because of what it *meant*—in other words, what it showed forth about the universe and humanity's place in it.

This approach to the monstrous only faded out with the Scientific Revolution, which began some three hundred fifty years ago in Western Europe. The thinkers who spearheaded that revolution saw traditional lore of all kinds as one of the most important roadblocks in the way of their dream of a wholly rationalistic approach to the world. Some of these early scientists, such as Francis Bacon, suggested that the old lore should be carefully searched for whatever real knowledge it contained. The majority, though, thought otherwise, and it was their view that ultimately triumphed.

That triumph was rooted in a profound change in the way people understood the world around them. Before the Scientific Revolution, most people saw the world as a living unity, one that communicated with the observant mind. With the new science came a radically different way of thinking about the universe: a way that saw dead matter moving in empty space as the only reality, and rejected everything else as fable, fraud, or delusion. Under the influence of this new philosophy, all the old monster-lore of the ancient and medieval periods (and a great deal more) was heaped up into one great pile, labeled "nonsense," and tossed aside without a second thought.

Depending on one's viewpoint, this shift in the way people understood the world may look like either common sense breaking through centuries of superstition, or a Faustian bargain in which an entire civilization sold its soul in exchange for material wealth and power. Our task here, however, is not to judge the Scientific Revolution but to understand it, and to make sense of the changes it made in our habits of thought—changes that have had a major impact on how we understand (or, more precisely, fail to understand) the appearances of monstrous beings in our midst.

## Theory, Evidence, and the Impossible

What set the new science apart from nearly all previous ways of thinking about the world was its insistence that everything *real* had to be *material*—that there was nothing in the universe except atoms and empty space. The most interesting thing about this claim is that no one ever proved, or even tried to prove, that it was correct. It was simply assumed, by the founders of modern science, without proof—and it is still assumed, without proof, by most scientists today.

It may come as a surprise to learn that the Scientific Revolution's rejection of magic, alchemy, and the like was based on rhetoric, not experiment. In all the arguments over the reality of these things, no one on the scientific side of the debate claimed to have done experiments proving that magic, alchemy, and other kinds of "rejected knowledge" were false. (This point can be looked up quite readily in contemporary sources, or in the very large modern historical literature on the period.) The early scientists assumed that these things were false because they didn't fit the new scientific and materialist image of the universe, not because anyone disproved them.

In the same way, the lore of monsters was tossed out with the trash, not because people didn't keep seeing monsters—they did—or because monster sightings all proved to have simple, straightforward, scientifically acceptable explanations—they didn't—but because the scientific model of the universe had no room for monsters. Monsters *couldn't* exist—this is how the logic went—and therefore they *didn't* exist.

By an extension of this same sort of thinking, anyone who disagreed with this sweeping dismissal was obviously either deluded or misinformed, and anyone who claimed to see a monster had to be either mistaken, dishonest, or crazy.

By any standard of logic, of course, this approach is impossible to justify. If the evidence contradicts one's theory, the reasonable thing to do is to throw out the theory—not the evidence! Still, the opposite habit has a long pedigree in scientific circles. It has even been raised to the level of a full-blown philosophical argument by David Hume, whose book *An Enquiry Concerning Human Understanding* (first published in 1748) was one of the first clear formulations of the philosophy of modern science. In that book, Hume argued that no amount of evidence could prove the reality of an event that violated the laws of Nature, since it was always more likely that the evidence was wrong than that natural law had been set aside.

This is an interesting claim. If we knew, with absolute certainty, what laws Nature follows, it might even be a reasonable one. Since we don't—scientific "laws," then and now, are simply the most widely accepted theories about how the natural world works, and they constantly change as our knowledge changes—dismissing relevant evidence because it doesn't agree with one's preconceptions is at the very least a questionable way to go about things. Nonetheless, this kind of logic has remained standard within the scientific community for more than three centuries now, and has shaped our culture's response to an astonishing array of phenomena.

Thus, for example, no less a personage than Thomas Jefferson reacted to reports of a meteorite impact—at a time when scientific theory stated that meteors were not made of rock and could not hit the Earth—by insisting it was more likely that an entire county full of witnesses had lied than that a stone had fallen from the sky. His logic was simple: the best scientific authorities said that there were no stones in the sky, and therefore stones couldn't have fallen from the sky. Meteorites couldn't exist, and therefore they didn't exist—no matter what the evidence said.

Similarly, until Nixon's trip to China brought acupuncture into a blaze of publicity that no amount of official condemnation could obscure, medical authorities in the West insisted that putting needles into a person's skin couldn't possibly cause anesthetic and healing effects. These statements were made, not because anyone had done experiments disproving acupuncture, but because Western medical theories couldn't (and still can't) account for it. Even now, after the publication of reams of experimental studies showing that acupuncture does in fact have the effects claimed for it, there are plenty of medical researchers in the Western world who still dismiss it as quackery because it doesn't fit their theories.

The same questionable logic, finally, continues to govern the way most scientists respond to more than a century of systematic research into extrasensory perception (ESP) and other unusual powers of human consciousness. As sociologist James McClenon demonstrated in his incisive study *Deviant Science*, most of the scientists who accept the reality of psychic phenomena do so on the basis of evidence. Some are familiar with the impressive results of parapsychological research over the last century, while others have had personal experiences with ESP. Most of those who reject the possibility of psychic phenomena, on the other hand, do so on the basis of theory. In McClenon's study, in fact, no less than 93 percent of scientists who rejected psychic phenomena referred to a priori arguments (that is, arguments based on theoretical principles) as an important factor in their opinions, while only 7 percent of those who accepted psychic phenomena did so.

The sort of thinking that considers theories more important than evidence is a major barrier to the study of monsters and monster lore, among many other things. If any sort of sense is to be made of traditions and experiences involving monsters, it's crucial to avoid this highly unscientific "scientific attitude."

At the same time, of course, it's important to stay away from the opposite extreme of complete credulousness. The realm of the monstrous has attracted its share of questionable cases and dubious characters down through the years; there have been lies, hoaxes, cases of mistaken identity, and other sources of confusion and misinformation. It's important not to forget these issues—but it's equally important not to fall into the trap of assuming that just because such things occur, as they do in every other field of research, the whole subject can be comfortably dismissed. Either of these attitudes misses out on what monsters have to reveal.

## Three Monstrous Questions

All of the above begs at least three difficult questions—monstrous questions, one might say—which need to be asked and answered before we go any further.

First, a matter of definition: over and above issues of the word's origin, what *are* monsters? What kinds of beings or phenomena properly fit within this shadowy category, and what kinds belong elsewhere?

Second, a matter of reality: do monsters actually exist? Does the monster lore found in the world's cultures come out of nothing more than ignorance and misunderstanding, or is there something more solid behind any of it?

Third, a matter of relevance: do monsters matter? Even if there are real beings or phenomena that correspond to the various monsters of legend and lore, what importance do they have to people living in a modern industrial society?

We'll take these questions one at a time.

## Defining the Monstrous

As mentioned, the word "monster" originally meant something shown forth, a revelation of the hidden side of things. While this definition still has relevance today, it's a good deal too broad for the present purpose. Closer to our needs here is the most common modern definition—that a monster is a strange and frightening being whose existence is doubted by most or all of the currently accepted scientific authorities.

Even this definition is too broad, though. There are many different kinds of beings that can all be put into this category, even though they have nothing in common beyond a habit of frightening people and a history of rejection by the majority of scientists.

### Undiscovered Animals

One such category consists of animals that, for one reason or another, have not yet been officially discovered by the biological sciences. The mountains around the Puget Sound country where I live are home to one of the more famous of these, a large

ape known locally as the sasquatch. Bigfoot, as it's also called, has been part of the animal lore of the local native tribes as far back as records go; it has been seen literally thousands of times in mountain forests along the West Coast, from northern California to British Columbia; tracks, droppings, hair, photographs, and even a short film have been collected by researchers. All this seems to point clearly in the direction of an actual, biological animal.

The sasquatch even has a likely pedigree. Paleontologists have uncovered fossils of a very similar creature called *Gigantopithecus*, dating back only a few million years—an eyeblink in evolutionary terms—on the other side of the Bering land bridge in Asia, and reconstructions of this big, upright ape look remarkably like eyewitness accounts of the sasquatch. The only thing no one has yet been able to produce is a specimen, living or dead.

The sasquatch is only one of a number of animals that appear to exist, but remain unrecognized by the scientific mainstream. This may seem surprising; still, since nearly all universities and grant-providing agencies assume that such creatures don't exist, it's all but impossible to get funding for the very expensive process of tracking them down systematically. A new scientific specialty, called cryptozoology, has emerged around the best cases, although—predictably—a majority of scientists and scientific organizations still dismiss cryptozo-oologists as crackpots.

Nearly all the creatures currently being studied by cryptozoologists would count as monsters under the modern definition of the word, and many of them are discussed in books that have the word "monster" some-where in the title. These animals are strange, or at least unfamiliar; many of them have been known to frighten people; all of them are considered nonexistent by most scien-tists. Still, the label seems inappropriate for creatures whose "monstrous" character is mostly a function of our ignorance.

Any one of them, after all, could lose its credentials as a monster instantly, by the simple process of being officially discovered. If a hiker with a cellular phone in his or her pack were to stumble across a recently dead sasquatch in the Cascade Mountains next week, for example, odds are that within a very short time Bigfoot would simply be another part of the local fauna, of interest chiefly to wildlife photographers, zoos hop-ing to expand their primate collections, and activists gearing up for another fight over the Endangered Species Act. Given that the sasquatch is rare, shy, mostly vegetarian, and far less dangerous to human beings than the average bear, it's hard to see it as a monster in any real sense of the word. The same is equally true of the other still-unknown ani-mals that appear to be hiding in various parts of the world. Whatever monsters may or may not be, these creatures belong in a different category.

### Fictional Monsters

Another set of creatures that qualify as monsters, at least by the modern defini-tion, are more of interest to the literary critic than to the zoologist (crypto- or otherwise). These are the purely fictional monsters of literature, movies, and televi-sion. Perhaps the best example of these is Frankenstein's monster—that extraordi-nary product of a teenage girl's imagina-tion, reshaped by way of one of the first great horror movies into an image that lurks behind every shadow of our modern technological society. Mary Shelley drew on what was then up-to-date scientific research, as well as on very old legends, as raw material for her monster; still, this is one monster that is wholly a work of fic-tion—at least for now.

The same thing is true of a great many other monsters whose images and stories are familiar to everyone raised in American culture. King Kong, for instance, was invented by a scriptwriter and never lived anywhere outside the silver screen. Equally, though, a good many monsters with a much longer history have similar origins. Unicorns, gryphons, cockatrices, and many other creatures who stalk through the pages of medieval bestiaries are also literary cre-ations; they were the product of an earlier

9

form of monster fiction, the traveler's tale, and passed from writer to writer over the centuries, picking up details as they went. Some of them probably started out as unfamiliar living animals—the earliest descriptions of the unicorn sound suspiciously like a rhinoceros—while others probably have nothing more solid behind them than Frankenstein's monster.

All of these creatures are strange; all of them are frightening, or at least produce the vicarious thrill of fear that makes horror movies so popular; all of them, with very good reason, are thought to be nonexistent by scientists. By the modern definition given earlier, they all qualify as monsters. Still, when the vast majority of the world's cultures have treated monsters as a significant part of the real world, wholly fictional creatures should properly go into a different category.

## Three Monstrous Features

With the cryptozoological and fictional "monsters" set off to one side, what remains are the monsters with which this book is centrally concerned—vampires and werewolves, ghosts and demons, as well as beings such as faeries, mermaids, and angels, which don't qualify under current definitions but would have counted as monsters under the older meaning of the word. It's worth noting that these entities don't just make up a grab bag of miscellaneous horrors. They have a number of important features in common, and these will form the basis for the working definition of "monster" we'll be using throughout this book.

The first of these common features is that the monsters of our third category are described, usually in great detail, in folklore. What is folklore? There are a number of definitions used in the academic field of folklore scholarship, but for our purpose it's most useful to think of folklore as the realm of *unofficial knowledge* in any culture.

Folklore, in other words, is the knowledge ordinary people learn from their friends, coworkers, and family members, and pass on in turn through the same sort of connections. Every culture and subculture has its own folklore, which differs to a greater or lesser degree from whatever official knowledge that the culture may pass on through formal methods of education—whether these latter take the form of tribal initiatory societies or graduate schools offering Ph.D. degrees in astrophysics and molecular biology. The official knowledge of any given culture may or may not include lore about monsters, but the folklore of most cultures includes lore about the most common monsters of our third category.

The second common feature is that this category consists almost entirely of beings that either do not have physical bodies of the usual flesh-and-blood kind, or that behave in ways that ordinary flesh and blood do not normally permit. (Ghosts are an example of the first type, werewolves of the second.) This feature has driven much of the official rejection of monstrous beings, since it has been an article of faith in our culture since the Scientific Revolution that material effects must have material causes. Still, if we are to consider the evidence rather than the preconceptions that have been used to interpret it, this aspect of the monstrous can't be avoided.

With the third feature, we approach an answer to the first of our three questions—what are monsters?—and at the same time throw open the second question, the question of their reality. To make sense of this third feature, we'll need to take another look at the way all three of our categories relate to the models of reality we normally take for granted.

## The Reality of Monsters

The "monsters" of the first category, that of undiscovered animals, however unlikely they may seem to modern scientists, offer no particular challenge to the scientific view of the universe. The sasquatch, for example, is no more "impossible" than the mountain gorilla or the orangutan, and the most drastic thing that would happen to modern sci-ence if sasquatches were to be officially discovered is that textbooks on the anthropoid apes would need a new chapter in a hurry. Many monsters of the second category, by contrast, could be real only if most current scientific knowledge is dead wrong—for example, the gryphon has the front half of an eagle and the rear half of a lion, which violates most of what we know about evolutionary biology—but there is no evidence whatsoever that these creatures are real in any sense, and sightings of them are very few! Monsters of the first category, then, are scientifically plausible and potentially real; those of the second category, by contrast, are scientifically preposterous but certainly (or almost certainly) unreal.

Our third category is more troubling. Ghosts, vampires, spirits, and demons, like many fictional monsters, would pose a stark challenge to the scientific view of the universe if they exist. After all, that was why they were relegated to the category of "superstition" at the time of the Scientific Revolution, and why they are dismissed as imaginary by most people today. The problem is that people see them. The monsters of our third category are encountered, not just now and again but quite frequently, by modern, educated, apparently sane people.

This fact—and it is a fact—stands in such flat contradiction to our usual assumptions that it's worth taking a look at the evidence. Fortunately, the last few decades have seen several capably done surveys on supernatural experience in America and elsewhere, and some of these dealt directly with monsters and monster-related experiences.

The picture painted by this research is an astonishing one. According to a Roper Organization poll in 1991, 18 percent of Americans report at least once waking up paralyzed with a strange person or being in the room with them—a fair description of a monster-related experience we'll be studying in much more detail shortly. Eleven percent had seen at least one ghost, and 7 percent had seen at least one UFO (Roper 1992).

A more extensive set of surveys on psychic phenomena carried out by the National Opinion Research Center in 1973 discovered that 28 percent of Americans reported having been in direct personal contact with a ghost; 58 percent reported having experienced telepathic contact with a living person; 24 percent had experienced clairvoyant visions of events happening at a distance; and 36 percent reported at least one ecstatic mystical experience (Greeley, 1975). Similarly, John Palmer's 1974 survey found that 17 percent of residents and students in Charlottesville, Virginia, reported seeing at least one apparition, and some three-quarters of those who had done so had seen more than one.

All of these experiences, it bears remembering, are labeled nonexistent by the official knowledge of our culture. Yet all of them happen routinely to millions of people.

Defenders of the scientific worldview have an explanation for unnerving facts of this sort. It's called the cultural source hypothesis, and it has dominated discussions about ghosts and other monsters of our third category for the last three centuries. The English writer Reginald Scot was already arguing for this point of view in a fine thunder of contemptuous prose as early as 1584, in his book *The Discoverie of Witchcraft*:

> But in our childhood our mothers maids have so terrified us with an ouglie divell having hornes on his head, fier in his mouth, and a taile in his breech, eies like a bason, fanges like a dog, clawes like a bear, and a voice roring like a lion, whereby we start and are afraid when we heare one crie Bough; and they have so fraied us with bull beggers, spirits, witches, urchens, elves, hags, fairies, satyrs, pans, faunes, sylens, kit with the cansticke, tritons, centaures, dwarfes, giants, imps, calcars, conjurers, nymphes, changlings, Incubus, Robin good-fellowe, the spoorne, the mare, the man in the oke, the hell waine, the fierdrake, the puckle, Tom thombe, hob gobblin, Tom tumbler,

boneles, and such other bugs, that we are afraid of our owne shadowes.

In the same way—although rather less colorfully—the cultural source hypothesis points out that traditional folklore includes detailed descriptions of various kinds of "imaginary" beings, such as ghosts, spirits, vampires, and so forth. When people are raised believing in such folklore, it's claimed, they are likely to mistake perfectly natural phenomena for the presence or actions of these beings. For example, they may see swamp gas and think that it is a spirit, or have a stress-caused hallucination about someone who has died and think that they have seen a ghost. Equally, people familiar with such traditions may use them as the basis for hoaxes of various kinds, and other people who are also familiar with the same traditions may take these fraudulent phenomena at face value.

Certainly such cases of mistaken identity do happen; a good many of them have been documented over the last century or so, since the beginning of systematic research on ghosts and other psychic phenomena. Certainly, too, frauds and hoaxes of many kinds are far from unknown in the same fields. The problem comes when one tries to turn these valid but limited points into a universal explanation. The assumption that all experiences of monstrous beings come from cultural sources, as the hypothesis insists, doesn't actually fit the facts very well.

What the evidence suggests instead is that, in a disturbing number of cases, the experiences aren't rooted in folklore traditions. Rather—in flat contradiction to our usual assumptions—the folklore traditions are rooted in actual experiences.

## The Old Hag

This was the central finding of an extraordinary study carried out by folklore researcher David Hufford, and described in detail in his book *The Terror That Comes In The Night*.

In 1971, while conducting research in Newfoundland, Hufford came across accounts of an odd figure in local folklore—the Old Hag. According to these accounts, the Hag was a spirit that attacked people as they lay in bed, usually at night. People spoke of waking up suddenly, unable to move or speak, as a spectral presence approached the bed and then seemed to press down, strangling or smothering. Such tales are found all over the world, and Hufford quickly recognized the connections with folklore. At the same time, he noticed that many of the accounts came from people who claimed to have had the experience themselves.

Intrigued, he put together a research questionnaire and gave it to groups of Newfoundland university students. The results were astounding. Nearly a quarter of the students surveyed reported undergoing the Old Hag experience themselves. Of those who did, a large proportion reported details that Hufford had found in folklore accounts, but hadn't mentioned in the questionnaire. Most astonishing of all, a significant number of students who reported the experience and described it in detail had no knowledge of the folklore tradition and had never heard of the Old Hag. Further research over the next several years showed that the same experience was common all over North America, with between 16 and 25 percent of all surveyed groups reporting it—*whether or not anyone in the group being surveyed had ever heard of a similar experience.*

It's important to keep in mind that this experience isn't simply a vague general category, or another name for sleep paralysis or some other simple medical diagnosis. It's a very specific type of event with a whole series of consistent details. The experience almost always happens with the subject lying on his or her back. The subject wakes up, and can perceive his or her actual surroundings, but cannot move or speak as the experience begins. A presence approaches the subject and then presses down, choking or smothering.

If there is enough light to see, this presence may appear as an indistinct, murky shape in the air, but it is more often invisible. Intense fear, often a fear of death, usually accompanies the experience. A peculiar rhythmic sound, like shuffling footsteps or sandpaper sliding over wood, often comes just before the attack. If the subject can force himself or herself to move even slightly, the sense of presence and all the other features of the experience vanish at once. Again, this very specific pattern of experience occurs whether or not the subject has ever heard of the Old Hag or any similar folklore tradition.

Clearly, the Old Hag phenomenon poses a challenge of shattering intensity to the cultural source hypothesis. Since people report the same experience whether or not they have encountered the tradition, it seems clear that the experience gave rise to the tradition rather than vice versa—in other words, that some actual phenomenon lies behind the legend of the Hag. Certainly this was Hufford's own conclusion, and it has been shared by most of the researchers who have followed him in attempting to understand the Old Hag.

What might that phenomenon be? Hufford himself simply commented that the Hag could not be adequately explained on the basis of existing knowledge, and left it at that. Others have been less cautious. The most common suggestion has been that the Old Hag is a combination of medical and neurological factors that produce the illusion of an attack by an immaterial being.

The problem is that none of these proposed factors explain more than a small portion of the total phenomenon. For example, sleep paralysis, a poorly understood but common experience, can account for the inability to move, and there are several proposed explanations for the difficulty with breathing; hypnopompic imagery, or some other leakage of dream imagery into waking consciousness, can be used to explain away the sense of presence and the visual dimensions of the Hag, and so on. Why, though, should sleep paralysis and breathing problems be associated with the same set of imagery, over and over again, in up to one quarter of the population? Why not imagery of drowning or burial, say, which might be expected to occur more readily to the dreaming mind of a modern American than the bizarre, archaic image of attack by a spirit? And what are we to make of details like the sound of shuffling footsteps?

There is another potential explanation for the Old Hag phenomenon, of course—one that neatly and efficiently accounts for the entire range of details reported by people who have experienced an attack by the Hag, or by her many equivalents in other cultures. This is the hypothesis that the Old Hag experience is, in fact, exactly what it seems to be: a visitation by a hostile spirit. For obvious reasons, this hypothesis has received no attention at all in academic literature, and in fact most writers who have dealt with Hufford's findings have taken

pains to distance themselves as far as possible from the idea.

Still, there is no valid reason why it should be dismissed out of hand. Despite three hundred years of rhetoric from the publicists of science, no known law of nature forbids the existence of spirits—that is, of beings without flesh-and-blood material bodies. The conviction that spirits do not and cannot exist is an assumption, not a proven fact, and if a phenomenon such as the Old Hag is best understood by throwing out the assumption, then out it should go.

## SUNDS and Dab Tsog

Hufford's research is not the only recent study of the Old Hag and her close relatives. Another set of explorations into this twilight territory will lead us from the second of our three questions—whether monsters are real—to the third: what difference they make to our lives.

These studies have their roots in one of the major human tragedies of the Vietnam War. Starting in the late 1950s and continuing until the war's end in 1975, the Hmong—a tribal people of the hill country of Laos—were recruited, armed, and equipped by the CIA as a guerrilla force to counter the Communist Pathet Lao insurgency. After the Pathet Lao victory in 1975, most of the surviving Hmong fled to refugee camps in Thailand. More than

100,000 of them ended up emigrating to the United States.

The traumas of war, exodus, and resettlement had barely begun to fade when, starting in 1977, dozens of Hmong began to die of an unknown ailment. The victims were nearly always male, usually in good health, and died silently in their sleep without warning and without any detectable cause. Baffled doctors labeled the epidemic SUNDS, Sudden Unexplained Nocturnal Death Syndrome, but were at a loss to explain what was happening. They still are; after many studies and twenty years of research, researchers have yet to find a definite cause for SUNDS or a way to prevent it.

One thing did come to the attention of researchers quite early on, however. A remarkable percentage of Hmong immigrants reported having a very specific kind of experience at night, one that seemed possibly related to SUNDS. As described by Dr. Neal Holtan, an epidemiologist in charge of one of the major SUNDS research projects, this "transient nocturnal event" has the following features: "(1) a sense of panic or extreme fear, (2) paralysis (partial or complete), (3) a sense of pressure on the chest, (4) a sense that there is an alien being (animal, human, or spirit) in the room, (5) a disturbance in sensation (auditory, visual or tactile)" (Holtan 1984; see also Adler 1995).

As a number of researchers realized, this list is identical with the core characteristics of the Old Hag experience as anatomized by Hufford's work. Folklorists knew already that Hmong traditions call experiences of the Old Hag type *tsog tsuam* (pronounced "cho chua"), and hold that they are caused by a monstrous being called *dab tsog* (pronounced "da cho"). Tsog tsuam, it has been argued, is the missing piece of the SUNDS riddle. To understand why, it's necessary to journey into the traditional worldview of the Hmong.

In their homeland in the mountains of Laos, the Hmong practiced a complex shamanistic religion in which many different spirits and monsters played a role. The ancestors of each family received offerings and ceremonies performed by the head of the household, and in exchange, protected the family from dangerous creatures such as dab tsog.

Dab tsog, who sits upon sleepers and suffocates them, is one of many kinds of *dab*—monsters who live in caves under the ground by day and venture forth by night. Usually held at bay by the ancestral spirits, dab are thought to be able to overcome this protection if the offerings to the ancestors are neglected or other religious rules broken. In older times, when someone was attacked by a dab, Hmong shamans would divine the cause of the attack, and special offerings would be made to turn aside the anger of the dab. If this was not done, the dab would return again and again, and sooner or later it would take away the soul of the offender and he would die.

When the Hmong fled their homeland, first to Thailand and then to the United States, the traditional rituals and sacrifices of their religion were profoundly disrupted. With village and clan groups scattered across a continent, it became difficult to find religious leaders to carry out some ceremonies, and since most Hmong in America ended up living in apartments where they could not legally raise or slaughter animals, there were major problems providing sacrificial livestock. Even architecture worked against the continuity of Hmong religious practice: the central pillar, a universal feature of Hmong village architecture and the dwelling place of Hmong ancestral spirits, is absent in American apartment and house designs. For this reason, nearly all Hmong in America had severe difficulties keeping the tenets of their traditional faith.

The dab, and especially dab tsog, responded accordingly. Surveys have shown that an extraordinary 50 to 60 percent of the Hmong population in America have undergone at least one Old Hag experience of the classic variety—a rate two to three times that of the general population. Of those Hmong who have converted to Christianity, and thus abandoned most or all of their native spiritual traditions, the rate is even higher: some 72 percent, according to one study, which would give Christian Hmong the highest rate of Old Hag experiences of any known population anywhere (Adler 1995, pp. 187–189).

To Hmong who still follow their own religious traditions, SUNDS is not a mystery. The role of ceremonies in keeping dab tsog at bay is common knowledge among them, and the role of tsog tsuam itself in causing sudden death by night is equally so. Hmong interviewed by folklore researchers have explained that the sudden deaths were unheard of in Laos, where ritual countermeasures could be readily put to work. Only in the refugee camps and in America did the traditional protections break down and allow the dab to kill.

The grim story of dab tsog and SUNDS has something like a happy ending. Within a few years of the exodus to America, many Hmong left the urban communities where they first resettled and moved to more rural areas, where traditional clans and extended families could be reunited and religious practices renewed. In response, SUNDS deaths—which had climbed steeply from 1977 to 1981—have decreased steadily ever since (Adler 1995, p. 198).

## Understanding Dab Tsog

The connection between dab tsog and SUNDS has been understood in various ways, when it has been accepted at all. (Predictably, there have been researchers who have rejected the connection entirely—on theoretical grounds, of course.) Many researchers have treated tsog tsuam as nothing more than a symptom of whatever underlying medical cause must actually be behind SUNDS, dismissing dab tsog as a mythical monster. A different approach, more attentive to the effects of mental factors on health, has pointed to a combination of Hmong traditions about dab tsog, the overwhelming stress suffered by many Hmong during and after the exodus, and the belief that dab will kill those who fail to keep Hmong religious obligations. According to medical anthropologist Shelley Adler, the major proponent of this latter theory, the combination of these three factors with the naturally occurring Old Hag experience has produced a situation in which Hmong who undergo tsog tsuam may quite literally be frightened to death (Adler 1995; see also Adler 1991).

The problem with both these approaches is that they fail to deal effectively with the relation between the Old Hag experience, which seems to be universal, and SUNDS, which is a syndrome that affects a very specific group of people in an equally specific situation. If the first approach is correct, and tsog tsuam is nothing more than a symptom of a potentially fatal medical condition, then SUNDS should be far more common than it is. After all, people all over the world report experiences just like the

Hmong tsog tsuam, and would therefore seem to be at risk from SUNDS. (A few SUNDSlike deaths have occurred in a handful of other Asian ethnic groups in this country, and a few other Asian cultures recognize a syndrome like SUNDS, but the point remains that the Old Hag phenomena occurs everywhere and SUNDS does not.) Since Hmong apparently die from tsog tsuam, but Newfoundlanders (for example) don't normally die from being "hagged," there must be another factor involved.

If the second approach is correct, in turn, it should be the case that something like SUNDS would occur whenever a group of people with traditions like those of the Hmong are placed under the same degree of cultural and personal stress. The ghastly history of the last few centuries has produced similar situations before, after all.

Why, then, was SUNDS such a total surprise when it first appeared among the Hmong? Why, to name only one of many possible examples, didn't the same thing happen among refugees from Slavic ethnic groups who fled the violence and oppression of Tsarist Russia in the late nineteenth century, and came to North America with their traditional beliefs intact—beliefs that included plenty of lore about an Old Hag-equivalent called *upir* or *vampyr*, and also included protective rites that could not be effectively carried out because of American and Canadian laws and customs?

A final point needs to be made about both of the approaches described above. Neither one provides an effective explanation for the fact that Hmong in America undergo the Old Hag experience two to three times more frequently than average, nor for the fact that Hmong who have converted to Christianity have an even higher rate of tsog tsuam—the highest rate, in fact, of any known population anywhere in the world. It's been suggested that many Hmong converts joined Christian churches for reasons that had little to do with changes in their actual spiritual beliefs, but it's hard to believe that all of them fall into this category, or that converts received no spiritual comfort or emotional support from the churches they joined. These variations in the frequency of the Old Hag experience are crucial pieces of the SUNDS puzzle, and yet no medical, sociological, or psychological theory has offered a plausible explanation for them.

There is, of course, one theory that does offer a clear explanation of these points, and of the rest of the SUNDS/tsog tsuam phenomenon. That theory is the one held all along by the traditional Hmong: that an entity called dab tsog exists; that it participates in a complex pattern of relationships—a kind of spiritual ecosystem—that also includes the Hmong, their ancestral spirits, and various other kinds of beings who do not have physical bodies; and that

when this pattern is disrupted because the Hmong are not able to carry out their traditional roles in it, the pattern shifts and people begin to die.

Such a theory would be completely acceptable to modern scientists if all the factors in it happened to have physical bodies. Compare it, for example, to the standard theory that is used to explain outbreaks of lethal tropical diseases such as Ebola fever. According to that theory, the Ebola virus is a natural part of the ecosystem of the central African tropical forest, an ecosystem that also includes human beings, chimpanzees, okapis, and many other creatures. When human beings disrupt the balance of the ecosystem—usually because their traditional cultures, which tend to hold the ecosystem in balance, have broken down—the ecosystem shifts and people begin to die.

If spirits—that is, beings without physical bodies—do exist, and if they are capable of interacting with living human beings, the Hmong theory makes a good deal of intuitive sense. That theory also corresponds closely to what we know about other kinds of complex systems in ecology, sociology, and economics. It deals efficiently with the entire spectrum of evidence surrounding the SUNDS epidemic to a much greater degree than any of the scientifically acceptable theories that have been proposed. The only problem with the Hmong theory is that it depends on the existence of beings who can't exist—at least not in theory.

When the evidence contradicts our assumptions, once again, challenging the assumptions makes much more sense than trying to hide from the evidence. The SUNDS epidemic points out another reason why this can be a very good idea—and also suggests an answer to the third of our original questions. If a monstrous being such as dab tsog can kill people, its existence, nature, and habits are arguably of more than academic interest, and assumptions that make it impossible to deal effectively with a potentially lethal being are questionable at best.

If dab tsog were the only monstrous being that appears to affect people in so drastic a manner, it might still be possible (for anyone but the Hmong, at least) to disregard the lore of monsters. For good or ill, though, dab tsog has plenty of company. As we've already seen, a very large fraction of Americans have come into direct personal contact with at least one supernatural being, and this may well be only the proverbial tip of the iceberg. Folklore traditions, concrete evidence, and an enormous collection of personal experiences all support the idea that monstrous beings actually interact with humanity fairly often. Not all these interactions have the same terrible results as that between Hmong refugees and dab tsog, but there is good reason to think that such deadly interactions happen far more often than most people suspect nowadays. Furthermore, according to the same body of sources, even less dangerous contacts with monsters can have major impacts on human beings—impacts that may be positive or negative in nature.

## Three Monstrous Answers

We are now in a position to propose tentative answers to the three questions asked earlier. To those comfortably settled within the modern scientific worldview, the answers suggested here will be at least as monstrous as any of the creatures discussed later on in this book, but that can't be avoided in the light of the material we've explored.

### What are monsters?

For the purposes of this book, the term "monster" describes beings that cannot exist, according to currently accepted scientific theories about the way the universe works, but which are routinely encountered by credible witnesses and described in traditional folklore.

### Do monsters actually exist?

Without getting into deep philosophical waters—it's actually impossible, in terms of strict logic, to prove beyond question that anything exists at all—it's reasonable to say that, for all practical purposes, some monsters appear to exist. Certainly, there are things that impact human life in ways that correspond closely to accounts in traditional monster lore, and theories that refuse to admit the possibility of monsters fail to account for these impacts as effectively as the traditional monster-based explanations do.

### Do monsters matter?

Once again, a useful answer to this question needs to avoid the deep places of philosophy. To those who are affected by them directly, such beings matter very much indeed. Given that a very sizeable fraction of people have such experiences at some point in their lives, any of us may suddenly find ourselves, or someone close to us, in this category. For this reason, if for no other, monsters and monster lore are anything but trivial subjects.

## Four Essential Points

In light of the evidence discussed above, furthermore, we can go beyond the questions just posed and answered to make four crucial points about monsters. These points will be central to everything that will be covered in this book.

1. The first point is that folklore is a much better source of information concerning monsters than modern prejudices would suggest. The accounts of the Old Hag in Newfoundland legend and folklore, for example, provide very good descriptions of the experience that Hufford's research uncovered. All of the major elements of the experience, and many of the minor ones, occur in stories and descriptions of the Old Hag passed down as part of Newfoundland's folk culture. Similarly, Hmong folklore about tsog tsuam corresponds closely to the same experience. Where the common modern habit is to dismiss folklore as inaccurate and confused, the folklore actually gives a clear and accurate account of the experience. The lesson here is that research about monsters needs to start with the traditional folklore and take it seriously, not simply try to dismiss it or force it into some Procrustean bed of theory.

2. The second point is that one of the best ways of checking the accuracy of monster folklore is to compare it to its equivalents in other cultures. Just as the experience of tsog tsuam or being "hagged" is by no means limited to Laos or Newfoundland, folklore relating to the same experience can be found all over the world. Students of ancient Germanic folklore have long known about a legendary being called the *mara*, which was believed to smother people as they slept; the English

word *nightmare*, and the term *mare's nest* for a tangle of hair found on waking, both come from this ancient tradition. Many other cultures, ancient and modern, have similar traditions; ancient Greeks spoke of nocturnal visitors such as the *ephialtes* ("leaper") and *pnigalion* ("strangler"), for example, and Romans of the *inuus* ("one who sits on"). The lesson here is that real monsters and monstrous experiences often cross cultural barriers. When details of monster lore from one culture match those from another, particularly if the two are widely separated in space or time, it's more likely that an actual experience lies behind both.

3. The third point is that an experience can be extremely common, and can affect many human lives, even though it has no place in our modern culture's view of reality, is ignored by education and the media, and does not even have a name. Until Hufford went public with his research, thousands of people in the United States and Canada, along with their families, friends, and doctors, had faced the same bizarre and terrifying experience without knowing that anyone else in the world had ever been through the same thing. The lesson here is that such events are by no means as rare as many of us tend to

think. In fact, it can be argued that they surround us all the time; it's simply that we've been taught not to notice them, or when we do notice, to either stuff them into some more acceptable category of explanations or simply shrug and go on with our lives.

4. The fourth point is at once the most crucial and the most disturbing of all. This is the fact that phenomena like the Old Hag cannot be kept separate from the realms of magic, religion, and the supernatural. All through his exploration of the Old Hag experience and the folklore surrounding it, Hufford kept running across connections between the tradition and the experience, on the one hand, and currents of folk magic and spirituality on the other. A number of the accounts that first caught his attention, for example, involved the idea that the Hag could be summoned by one person and sent to attack another. Many of the people who knew of the tradition recounted ways to "hag" another person, as well as methods of supernatural self-defense that could deal with the Hag or her summoner.

More generally, people all through Hufford's research tended to treat the Hag experience as a supernatural event (rather than, say, a medical or psychological condition) whether they knew about the tradition or not. This was true of people with no particular spiritual beliefs as well as of those with strong religious convictions, and it occurred often enough that Hufford came to include a "numinous" (in other words, supernatural) quality in his list of common features related to the Hag. Certainly, too, the Hmong understand tsog tsuam as a process linked directly to the spiritual realm, and used ritual methods to keep dab tsog at bay.

The lesson here is that it's rarely a good idea to demand that monster-related experiences or traditions should fit the prejudices of modern materialism. Our third category of monsters is "spooky," straying outside the borders of ordinary experience. If we ignore that spookiness, we risk falsifying what we are trying to understand. If we face up to it, we may find that the resources for understanding that are offered by magical traditions and teachings may offer us valuable tools and unexpected insights.

## Val and the Watchful Planet

In his groundbreaking book *Daimonic Reality*, which belongs on the required reading list for any student of monster lore, Patrick Harpur recounts a story that makes this last point with clarity. He and other attendees at an English UFO conference in the 1980s had tuned in to a talk-radio program on flying saucers that happened to be on the air that day. A woman calling herself Val phoned in from Peckham, reporting that she had sighted a weird light in the sky. According to her account, the light seemed to be watching her and showed definite signs of intelligence, and she had felt all funny as she watched it. From her description of the light's appearance and position, on the other hand, it was clear at once that her "UFO" was actually the planet Venus.

Such astronomical "UFO sightings" have happened millions of times since Kenneth Arnold's 1947 sighting ushered flying saucers into modern consciousness, and they are routinely tossed aside by more literal-minded UFO researchers as simple mistakes. As Harpur points out, though, Val's experience was something more than a misperception. She didn't just mistake a planet for a spacecraft; she perceived the planet through the sort of awareness that anthropologists call *animism*—that is, the perception of life, intelligence, and meaning in some part of the universe that our culture normally labels "dead matter." That perception needs to be taken into account as a factor in its own right; it represents a very ancient and widespread way of experiencing the world, and it's not disproved or made irrelevant just because the light that triggered it turned out to be a planet rather than a flying saucer.

This is a crucial understanding, and it's relevant to much more than UFOs. Val, after all, is hardly the first human being in history to experience that particular light in the sky as a living, watchful, intelligent presence. To societies around the world and throughout time, the planets have been either the homes of gods or spirits, or gods and spirits themselves. We're taught that the rejection of such "primitive superstitions" is one mark of science's superiority over all previous ways of thought. Yet Val's "UFO sighting" reminds us that the planets as conscious, watchful powers can be a matter of direct personal experience.

It's in this light that Val's "misperception" needs to be understood. Raised to believe that planets are dead lumps of rock spinning through empty space, and taught that intelligence only exists within the brains of human or humanlike beings, Val interpreted the unearthly living presence that shone down from the night sky over Peckham as a technological device piloted by humanoid entities from another planet. It's hard to see how she could have done anything else—unless she happened to have a background in one of the traditions that offer a more useful way of understanding her experience.

Among the richest of those traditions come down to us by way of the surviving magical teachings of the West. In the lore of ceremonial magic, for example, the planet Venus is associated with an entity known as Kedemel, who is known as the Spirit of Venus. Had Val been a student of this lore, and known about these particular traditions, she would have been far less likely to confuse a planet with a spacecraft, and far more likely to identify the planet as a planet—but a planet in the magical sense, a celestial body whose rays and subtle energies are linked with various powers in the subtle realms of being.

Her options would not have been limited to the act of understanding, though. According to its own traditions, at least, magic is a way of acting as well as a way of knowing. If Val had developed the necessary skills through magical training and practice, she could have set out to commune with the spirit, turning the experience of contact into a vehicle for communication. Or she could have called down power from the spirit for some work of practical magic, turning it into a vehicle to reshape the world of her experience through the energies traditionally assigned to Venus. As a result, what was simply a baffling experience might have become an opportunity for magical transformations.

## The Advantages of Magic

All this may sound very strange to those who have had no contact with the living magical traditions of the West, but this is the way that magicians deal with the world.

Strange as it may seem, it has at least two important advantages that the scientific approach lacks in dealing with the realm of monstrous beings.

The first of these advantages is that the magical ways of knowing allow the whole of Val's experience to be taken as the starting point of investigation, while the scientific one does not. From a modern scientific viewpoint, Val's perception of intelligence and watchfulness in a light in the sky has to be read in one of two ways; either the light was behaving in an intelligent and watchful fashion, in which case it could not have been the planet Venus, or it was the planet Venus, in which case it could not have been behaving in an intelligent and watchful fashion. Yet what Val experienced was the planet Venus behaving in an intelligent and watchful fashion—a possibility the scientific worldview cannot contain.

This does not mean that her experience necessarily has to be taken at face value. In any case of this sort, it's possible that the person reporting the experience may be lying, for one reason or another, or may be suffering from sensory or mental defects that interfere with perception. It's possible that the experience in question is a matter of delusion—although too often, this term is nothing more than a convenient label for any experience that doesn't fit our culture's expectations about the universe. In some such cases, though not Val's—manipulating

the planet Venus is still beyond the means of human pranksters—it's also possible that the witness is completely honest, clear-sighted, and sane, but that the experience is being faked by someone else.

Still, the experience itself has to be taken as the starting point of investigation, and it needs to be taken in its completeness, not simply stretched or hacked until it fits the framework of some established theory. Modern scientific thought, because of its overly rigid theoretical structure, can't do this in cases like Val's; by contrast, magical thought can.

This first advantage is relevant in situations far less subjective than that of Val's watchful planet. In his book *Lake Monster Traditions*, for instance, Michel Meurger argues that most approaches to monsters of the Loch Ness variety take a partial and limited sample of the total evidence in order to bolster a case for such beings as flesh-and-blood biological creatures. Material relating such monsters to the world of magic, prophecy, and portent, for example, is routinely tossed aside as irrelevant—even though such connections make up an important facet of the lore of lake monsters around the world.

Meurger himself, as it turns out, is vulnerable to the same sort of argument; a solid partisan of the cultural source hypothesis, he has to make use of an array of rhetorical devices to evade the point that lake monsters are a matter of direct, concrete personal experience, not simply a subject of folklore traditions and friend-of-a-friend stories. Just as the cryptozoological approach ignores the mythic and magical context of lake monsters and focuses on their physical (or quasi-physical) manifestations, Meurger's folklore approach ignores the manifestations and focuses on myth and narrative. To deal with the entire lake monster phenomenon, on the other hand, it's necessary to take both these aspects as serious and relevant. A magical approach to the evidence can do this; to judge by past examples, certainly, an approach based on modern scientific ideology cannot.

The other principal advantage that magical approaches have over the modern scientific one is that they allow such experiences to be put to practical use, while the scientific model does not. As mentioned above, had Val been a magician with the appropriate knowledge and training, she would have been able not only to make sense of her experience but to do various things with it, some of them quite practical. This aspect of magical thought isn't limited to Val's case, of course; as the cases of the Old Hag and dab tsog point out, magical ways of action are the standard approach in nearly all cultures when monstrous and supernatural beings are to be dealt with.

Few ideas have been so thoroughly denounced by the spokespeople of modern science as the notion that magical workings are able to have concrete, practical effects. Still, those who have never studied or practiced a subject, and know effectively nothing about it—and essentially all scientific critics of magic fall into this category—are hardly in a position to say what the technical methods of that art can or cannot do. This point is even more valid when the critics in question make sweeping statements on the basis of theory rather than evidence; with magic, just as with monsters, this is precisely what most scientific critics do.

Since this book is primarily about monsters rather than magic, the question of the practical effects of magic will be dealt with here only briefly. Certainly, it's clear that traditional cultures around the world and throughout time have used magic for a wide array of purposes (including dealing with monsters). It's equally clear that people within the Western industrial societies themselves have continued to preserve and use magical traditions in the face of unyielding opposition from scientists, educational institutions, and churches.

Maybe all of this marks nothing more than the extraordinary persistence of a delusion, as the propagandists of modern science have claimed. On the other hand, in the light of some of the evidence we've reviewed already, it's at least possible that making such a sweeping assumption may be not only unjustified, but potentially dangerous as well.

## Magic and the Levels of Being

The magical traditions of the Western world include, among a great many other things, detailed information about various kinds of monsters. Just as the traditional Hmong relied on rites and sacrifices to keep dab tsog at bay, people in the Western world have relied on various magical, religious, and quasi-religious practices to drive off the more dangerous monsters of their supernatural environments, and much of that lore has been preserved in the surviving magical traditions.

But the link between the realm of monsters and the realm of magic goes deeper still. Central to magic in all its forms is the idea that beside the aspect of the world we perceive with our ordinary senses, there are others, subtler and stranger, which interpenetrate our ordinary world at every point and shape it by means of hidden connections. Magical theory speaks of various realms or levels of being, all of them interconnected, all present at every moment and in every phenomenon. These realms or levels aren't the sort of alien dimensions one reads about in science fiction; rather, they are other aspects of the world we inhabit.

Only our culture's obsessive material-mindedness keeps us from paying attention to the subtler realities that surround us at every moment. Each of these levels are also part of the totality of each individual human being, and only the same habit of material-mindedness keeps us from perceiving the many-leveled complexity of ourselves.

There are various different ways of classifying these different levels, but the scheme given below is common to many branches of the Western magical traditions. It's common and convenient to speak of these as "higher" and "lower" levels, although this is purely metaphor—in the same way that one doesn't have to climb stairs in order to study higher mathematics. The five levels of this scheme are as follows:

### Physical Level

The densest and "lowest" of the levels, identical to physical matter as we perceive it with our five ordinary senses. In human beings, this level corresponds to the physical body, the ordinary body of flesh and blood.

### Etheric Level

The level of life force, closely linked with breath and living matter, and also the framework of subtle energies on which all physical substance is arranged. In human beings, this level corresponds to the

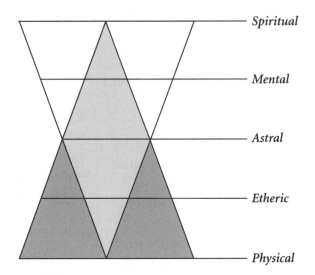

*The Levels of Being*

etheric body or aura, the subtle body of vital energies.

### Astral Level

The level of concrete consciousness, the realm of dreams and imagination (understood by magicians as objective realities in their own right), and of ordinary mental activity. In human beings, this level corresponds to the astral body, or the subtle body of imagination and the personality that is the vehicle for most out-of-body experiences.

### Mental Level

The level of abstract consciousness, the realm of timeless and spaceless meaning, the laws of logic and mathematics, and the fundamental patterns of the cosmos. In human beings, this level corresponds to the mental body, the essential and immortal pattern of the self.

### Spiritual Level

The level of primal unity, from which all the other levels emanate and to which they return. In human beings, this level corresponds to the spiritual body or monad, the transcendent core of the self.

The physical level is relatively familiar to us nowadays, and few magicians have much argument with the findings of modern science concerning its structure and properties. (The problem with current scientific thought, from a magical perspective, is not that it's inaccurate but rather that it's radically incomplete.) The spiritual level has a certain degree of familiarity as well, for it remains the primary focus of the Western world's surviving religious traditions. It's the intermediate levels—etheric, astral, and mental—that are largely unexplored in the present, and that most need to be understood if the magical approach to monstrous beings is to be grasped clearly.

The etheric level is in many ways the most important for our present purposes. It has a number of characteristics that need to be kept in mind as we proceed. First of all, the etheric level is very close to ordinary matter. It exists in space and time, just as matter does, and can affect the physical level directly. It's by learning to channel and concentrate etheric force—*ch'i* in Chinese, *ki* in Japanese—that masters of the more subtle martial arts, such as t'ai chi ch'uan and aikido, accomplish their more spectacular feats.

The energies of the etheric level serve as a vehicle for different kinds of consciousness, and can be shaped and reshaped by conscious imagination and will. They can also be concentrated or diffused by various methods. When concentrated, they take on a certain degree of apparent solidity, and (for example) can be felt directly by the nerve endings in human skin; they can exert pressure on physical objects, and appear to have physical weight and inertia. In this

state they can even sometimes be mistaken for solid (or semisolid) matter. When diffused, on the other hand, etheric energy becomes intangible and almost impossible to detect, unless the necessary disciplines of awareness have been mastered.

The astral level, the level of concrete consciousness, is nearly as important as the etheric in the magical approach to monster lore. This level is actually quite easy for human beings to experience directly—in fact, every one of us does so for several hours every night, during our dreams. The detailed studies of dream structure and logic carried out by psychologists have much to offer in this context. Where the magical traditions break from modern psychology is in suggesting that the astral realms of dream, imagination, and vision are concrete realities in their own right, and are not limited to the inside of any one human head.

Furthermore, central to magical teaching is the idea that the astral shapes the etheric just as the etheric shapes the physical. A pattern formulated with enough intensity on the astral level will tend to reshape the subtle substance of the etheric level, which in turn will tend to reshape the material substance of the physical level; this is the basic formula of magic. In turn, any event that occurs on the physical level echoes patterns already established on the etheric and astral levels, and those patterns can be perceived in advance of the physical event by those attuned to these higher levels; this is the basic formula of divination.

The astral level is often divided, for practical purposes, into lower and upper sublevels. (Again, "lower" and "upper" are convenient metaphors, not spatial descriptions.) The lower astral has more in common with the etheric and physical levels, while the upper astral more clearly reflects the mental and spiritual levels.

The mental level, in turn, is half familiar and half veiled to the modern mind; it plays a central role in current scientific ideologies, even though that role is rarely mentioned. This is the level where natural laws exist as concrete realities. Spaceless and timeless, it provides the fundamental patterns on which all manifestation on the lower levels is based. Those patterns are combined and interwoven by the processes of the astral level, which is neither quite in time and space nor quite out of them—again, dream experience is the best example here—and then reflected in various complex forms into the etheric level, which is entirely in space and time as we know them.

## Monsters and Magical Tradition

According to magical teachings, the spiritual level is the source of all patterns of being, and these patterns cascade down the levels until they reach their level of final manifestation. The material level, in turn, is a level of effects, not of causes. Everything that exists on the material level also exists in some form on all of the other levels. These same teachings, though, suggest that there are things and beings that exist on these other levels but not on the material one, and others that have only a very subtle foothold in the realm of matter. These things and beings can affect us, since we exist on all the levels, but our usual methods of understanding and shaping the material world do a poor job of affecting them.

Only methods that take into account the laws that govern these other levels—that is to say, magical methods—work well in dealing with these nonmaterial and quasi-material beings. Since (as we've already seen) such entities can sometimes have drastic and terrifying effects on human beings, a good deal of work in magical tradition has gone into understanding these entities and figuring out how to deal with them.

In one way or another, then, the lore of magic has a good deal to say about the lore of monsters, and many different branches of magical lore can contribute to the project of understanding the realm of monstrous beings. Magical understandings of death, the afterlife, and the pathologies of the dying process have a good deal to teach about ghosts, vampires, and similar monsters; magical lore about nonhuman entities is relevant to the folklore of faeries, angels, demons, and various other nonhuman beings; even legends as seemingly bizarre as those about werewolves make sense in the light of traditions concerning etheric bodies of transformation.

All of these, and more, will be covered in the main body of this book. So will a certain amount of the basic theory of magic—although there are limits to what can or should be covered in a book of this kind. The magical traditions of the Western world have evolved over several thousand years, after all; in their complexity, as well as their methods and purposes, they can stand comparison with the vast mystical systems of the Orient. For sheer reasons of space as well as relevance, then, we'll be concentrating on the particular aspects of magical lore that bear directly on monstrous beings and their effects in the world we know.

We will also be covering some of the basic techniques of magic that have direct bearing on monsters and their effects. This has quite practical motives. Some of the readers of this book may experience contact with monstrous beings at some point in their lives. Since some fairly simple magical practices can help keep such contacts from turning harmful or fatal, it seems reasonable to cover them here.

## Facing the Dark Places

In the pages that follow we will be exploring the monstrous realm from the magician's perspective. Our tools are folklore, history, and the traditional teachings of Western magic (primarily those of the Golden Dawn tradition, the principal system of magic in which I have been trained and which I know and teach). We will examine different monsters one at a time. We'll look over modern ideas about the monsters in question, to sort out sources of confusion; we'll trace monsters as they appear through history, concentrating on historical sources from the Western world to limit the sheer volume of material to be covered, but going further afield when relevant; we'll examine the traditional folklore surrounding monsters; then, with the help of magical lore, we'll set out to make sense of the monsters in question, discuss how the monster can be accurately identified, and suggest ways of dealing with the situation when humans and monsters interact.

By the very nature of the subject—monsters do not usually show up on demand to be observed or experimented on—much of what follows must be somewhat speculative. Equally, much of what follows will seem pretty strange to those who inhabit the scientific worldview of the modern West. The reality of the impossible can be a difficult pill to swallow.

Still, the circle of light cast by our culture's currently accepted ways of knowing is a narrow one. Outside it, even in our "enlightened" age, there are ancient shadows moving through the darkness. Our unwillingness to look at them, or even admit their existence, will not help us much in those terrifying moments when the world we think we inhabit tears open, and something impossible comes in through the gap.

In such moments, knowledge is the only source of power. It is with this in mind that the following pages have been written.

*Part II*

# A FIELD GUIDE
# TO MONSTERS

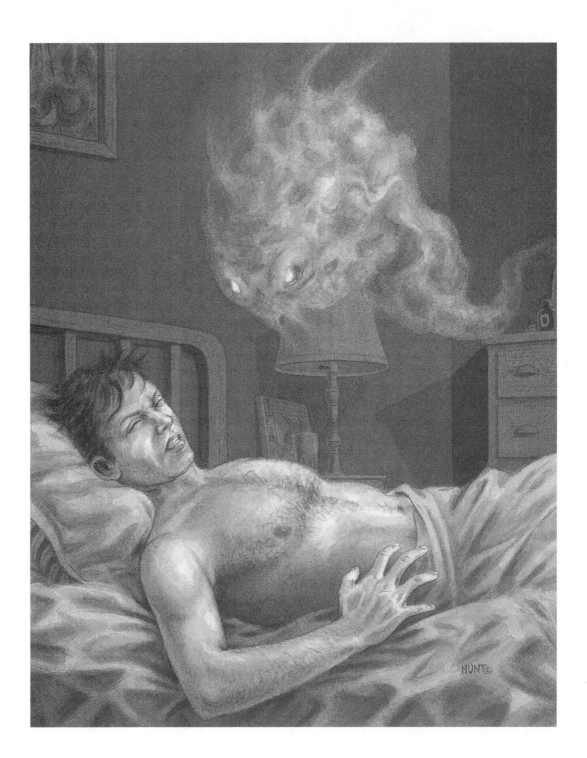

# VAMPIRES

In modern American culture, the vampire is far and away the most famous (or infamous) of all monsters. Vampire movies and vampire novels share space in today's zeitgeist with *Vampire: The Masquerade* trading cards and *Buffy the Vampire Slayer* reruns. It's a very rare Halloween party nowadays that doesn't get at least one guest in the standard Bela Lugosi kit of evening dress, scarlet-lined black cape, white face makeup, and glow-in-the-dark plastic fangs. The vampire's popularity has reached such a pitch that there is now a sizeable vampire subculture in many American cities, made up of people who have adopted modern notions of the vampire identity for their own.

All this publicity means that everyone who hasn't spent the last fifty years sound asleep in a coffin has a collection of "facts" about vampires tucked away in their crypts of memory. This list of generally known vampire lore runs more or less as follows: that vampires are dead (or "undead") people, usually long-dead aristocrats, who physically climb out of their graves at night, bite people on the neck, and drink their blood; that they can turn themselves into bats; that they fear garlic, sunlight, and the sign of the cross, and have to sleep in their native soil; that anyone who dies from a vampire bite becomes a vampire in turn; and that the standard way to eliminate a vampire is to drive a wooden stake through its heart.

This list casts an interesting light on our present culture, but it has little to do with vampires themselves, for only two of these "facts" about vampires are part of authentic vampire lore. According to tradition, vampires don't normally bite people on the neck, and many don't drink blood at all. The typical vampire of folklore lived life as a peasant, not an aristocrat, and died recently, not in the distant past. Vampires have nothing whatsoever to do with bats, ignore religious symbols and artifacts, and have no need for their native soil. Most victims of vampire attacks die and stay dead, although it's true that vampire victims are somewhat more likely to become vampires themselves. Cremation, with or without staking, is the classic way to deal with a vampire. Even the most basic element of the modern American definition of vampirism—that vampires are "undead" corpses that physically walk around at night—is contradicted by many traditional accounts insisting that the vampire travels about in a ghostly form while its corpse remains secure in its tomb. Nearly the only point common to modern vampire imagery and traditional vampire lore alike is the idea that garlic and sunlight are effective vampire repellents.

What all this demonstrates is the power of a single work of literature to shape the ideas and expectations of a whole culture. The work in question, of course, is Bram Stoker's novel *Dracula*. Nearly all of our current notions about vampires come straight out of Stoker's vivid imagination, which was inspired but by no means limited to the few folklore sources he had at his disposal, and which also drew heavily on the literary antiheroes of the Romantic movement in its portrayal of the sinister Count. As a result, *Dracula* is a great work of fiction but a poor source of accurate information about vampires. As it happens, it's an equally bad source of information about the historical "Dracula" himself, who was a prince rather than a count, lived in Wallachia rather than Transylvania, has no reputation for vampirism anywhere outside of Stoker's book, and spelled his title—on the rare occasions when he used it at all—"Dragwlya." His real name was Vlad Tepes, and Romanians recall him to this day as a hero in the wars against the Turks.

All this is important to the student of monster lore, for reasons that go beyond simple accuracy. The modern vampire of horror fiction and the media has come to be seen as an appealing, seductive figure who offers eternal life in exchange for a voluptuous, quasi-sexual sharing of blood. It's no wonder that people find the image an attractive one, even to the point of trying to adopt it for themselves.

The reality is a good deal less pleasant. Actual vampires are about as appealing as bubonic plague and as seductive as blood-sucking leeches. A predatory ghost who murders people to prolong its own unnatural existence, the vampire is perhaps the least attractive and most destructive of all monsters. All the other entities discussed in this book, even those that are highly dangerous to human beings, can be dealt with in ways that stop short of annihilation—by means of magical protections and banishings, ordinary caution, or a simple willingness to live and let live. Not so the vampire: it must be destroyed or it will kill, over and over again. The harsh treatment meted out by Eastern European peasants on actual or suspected vampires makes perfect sense in the light of actual vampire lore.

## The Authentic Vampire

In order to make sense of the vampire, then, the first and most crucial step is to forget everything you think you already know about vampires. As just mentioned, nearly every detail in the modern image of the vampire comes from fiction, rather than from authentic folklore. The shadow of Bela Lugosi's cape reaches far.

To examine the authentic folklore of the vampire is to enter a different world, one governed by the rules of magic rather than those of Hollywood scriptwriting. To begin with, the standard way of becoming a vampire in fiction—being bitten by one—is only one of many options available in the traditional lore, and far from the most

effective one. According to the authentic sources, to become a vampire, it's enough to be a werewolf, practice sorcery, be excommunicated by whatever church is standard in the area, or commit suicide; no bite is necessary.

In some areas, there are still other options. In the Slavic countries, for example, it's believed that if a cat jumps onto a corpse before it is buried, the dead person will automatically become a vampire. (This may have connections with old traditions regarding the animal familiars of sorcerers.) The range of potential ways to become a vampire are extensive enough that nearly any corpse was suspect, and in many areas the bodies of the dead were automatically dug up after a year or so, checked to make sure they had decayed properly, and then buried in a permanent grave.

An equal diversity of options surrounds the activities of vampires once they come into being. In most of central and eastern Europe, it's held that a vampire will first seek out and attack the members of its family, then go on to neighbors and friends, before finally feeding on anyone within reach. Other traditions, though, hold that a vampire's targets are chosen more or less at random, or starting with whomever lives the closest to the vampire's grave. In some areas, vampires are held to drink blood, usually by biting the chest of their victims; in others, vampires are believed to strangle or smother their victims, or simply to spread illness and death by their presence alone.

Some folk traditions hold that vampires physically leave their graves and stalk through the night, in much the same way as their Hollywood equivalents, but this view seems to be a minority one. More common is the idea that what leaves the grave is a good deal less solid: a cloudy, blurred shape, tangible but soft to the touch. One source in this latter tradition describes the vampire as being like a leather sack full of blood, featureless except for red, glowing eyes.

In the southern Balkans and Greece, where this latter view is especially common, folklore goes into more detail about the processes by which a vampire's new body takes shape. At first, according to the lore, a vampire is a soft, shapeless thing with no bones. If the vampire can survive for forty days after death, its new body develops bones, and from that time onward it is far more dangerous and harder to kill.

It's interesting to note that, despite all the variations between the vampire beliefs of different areas, some details are almost universal. Among them are several of the basic limits with which vampires have to deal. All through vampire country, it's held that vampires cannot endure the light of the sun and cannot cross running water, and it's generally believed (despite media-vampire mythology) that they can easily be wounded or killed by sharp metal objects. These all have to do with the etheric nature of vampirism, as we'll see, and make perfect sense when the laws governing the etheric world are kept in mind.

Methods for killing or warding off vampires make up a very large percentage of the total body of authentic vampire lore, for obvious reasons, and here the variations common to other parts of vampire lore are far fewer. People all through the homelands of the vampire seem to have relied, sensibly enough, on a few proven approaches. For warding vampires off, the standard methods were the use of garlic and a few other protective plants, on the one hand, and the habit of scattering seeds on the ground outside one's house, on the other; it was claimed that the vampire would have to stop and count every one of the seeds before going on, and might be forced back to its grave by sunlight before it could go on to attack anyone. (As we'll see, this actually may have had a different and much more straightforward purpose.)

For killing vampires, the essential method was much the same everywhere: dig up the suspected vampire, drive a sharp stake through its heart, and burn the corpse to ashes. There were a few other approaches that were used in some regions—for example, it was customary in parts of Greece to cut off the vampire's head and put it between its feet, and in many Slavic countries it was considered sufficient to turn the corpse over so that the vampire, trying to rise out of the grave, would actually descend even further into the depths of the Earth and become lost. Still, even where such approaches were used, they were thought by many to be second-best measures, and there are recorded cases where vampires continued their depredations after such treatment, and had to be dug up again and burned to lay them to rest once and for all.

## The Quest for Immortality

These patterns of folklore, like the vampire itself, have deep historical roots, and a glance at these roots will lay the foundation for a clearer understanding of what actually lies behind the vampire legend.

Many historical studies of vampire lore begin by surveying the wide range of predatory spirits in the traditions of cultures around the world. Even though some of these spirits have certain vampirelike qualities, this sort of approach is misleading at best. The vampire is not a nonhuman spirit, as most of these other entities are. Predatory nonhuman spirits are classified with demons (see pp. 161–174) or spirits (see pp. 131–144) or in some cases, with fays (see pp. 83–107), not with vampires. Central to vampirism is the point that the vampire was once a living human being, and only entered the vampiric state after passing through the process of physical death.

To grasp the deeper historical roots of vampirism, it's necessary to take a different approach. Such an exploration must necessarily be speculative in places, since the origins of the vampire tradition date back to eras well before written history; still, there are signposts on the way, ranging from certain odd details of history and archeology to occult lore concerning death. Our search will begin in neither of these places, though. Rather, we will start in the country that is now called Egypt but was once known as Khem, the Black Land, the gift of the Nile.

When we think of ancient Egypt nowadays, nearly all of what comes to mind relates to the Egyptian obsession with the secrets of the afterlife. Few societies in all of history have been so intently focused on the mastery of death and the attainment of immortality. The largest single body of surviving ancient Egyptian literature consists of handbooks to help the dead escape the dangers of the *Duat*—the underworld where the sun went at night—and achieve eternal life. The *Pert em Hru* or Book of Coming Forth By Day, better known nowadays as the Egyptian Book of the Dead, is the oldest and most famous of these handbooks, but there were many others.

Central to this lore was a set of teachings about the different souls or spiritual aspects of each human being. The two most important souls in Egyptian thought were the *ba* and the *ka*, which correspond almost exactly to the modern magical concept of the astral and etheric bodies, respectively. The ba, according to Egyptian lore, was not bound to the physical body, and could travel to distant places—its emblem in Egyptian art was a human-headed bird, representing its powers of astral flight—while the ka was linked to the physical body; it could travel for short distances away from it, but had to return regularly and could not survive if the physical body decayed or was destroyed.

To maintain life after physical death, Egyptian teachings held, the critical point was to preserve the ka in working order. This required, first of all, the permanent preservation of the physical body—a requirement that led to the development of ever more complex technologies of mummification; second, magical processes to "open the mouth" of the ka and enable it to take in nourishment; and third, regular offerings made to the ka so that it would not wither away from starvation. In the language of modern magic, food and drink were used to provide the ka with a steady source of etheric energy so that it would be able to maintain its existence and avoid the Second Death (the process through which the human soul sheds its etheric body after death, and goes on into the afterlife). The tomb of every Egyptian who could afford mummification thus had a ka temple connected to it, and each of these temples had at least one ka priest, whose job it was to feed the ka of the dead with sacrifices every day.

If the ka no longer received these offerings, it faced a peculiarly unpleasant fate. As chapters 52 and 53 of the Pert em Hru make clear, a ka who did not receive offerings had to venture out of its tomb at night to find what nourishment it could—and that normally added up to excrement and urine, two readily available sources of low-grade etheric energy. These starving ka wandered at night, naked or clad in their funeral clothes, and the pale light they gave off led them to be called *khu*, "luminous ones." Not all khu restricted themselves to filth; some invaded the houses of the living, causing physical or mental illness. There is even a passage in the Pert em Hru that seems to indicate that khu could attack the living directly and drink their blood. Once the system was well established, therefore, it was very hard to stop safely. The cost of sacrifices and the upkeep of ka priests became an economic burden large enough to play a major role in the collapse of several Egyptian dynasties, but the system continued solidly in place until Egypt fell under Persian rule in the sixth century before the common era, and even then lingered on in places until the coming of Christianity.

Egypt was not the only part of the world where the quest for personal immortality was followed in this way, however. Rather, it's the best-documented example of a very widespread set of traditions. Over much of the world, in very ancient times, burial mounds of packed earth or stone were raised above the tombs of kings and nobles, various kinds of mummification were used to preserve their bodies, and offerings were made to their spirits to maintain them in a state different from those of the ordinary dead.

Over much of the world, in turn, these traditions were replaced in more recent times by a very different set—one that focused on destroying the bodies of the dead rather than preserving them. The details of the transition from one approach to the other seem to have varied from place to place. In some cases, societies seem to have collapsed under the economic burden of supporting past generations, or were conquered by less overloaded neighbors. In other cases, violent uprisings—in effect, revolutions of the living against the dead—shattered the ancient system, while in other cases, the causes of the transition are uncertain. Still, the impact was dramatic, and it can be traced across the world in the archeological record.

By Roman times, for example, the dead in most Mediterranean countries were cre-mated, and even when the coming of Christianity ended this custom the dead were buried in simple graves in the earth, where decomposition would set in quickly. Further east, in India, cremation replaced mound burial at a very early date, and spread by way of Buddhist missionaries to Japan and other east Asian countries. Even in North and Central America, where megalithic burial mounds (and even a few burial pyramids) were still in use a thousand years ago, most of the native peoples at the time of European contact used ordinary burial or exposure—placing the bodies of the dead in platforms atop trees, or the like—to ensure the quick dissolution of the body.

There were two main areas of the world where the older traditions survived into much more recent times. One of these was in northern, central, and eastern Europe, where mound burial remained standard for kings and aristocrats until 1000 C.E. or later. The other was in China, where the traditional Confucian cult of the ancestors made it unthinkable to destroy the bodies of the dead, and where the pursuit of immortality remained a major cultural force until the Communist takeover in 1949.

These areas have something else in common, of course. They are the two regions where vampires have been reported in large numbers in historical times.

In the traditions and phenomena of vampirism, in other words, we are dealing with the last survivals of an ancient technique aimed at personal immortality. That technique once had a deeper and more spiritual meaning, according to magical tradition; those who took part in it did so as an act of sacrifice, removing themselves from the cycle of reincarnation for a time in order to serve some purpose that required more than a single lifetime. In ancient times kingship was deeply intertwined with traditions of service and sacrifice, which did not stop at the boundary of a single life. In the earliest Egyptian dynasties, similarly, the pharaoh's task of mediating between Egyptian society and the divine powers merely underwent a change of form at death. It was only much later, when the original purpose of the system had been lost, that it fell into the hands of the selfish and greedy, and turned into an attempt to cheat death altogether.

By the time it appears in the historical record, though, the system was basically parasitic, exploiting the living for the sake of the dead. Only those wealthy or powerful enough to provide for a tomb and regular sacrifices could have any hope of making use of it. When new traditions and the collapse of ancient cultures cut the ground out from under the system, and made it impossible to arrange for the specific forms of burial and the regular sacrifices that were

necessary parts of it, it became parasitic in a far more obvious sense.

It's easy to trace what must have happened. Like the starving khu of Egyptian lore, the etheric bodies of those who followed this ancient tradition had to venture out by night, looking for nourishment. As the tradition developed and took on increasingly corrupt and destructive forms, the nourishment in question came increasingly from living human beings. The end result of these developments was the vampire.

There seem to have been two somewhat different traditions of vampirism, both driven by the same set of historical and magical forces, but shaped by the different circumstances of the two major areas where vampirism flourished. The Chinese vampire or *ch'iang shih*, with its staring red eyes and long crooked claws, is not identical to the *nosferatu, nachzerer,* or *wampyr* of central and eastern Europe. Still, the material on ch'iang shih in the huge traditional Chinese literature of monsters makes it clear that the two kinds of vampires are variants of the same basic type of monster. (To mention only one point, ch'iang shih are just as effectively repelled by garlic as any Western vampire.)

While China and the central and eastern parts of Europe were the homelands of the vampire, the traditions seem to have spread geographically over a fairly large area—the Chinese vampire through much of east Asia, and the central European type west to France and England, and even across the Atlantic to New England, where several credible cases were recorded in the eighteenth and nineteenth centuries. Still, along with vampirism itself, the knowledge of how vampires are killed spread to these new territories, aided by the printing press and the first stirrings of what we now call parapsychological research. Even the New Englanders afflicted by vampires in the nineteenth century knew enough to dig up the suspects' graves and let fire solve the problem.

Recent vampire cases are thus few and far between, particularly in North America. The massive cultural disruptions of the last century, especially but not only in the vampire's historical homelands, have caused many other folk traditions to be forgotten, and it may be hoped that the rites and practices once used by would-be vampires have gone the same way. As we'll see a little further on, too, shifts in the way people in the developed world deal with corpses have also had a major impact. Still, it's possible that the old lore is not wholly extinct, and as long as the possibility of its survival remains, there's reason to keep watch for the telltale signs of the vampire.

## Understanding the Vampire

What lies behind the legends and lore of the vampire, then, is the remnant of an ancient magical technique, one that aimed at personal immortality through the construction of what modern magicians call an *etheric revenant*. The process has been understood in occult circles for a very long time now, and the general outlines of the technique have been published in occult literature several times over the last century and a half. (Those who seek detailed information on the technique, though, will not find it in such sources, or in this one. Some kinds of knowledge are better off forgotten, and the technical methods of constructing an etheric revenant have earned a place high up on that particular list.)

In general terms, though, the technique is a way of deliberately evading the Second Death. It's when the Second Death doesn't take place properly that the soul stays within reach of the world of the living.

Ghosts, as we'll see a little later on, fall into this state by accident. In the case of the vampire, by contrast, the failure to pass through the Second Death happens intentionally. In some cases, would-be vampires begin the process of evading the Second Death while still alive, using exercises to strengthen and condense the etheric body, and thus helping it resist the disintegrating processes of the Second Death. In other cases, types of magical practice that aren't specifically aimed at vampirism can produce the same changes in the etheric body as a side effect, and make vampirism a possibility. In still others, the transformation of the etheric body begins after physical death; a soul that is strong enough to remain conscious in the twilight of the after-death state, and frightened enough to try to avoid the transition out of that realm, may learn (or may already know) the trick of stabilizing the etheric body and may be able to put it to use before etheric disintegration has gone too far.

As long as the etheric body stays intact, the Second Death cannot begin; and so the goal of the vampire is to keep the etheric body strong enough to resist the natural process of disintegration. This can be done for a time by using the methods just described, but there are two further requirements that have to be met if the etheric body is to stay intact for very long.

The first is the preservation of the vampire's corpse in a state that can sustain some etheric functions, for if the physical body is destroyed, the etheric body is destabilized and quickly unravels. The second is a regular source of fresh etheric energy to replace what is used up or lost in the course of the vampire's day-to-day (or, rather, night-to-night) existence, for the sources used by living people—mostly connected to breathing—are closed off permanently once the first stage of death begins.

Each of these requirements involves the vampire in further complications. The funeral customs of ancient Egypt made the first requirement easy for the etheric revenant. Mummification worked by drying the body without disrupting its chemical or etheric structure; soft tissues that might easily rot were removed but kept nearby, in sealed stone jars. Burial in pyramids or deeply buried tombs also had an important role in this context, since stone and soil both function as etheric insulators, sheltering the revenant from outside forces (such as the subtle radiations of the sun) that might gradually disrupt it. While few other cultures managed quite so impressive a development of the basic technology, nearly all used burial mounds of earth and stone to shelter the phantoms of the dead, and a good many worked out ways of preserving the physical body that helped make the revenant's job easier. The vampire, by contrast, normally has no such support system in place, and must make do with the limited shelter of six feet of loosely packed soil, even when funerary customs allow the body to stay etherically functional at all—which, as we'll see, is far from common nowadays.

With the second requirement—the need for fresh etheric energy—matters are similar. In ancient times, because of the protective effects of mummification and deep burial, fairly small infusions of low-grade energy were enough to keep etheric revenants fed; the ka priests of ancient Egypt, for example, simply cooked and offered ordinary meals to the ka they served. For a vampire's more extreme needs, by contrast, the only sources that are of sufficiently high quality are the etheric bodies of living human beings. The amounts that have to be taken are usually enough to cause severe damage to the etheric bodies of the victims—damage that normally results in serious illness or death—and these depredations have to be repeated on a regular basis in order for the vampire to survive. This understandably makes the living more than a little averse to having a vampire in the neighborhood, and explains the harsh treatment visited on so many vampires in the past.

From these two basic requirements of vampire existence, in turn, the reasons behind most traditional vampire lore can easily be understood. Since the vampire survives only so long as its physical body remains intact, this provided the obvious point of attack for vampire hunters, who could simply dig up the corpse in broad daylight and burn it to put an end to the trouble. Identification was made easier by the fact that the etheric body of the vampire would tend to preserve his or her physical body long after an ordinary corpse would have rotted away.

Equally, most of the methods used to drive off vampires in authentic folk tradition have a clear etheric basis. Sunlight and running water are both etheric erasers, and so is allicin, a compound found in high concentrations in garlic and other plants of the onion family; all three of these threaten a vampire with a sudden passage through the Second Death. (Surprisingly enough, all those jokes about vampires' fear of Italian cuisine have a basis in fact; folklore in Italy contains plenty of other monstrous beings, but vampires as such are almost entirely unknown there.) Highly conductive substances such as metals have a similar effect, just as folklore would suggest. Even the odd notion that seeds scattered on the ground might distract a vampire becomes plausible from an etheric standpoint; sprouting seeds contain very high levels of etheric energy, and it's easy to imagine that a hungry vampire might well be distracted by a free lunch of this sort.

On the other side of the equation, folk misunderstandings of the vampire's thirst for etheric energy easily gave rise to the idea that vampires drank blood. After a vampiric attack, the victim would be left in deep shock from loss of life-energy, and the waxen pallor that comes with this condition would make it look as though the blood had been drained from his or her veins. Furthermore, the very common human tendency to think about the world in purely material terms—a tendency that reached maximum with the coming of the Scientific Revolution, but is found in most if not all human cultures—explains the notion that vampires physically rise out of their graves, especially in Christian societies where the idea of physical resurrection was an important part of religious teaching.

It's important to understand, finally, that the vampire's hold on existence is a precarious one. As our society is finally beginning to learn in so many other contexts, it's rarely possible to go against the cycles of nature for very long. Even when a mob of villagers armed with shovels and firewood fail to show up, few vampires apparently last as long as a year after physical death; between the constant struggle to keep the etheric revenant fed, the magical countermeasures known to all cultures that have suffered from vampire depredations, and the pitiless natural processes of time and decay, the odds for vampire survival are not good.

The situation has become even more difficult for vampires in modern times, at least in America, on account of our culture's ways of dealing with the dead. In many states, the laws governing disposal of the dead require all corpses to be either embalmed or cremated; while there's no reason to think that these statutes were passed with vampires in mind, they certainly make matters difficult for the would-be revenant. Cremation, of course, is the classic way to destroy a vampire, while modern embalming technology uses formaldehyde and other highly toxic compounds that

bring cellular life to an abrupt halt and make it impossible for the etheric body to stay connected to the corpse. Metal caskets and steel burial vaults, both of which are very common in modern funerary arrangements, put an additional etheric barrier in the way of a vampire's activities.

## Identifying Vampires

For these reasons, vampires are far from common nowadays in America—certainly far less common than they once were in Central Europe, China, and a few other places—and your likelihood of running up against one is pretty small. Furthermore, there are several other types of beings, natural and supernatural alike, that can be mistaken for vampires by the uninformed or the unwary. For this reason, the process of identification needs to be carried out carefully, even when the obvious signs seem to point to a case of vampirism.

For example, vampire attack has a good deal in common with the Old Hag experience described earlier. Vampires, however, are not the only kind of preternatural beings that can attack a human being in this way; the same thing can be done by ghosts of the more usual type, as well as by faeries and demonic spirits. (In fact, there's good reason to believe that hagging is simply the way human beings experience a direct attack on their etheric bodies by any nonphysical being.) Even a hagging that proves fatal may be the work of some other kind of monstrous being, rather than a vampire; there's no reason to think, for example, that dab tsog—the demonic spirit apparently responsible for SUNDS among the Hmong—is a vampire. The world of monsters is a complex one, and simplistic theories and assumptions do not survive well there.

One classic way to detect a vampire, of course, is to examine the corpse of the suspected revenant and check for the signs of natural decomposition—a process much more familiar to our ancestors, who encountered death and its results on a regular basis, than it is to most of us. Such tests can rarely be applied nowadays, since it's unlikely that any American court would order a grave to be opened to test the occupant for vampirism! For the same reason, the classic and very effective Eastern European way of disposing of a vampire—driving a wooden stake through its heart, cutting off its head, and burning its body to ashes—is not normally a suitable remedy for vampirism nowadays. Tampering with the dead, after all, is a serious felony in most jurisdictions.

In order to properly identify a case of vampirism, it's necessary to test for and exclude the other possibilities, and to make sure that the case meets a set of specific criteria. Just as a competent physician rules out common ailments before considering more exotic syndromes, so the intelligent monster hunter will always remember that rare monsters are exactly that—rare—and less likely to be responsible for a given situation than more common ones.

## Other Beings and Phenomena that Can Be Mistaken for a True Vampire Include These:

### Living "Psychic Vampires"

The trick of absorbing life energy from other people is not limited to etheric revenants. Some living people learn how to do the same thing. Their depredations are usually a good deal less drastic than a true vampire's, producing general ill-health or simply unnatural exhaustion in their victims rather than the sudden collapse of life force that is the most common result of true vampire attacks. These "psychic vampires," as they've come to be called, are especially common among invalids and the elderly, and many nursing homes in particular have their resident example—usually well known as such to the staff, who will often go to great lengths to avoid spending time in the room of the "vampire."

Most psychic vampires have little real knowledge of the etheric realm, and learn to feed on other people's energy by instinct alone. They normally have to come within a few feet of their victims in order to draw any significant amount of life energy to themselves. The most effective way to deal with such people, therefore, is simply not to spend time around them. Other protective measures, which are covered in Part IV of this book, can also be used with good effect to keep psychic vampires at bay.

When a psychic vampire dies, there is a chance that he or she will begin the transformation into a true vampire; after all, the psychic vampire already knows the trick of feeding on other people's etheric energy, and may be sensitive enough to etheric processes in general to attempt to hold his or her etheric body together against the Second Death. Relatives of a psychic vampire, and people involved in providing medical and personal care to one, would be well advised to take protective measures as soon as possible after the person in question dies, and should keep them in place until a few days after the corpse has been cremated or embalmed.

### Larvae

Larvae, in magical terminology, are etheric parasites who normally feed on cast-off etheric shells but sometimes fasten onto the damaged etheric bodies of the living. Their activities can sometimes produce symptoms resembling a mild case of vampirism (see Spirits, pp. 131–144).

### Vampire Fans and Cultists

The current popularity of the modern fictional vampire, as mentioned above, has spawned a whole subculture of people who have adopted the vampire identity as their own to a greater or lesser degree. Some of these people are simply playing an adult version of make-believe, in much the same way that Star Trek fans dress up in Federation uniforms and say "Beam me up, Scotty" into plastic communicators. Others are drawn by the vampire aesthetic, with its mix of nineteenth-century Romanticism and stylish fin-de-siècle decadence. Still others use the vampire scene as a context in which to deal with (or avoid dealing with) various psychological and sexual issues. As with any modern subculture, it's a very mixed bag.

The vast majority of these would-be vampires are pretty harmless, and limit any blood-drinking they might do to consenting adults. There are some, though, who are seriously crazy, seriously evil, or both. The imagery of death and blood that surrounds the vampire, even in its modern fictional form, can attract some very dangerous people, and some of these have already tried to project their vampire fantasies out into the world of everyday life, with highly unpleasant results.

Fortunately, detecting a human being who is trying to imitate a vampire is fairly easy. Real vampires, since they travel in an etheric form, are free from the limitations that come from having to carry around a physical body; they can pass through solid objects, turn invisible, float in midair, and so on. They do not leave footprints or fingerprints, pry open windows, or engage in other physical activities. Furthermore, since the vast majority of vampire wannabes get all their information about vampires from horror fiction or the media, their activities nearly always bear the telltale marks of the modern fictional vampire. A "vampire" who wears a billowing cape and flashes gleaming white fangs is a human being playing at being Dracula or Lestat, not an authentic revenant. Should he or she stray over onto the wrong side of the law, the best response is a quick call to the police, not garlic or a wooden stake.

## Undiagnosed Medical Problems

This is one of the most common and serious sources of error in detecting and identifying a vampire. A wide range of illnesses—including tuberculosis, many cancers, and AIDS—can produce the pallor, weakness, and wasting symptoms that are also produced by vampire attacks, and hunting for a vampire won't do much good if what the "victim" actually needs is prompt medical attention. *The first thing that should be done in any case of suspected vampirism is to have the apparent victim get a thorough medical examination, including blood tests.* To neglect this step is quite possibly to put a life unnecessarily at risk.

## The Signs that Point to a Case of Actual Vampirism Are These:

- An outbreak of several cases of unexplained sickness, severe and potentially fatal, untreatable by ordinary medical practice, and involving symptoms such as shock, pallor, weakness, loss of energy and wasting, beginning days or weeks after the burial of the suspected vampire;

- Victims of this sickness independently report nocturnal attacks by a presence similar to the Old Hag described earlier, and those who see the presence may identify it as having the image of a person recently dead;

- The sites of these attacks are not separated from each other by running water, and if the grave of the suspected vampire can be located, all the sites of attacks can be reached from the grave without crossing running water;

- Those who use traditional protective methods, such as garlic, are not attacked even if they are in close contact with victims, and victims who survive an initial attack and then start using such methods recover fully;

- The suspected vampire, if it can be identified, has been buried, not cremated, and has not been embalmed or placed in a metal casket or vault;

- Other psychological, criminological, and medical explanations have been effectively ruled out.

*All* these symptoms must be present in order to justify a tentative diagnosis of vampirism. Vampires have become very rare in the last century or so, for the reasons described above, and it's wise to rule out every other possibility before settling on this one. In particular, psychological disturbances on the part of the "victim" should be considered, and the other possibilities listed above should also be kept in mind.

## Dealing with Vampires

As mentioned above, vampires are very rare in North America at present, and are likely to remain so for the foreseeable future. Should you end up actually dealing with one, though, this may be small consolation. Except in unusual circumstances—for example, when the vampire's next of kin are aware of the problem, able to deal with the reality of vampirism, and willing to arrange for the disinterment of the corpse—the classic remedy of cremation can't be used to put an end to a vampire's activities, and many of the other traditional responses to vampirism are also generally out of reach. Fortunately, though, there are fairly effective ways to interfere with a vampire's nasty habits that can be done with perfect ease in a modern setting.

The simplest strategy, given current social and legal factors, is to concentrate on protecting potential or actual victims of vampirism. Here natural magic is the most important tool, and the old standby of a hundred bad vampire movies—garlic—is perhaps the best place to start. If you've ever been around someone who ate a meal heavily seasoned with garlic several hours before, you already know that allicin (the most important active ingredient in garlic) shows up on the breath and in the sweat glands for quite some time after the garlic has been eaten. If there is any reason to suspect vampire activities, and the victim or potential victim can stand the taste of garlic, it should be added in fairly substantial doses to at least one meal each day. Peeled cloves of garlic can also be hung in cloth bags inside the house as a vampire repellent.

Other methods of natural magic can be put to good effect in the same context. Anything that interferes with the condensation of etheric patterns will interfere, often fatally, with a vampire and its activities. Basic ritual magic, similarly, can be put to use to drive vampires away, and the Rose Cross ritual given in Part IV of this book would be a good place to start.

These are all defensive measures, of course, and they do little to keep a vampire from looking for easier prey. To go on the offensive and hunt down the vampire is a far more demanding task, and one that has been made much more difficult in the last few centuries by a whole series of social and legal factors. It's no longer possible simply to dig one's way through a graveyard until every potential vampire has been uncovered and, if appropriate, burned. Other methods must be used.

Unfortunately, most of the really effective methods that can be used to locate and get rid of vampires in our present social climate require a solid practical knowledge of ritual magic, and so aren't really suited for a book like this one. If a vampire is at work, scrying mirrors and crystals, horary astrology, geomantic divination, magically trained clairvoyance, and astral projection can be used to locate it, and talismans, consecrated magical weapons, and similar devices will destroy it. If you intend to make use of such things, though, you need to pick up at least one good book on ritual magic and spend the next few years studying and practicing. If a vampire is already in the area, you don't have enough time for that.

Less demanding approaches do exist, and can be used if there is good reason to believe that a vampire is at work. For example, if the grave of the suspected vampire can be identified and located, sharp metal objects such as nails can be pressed down as deep as possible into the soil around the grave, in the hope that the vampire will blunder into one on its way out to hunt. In the same situation, a bunch of flowers that also happens to contain several peeled garlic cloves could be laid upon the grave without anyone being the wiser. None of these are foolproof by any means, but they throw an additional danger in the path of the vampire and may be worth using for that reason alone.

# GHOSTS

Ghosts are a constant presence in modern media culture, and not only around Halloween. Among the most common of all monsters—surveys, as we've seen, suggest that up to a third of the living population has encountered one—they are also among the most clearly understood, even among people who know little about the subject. Many monsters have passed through wild distortions in the popular imagination, and others are all but unknown outside of certain very specialized circles. Nearly everyone, though, knows that a ghost is the spirit of a dead human being that becomes visible to the living. As far as it goes, this is quite correct.

Nonetheless, ghosts have an oddly fragmented image in the popular mind. First of all, there is the generic Halloween ghost—a featureless white blob, with arms and sometimes legs as well, its flat black eyes and mouth generally pulled down into a stereotyped moan. The Halloween ghost haunts a graveyard or appears in the window of a ramshackle haunted house tenanted by witches, black cats, vampires, mummies, and the like; its only occupation is scaring people. This first image derives less from ghosts themselves than from people pretending to be ghosts; it's hard to miss the suggestion of a bedsheet with blacked-in features in the image itself, and while graveyards and abandoned houses are common sites for ghost hoaxes they are actually not very common places for real ghosts to be seen.

Secondly, there is the image of the ghost as defined by Hollywood horror movies and the occasional ghost-related television show. This has a potent influence on the way people imagine ghosts; after the theater run of the movie *Ghostbusters*, for example, parapsychologists all over North America found themselves being asked how many times they'd been slimed. (Fortunately, this isn't a real hazard of ghostly encounters.) The problem with ghost imagery out of movies and TV is simply that the people who create them know much more about entertainment than about ghosts; what appears on the screen is a product of the producer's and scriptwriter's vision and the current state of the art in special effects technology, rather than a reflection of authentic ghost lore.

Finally, there is the much less well-defined ghost image to be found all through our society in surviving traditions of ghost-related folklore. Take the famous urban legend of the Vanishing Hitchhiker. Some solitary driver sees a young woman standing by the side of the road, thumb out, hoping for a ride. The driver pulls over and picks up the hitchhiker, who asks to be taken to an address not too far away along the same road. When they reach the spot, the hitchhiker suddenly vanishes. The astonished driver investigates, and finds out that the "hitchhiker" looks exactly like a girl who was killed in a car accident on that same date some years back, and whose ghost tries to hitch a ride home every year on the anniversary of the accident. The place of the accident, of course, was the place where the "hitchhiker" waited by the side of the road.

Urban legend or not, this tale has a great deal in common with actual ghost reports. The "vanishing hitchhiker" is not a blobby white shape out of *Casper the Friendly Ghost*, much less the sort of glow-in-the-dark green phantasm beloved by special effects designers. She looks and acts like an ordinary human being, until the moment of her disappearance. Similarly, most authentic ghosts look like living people. The first clues that something extraordinary is going on are often subtle ones: clothes several generations out of style, for example, or movements and activities oriented to things that no longer exist. In many cases, it's only when a ghostly figure vanishes suddenly or walks through a wall that it becomes clear something outside of ordinary human experience is at work.

Several other elements of the Vanishing Hitchhiker story also appear frequently in authentic ghost sightings. The link with violent and untimely death is one of these. Traditional folklore and modern research both connect the majority of ghostly phenomena to events of this sort. Connections in time and space to the death are another; despite the Halloween imagery, ghosts are far more likely to show up in the places where they lived or died than to haunt a graveyard, and ghosts that reappear on the anniversary of their death each year are quite common.

One other similarity between legend and reality is worth citing. The ghost in the Vanishing Hitchhiker legend is not a frightening being. She repeats the same unfinished journey over and over again, as though caught up in a dream from which she cannot wake. This point is true of the great majority of ghosts nowadays. While there are dangers that can arise from dealings with ghosts, most of these spectral beings deserve pity from us rather than fear.

## A Little Ghostly History

Ghosts are a constant presence in history and anthropology. There seem to be a few tribal cultures in isolated parts of the world that have no tales or beliefs about unquiet spirits of the dead, but these are rare exceptions. In most societies, ghosts are a familiar part of the mental landscape, and the interactions between humans and ghosts are structured by traditions of ritual and taboo that enable the living to deal gracefully and effectively with the restless dead. The nature of those traditions, though, have varied sharply over the centuries.

The city-states of ancient Mesopotamia, where the oldest known system of writing was invented, also have the oldest recorded ghost traditions. Ideas about ghosts closely related to these Mesopotamian traditions can be traced all over the ancient Middle East; it's clear that these traditions were old, widespread, and firmly established by the time that the oldest clay-tablet records refer to them.

Some of the details of this ancient lore may sound very familiar in light of material we've already explored in this book. In Mesopotamia, and all through the ancient world, special burial rites and regular offerings of food and drink were used to keep the dead where they belonged. If these were neglected, a dead person might become an *etimmu* or *ekimmu*, a hostile ghost who could bring misfortune, disease, or death to the living. A large and important part of Mesopotamian ghost lore thus involved rituals of exorcism designed to drive ghosts back to the underworld where they belonged. Here, once again, we are back amid the traditions at the source of later vampire lore.

The collapse of these ancient traditions, and the coming of funeral methods that helped prevent etheric revenants from surviving, seems to have changed the nature of the unquiet dead substantially for the better. The result was what we might call the "modern ghost." This is the type of ghost we'll be studying here, since it's the type to which essentially all ghosts nowadays belong.

Writings from ancient Greece show the transformation from the ancient vampire-ghost to the modern type with some clarity. The oldest Greek literature dates from an age when mound burial and funeral sacrifices were still standard for the aristocracy, but by the coming of the classical period these had been replaced by cremation and the very occasional libation of wine. Thus a handful of solid and extremely dangerous ghosts can be found in the Greek sources, but as time went on more and more Greek ghost lore dealt with ghosts who would not seem out of place in a modern setting.

A good example of the first kind comes from Pausanius' tourist guide to Greece, written in the second century of the common era. Pausanius covers the traditional lore and legends of nearly every small town in ancient Greece; his entry for the little community of Temesa recounts the story of the famous boxer Euthymus of Locris, who boxed with a ghost there and won the match, rescuing (and later marrying) a local girl in the process. Though there are obvious elements of mythology and fairy tale in Pausanius' account, Euthymus was a real person—he won the prize for boxing at the Olympic Games in 484, 476, and 472 B.C.E.—and details of the story are attested in other ancient writings. Whatever the details, it's entirely possible that Euthymus may have helped bring a destructive haunting to an end. He was by all accounts an extraordinarily brave man, and nothing in this world or the next would have been likely to faze him.

Other Greek ghosts were of a much more modern type, however. One of the letters of Pliny the Younger describes the haunting of a house in Athens by the sound of clanking chains and the phantom of a lean old man in fetters. The owners of the house, which was a rental property, lowered the rent far below market value in the hope of finding a tenant, but it stayed vacant until the philosopher Athenodorus came to town, decided it met his needs, and rented it.

The night after Athenodorus moved in, he stayed up late writing a philosophical treatise. The noise of rattling chains duly began. The philosopher kept writing. A little later, the ghost itself appeared and beckoned to him. Athenodorus calmly motioned to the phantom to wait, and kept on writing. The ghost stood there, rattling its chains and gesturing, until finally the philosopher got up, took his lamp, and followed. The ghost led him out to a particular spot in the courtyard and vanished. Athenodorus marked the spot and went back to his writing. The next morning, when he had his servants dig up the spot, they found human bones and old rusted chains. The bones were buried in a cemetery with the proper rites, and the haunting stopped for good.

While this account is nearly two thousand years old, every one of its elements—from the theme of a ghost seeking proper burial down to the economic realities of renting out a haunted house—are standard throughout traditional ghost accounts. Change the names, in fact, and the same story would fit perfectly among the ghost lore of ancient China, medieval Japan, Renaissance England, or twentieth-century America. Since the emergence of what we've called the "modern ghost," in fact, the details of ghost lore have remained remarkably stable.

This can be checked by referring to the enormous literature on the subject, from classical times to the present. Ghosts and their activities were of great interest all through history; the afterlife has always been a subject of much interest, after all, and ghosts and ghost lore have often been treated as an important source of information about it. The Middle Ages and Renaissance in particular are a rich mine of ghost lore; with the coming of the early modern period, interest in ghosts became even more intense, as Protestant and Catholic writers turned accounts of ghost sightings into ammunition for their theological debates.

The level of interest in ghosts declined in the early years of the Scientific Revolution, but books on ghost lore have remained popular all through the heyday of scientific materialism. In the nineteenth century, the emergence of folklore studies as a scholarly discipline, the birth and explosive growth of spiritualism, and the first efforts at scientific parapsychology all focused new attention on the nature and activities of the restless dead. All this effort and energy has given rise to an enormous body of information—not all of it easy to locate or interpret, but most of it useful to the student of monstrous phenomena.

## Sorting Out the Evidence

In trying to make sense of the ghost lore that has come down to us from the past, the sheer volume of material may be the most serious obstacle. Any statement one cares to make about ghosts based on this material can be contradicted by equally reliable sources elsewhere in the literature. The central reason for this is that ghosts need to be divided into more than one category.

There have been various different classifications proposed over the years. In his 1953 classic *Apparitions*, for example, G. N. M. Tyrrell devised what is now the most common system for classifying phantoms. Tyrrell's scheme has four different categories:

### Experimental Apparitions

These are cases in which a living person consciously sets out to appear to another person some distance away. Many examples involve astral projection, in which the conscious self leaves the physical body behind—usually in a state of trance—and travels to other places. This class of apparition has little to do with ghosts as such, since the people involved are still alive.

## Crisis Apparitions

These are cases in which the image of a person who is undergoing a major crisis—an accident, an injury, an emotional trauma, or death—appears to friends or relatives at the time of the crisis.

## Postmortem Apparitions

These are cases in which the image of a dead person appears to the living after the person in question has died.

## Continuing Apparitions

These are cases in which the image of a dead person is seen by different people over an extended period, usually in a place frequented by the dead person during life. Continuing apparitions are commonly called hauntings.

This system of classification is good as far as it goes, but it suffers from several drawbacks for our purposes—understandably, since it was developed to categorize the whole range of apparitions, rather than the specific class of apparitions of ghosts. It includes many phenomena (such as astral projection and crisis apparitions of the living) that don't have anything directly to do with ghosts, and it leaves out some important elements of the picture. In its place, we'll be using a somewhat different classification system, based squarely on ghost lore itself. This scheme has five main categories:

## Transitional Ghosts

These are the fraction of Tyrrell's "crisis apparitions" that involve people who are dead at the time of their appearance. This type is extremely common, both in folklore and in reports of present-day ghost experiences. There are apparently few families that can't offer at least one tale of a family member hearing the voice or seeing the image of another when the latter had just died in another town, state, or country. As this might suggest, transitional ghosts almost always appear to family members, close friends, loves, or others with whom they share a close emotional link. The typical appearance lasts only a few minutes at most, and may involve nothing more than the dead person's disembodied voice repeating the name of the witness, or his or her image appearing unexpectedly in a doorway and then vanishing.

## Purposeful Ghosts

These are ghosts that appear to have some specific reason for returning from the grave. The reason can be almost anything that might motivate a human being. One type of purposeful ghost, a type very often reported in modern accounts, is the dead parent who returns at night shortly after death to visit his or her children one last time. Another type is the dead person who hid a document or a sum of money and wants to communicate its location to the living. Another far more dangerous type is the vengeful ghost, who seeks revenge on someone and will not rest quietly until its victim meets an unpleasant fate.

## Graveyard Specters

These are a very specific class of ghostly phenomenon, a humanlike apparition seen in the vicinity of a cemetery in the days or weeks immediately following a new burial. More often found in folklore than in reports of present-day sightings, graveyard specters are the subject of many old stories. It's claimed in some parts of England and northern France, for example, that the most recent person buried in a graveyard has to stay there as some sort of ghostly watch-man until someone else dies and takes his or her place. Graveyard specters rarely speak or produce other sounds; they seem content merely to hover in the air near their graves.

## Entity Hauntings

These are the most famous and most spec-tacular of ghost phenomena, in which one or more ghosts haunt a particular place for an extended period. Entity hauntings tend to follow a very specific pattern. Normally an entity haunting is the end result of vio-lence, madness, or some other form of tragedy, and one or more of the people involved will end up haunting the scene of the events after death. Their images, pale or shadowy, will be seen walking through the area, usually at night. The whole range of ghostly phenomena may occur around them, or appearances of the specter itself may be the only ghost-related event involved. Notable in the case of entity hauntings is a definite sense that an actual personality is present, capable of some degree of thought and of responding to the actions of people who are present.

## Replay Hauntings

These are a different phenomenon alto-gether—a situation in which a set of events from the past replays itself in the presence of people who are psychically sensitive. The most striking point about replay hauntings is that an event or a sequence of events is seen, in many cases over and over again, as though a videotape was being replayed. There is often no sense of a spirit or soul being present, and the images typically do not respond to anything the witnesses do or say; the haunting is simply an endless repe-tition of the happenings of an earlier time.

There are many old battlefields in Eng-land, for example, where soldiers in ancient gear have been seen marching or galloping into battle, centuries after they and the causes they fought for had turned to dust. Some scenes of crimes of violence and passion, similarly, become places where the same events play themselves out in ghostly form, over and over again, before generations of witnesses. Where the ghosts in entity hauntings often have a range of activities, the images seen in replay hauntings go through the same motions endlessly.

## Ghostly Activities

Beyond these five basic categories, it's also important to remember that ghost phenomena can take different forms. At least four of these are important enough to deserve comment:

### Apparitions

This is the classic type of ghost-related phenomena, the intangible image of a human being. Apparitions typically appear at night, and in most cases make no sounds and leave no tracks or other physical traces. Despite the Halloween and horror-movie images of ghosts, most apparitions look like living people, and it's only when the apparition walks through a wall or suddenly evaporates in the middle of a room that it's clear the visitor is a ghost rather than a burglar.

### Sounds

The old Scottish prayer asking for protection against "things tha' gae bump in the nicht" pays tribute to one of the most common ghostly phenomena, the sudden knock or thump with no observable cause. By contrast, very few ghosts moan, even fewer talk, and I have yet to find a single account in traditional folklore or modern experience of one who said "Boo." One sound sometimes associated with ghosts is the same sliding, scuffing, or sandpapery rhythmic sound, like footsteps, that is also commonly reported by victims of Old Hag attacks.

### Atmosphere

This is another common factor, especially in entity hauntings and replay hauntings. "Atmosphere" refers to a general emotional tone or mood that pervades an area, either at all times or when some other ghostly phenomenon is in process. In cases that start with some set of tragic events, the emotional tone of the events themselves shapes the ghostly atmosphere; a haunting linked with murder may create an atmosphere of threat or terror, one that began with a suicide may give rise to an atmosphere of severe depression, and so on.

### Poltergeists

Less common, but important enough to deserve a category of their own, are those ghost-related events in which physical objects are moved in various ways. The term *poltergeist* is a German word that means "noisy spirit," and refers to a very distinctive set of phenomena in which some invisible force causes objects to move about, sometimes dramatically, in a specific area. In a full-blown poltergeist haunting, objects may be flung around or broken, furniture may be turned upside down or rearranged, and people may be attacked in ways ranging from the amusing to the potentially deadly.

Many poltergeist accounts during the last few centuries relate this sort of behavior to ghosts, but this is a fairly recent idea. Old accounts of poltergeist activity tend to associate it not with ghosts but with non-human spirits, faeries, minor deities, and the like. In a dialogue by the Greek satirist Lucian, for example, the poltergeist activity in the household of a physician is blamed on the small bronze statue of a god. Comments the physician: "As soon as the light is out, the statue goes around the house making noise, emptying the pots, mixing up the medicines and overturning the mortar, especially when we're late making our annual sacrifice to him."

More recently, many students of poltergeist phenomena have suggested living human origins for these events. It has been noticed that in many cases, the events center on a child or teenager who is profoundly angry or unhappy, but unable to do anything directly about the sources of his or her feelings. Researchers have suggested

that in these cases, the bottled-up emotional energy finds a psychic outlet. Others have challenged this idea, and the matter is still more or less up in the air. At present, certainly, the possibility that poltergeist phenomena may be related to a ghost of one type or another should not be ruled out in advance.

It's worth noting, finally, that ghosts will shift from one to another of these categories of activity. Sometimes these shifts seem to have no rhyme or reason, although attention to the phases of the moon or the planetary cycles tracked by astrologers often will reveal correlations. Two particular patterns, though, deserve special attention.

The first of these is escalation—that is, a situation in which ghostly activities start off with one of the less striking manifestations and gradually add others, until what started out as a puzzling sense of presence or an occasional noise turns into a nightmare of apparitions, poltergeist phenomena, and other activities. This can be an extremely dangerous sign; hauntings that escalate often turn violent, and people have died as a result.

The other, opposite pattern is dissipation—that is, a situation in which ghostly manifestations gradually fade away. This seems to be a sign that a haunting is coming to an end. English ghost hunter Andrew Green describes a case in which a haunted mansion gradually lost its resident ghost. Originally in the eighteenth century she was described as a woman in a red dress and a black hat; by the later part of that century, the dress had become pink and the hat gray; in the mid-nineteenth century, the dress was white and the hat had given way to "gray hair." Just before World War II, witnesses heard the sound of footfalls and the swish of an old-fashioned dress. In 1971, as the mansion was being demolished, workers felt a presence in one of the old corridors, but nothing else occurred.

## The Inner Side of Death

It is clear from the evidence, then, that the lore and experiences associated with ghosts form several very specific, well-defined sets of phenomena. From the standpoint of magical philosophy, these phenomena have their source in the way that human beings pass through death.

Magicians divide the dying process into three main phases. The first, called the First Death, is the separation of the physical body from the other levels of the self. Depending on the cause, it can be a very quick process or a relatively slow one. Violent deaths bring about an abrupt separation, while natural deaths often involve a period of weeks or months in which the links with the physical body gradually and gently break down. The next stage, which is

called the Second Death, is the shedding of the etheric body. The Second Death normally happens within three days or so after the first, but can sometimes be delayed much longer. Its timing depends mostly on the strength and health of the etheric body itself, but it can also be influenced by the attitude of the dying person. Once the Second Death happens, the dying person moves onto the astral level and undergoes the third stage of the dying process; this varies sharply from person to person, depending on a wide range of factors, and isn't relevant to the present discussion.

Recent studies of near-death experiences (NDEs)—those cases when clinically dead people come back to life—offer some interesting corroboration of these teachings. The first phase of most NDEs is a standard out-of-body experience, in which people having the experience find themselves looking down at their physical bodies from outside. In this phase, physical surroundings are perceived accurately—for example, people undergoing NDEs in hospital emergency rooms are often able to describe the medical procedures being performed, even when these happen out of sight of their physical eyes. Some NDEs remain at this level.

In other cases, this phase gives way to another, in which physical surroundings disappear and other scenes—the dark tunnel, the realm of light beyond it, and so on—are experienced. The first stage, in which the person having the experience is out of his or her body but not out of the ordinary world, closely matches traditional descriptions of the period between the First and Second Deaths, while the second stage fits descriptions of the Second Death and the transition to the astral realm that follows.

In terms of ghosts and ghost lore, the Second Death is the critical point, for it's in the interval between the two deaths that ghostly phenomena can occur. The First Death cuts off all conscious connection with the physical body—subtle links between the physical and etheric bodies remain for some time after the First Death, and play a role in some of the phenomena we'll be considering—but the etheric body is more or less intact and can be used freely until it, too, falls away. Like physical bodies, etheric bodies exist in space and time, and etheric senses (which are subtle versions of the physical senses) give the dead the power to be aware of their surroundings. The dead can see and hear, and they can also move around freely, passing through physical matter at will. The dead who are between the two deaths can also affect the physical world in certain ways, and they can be seen by living people who are in certain states of heightened perception.

## Trapped Between the Worlds

All this should sound very familiar in terms of the ghost lore covered earlier in this section. A person between the First and Second Death is, in fact, a ghost, although most such "ghosts" never appear to the living. In most cases, according to tradition, the recently dead are in a state of consciousness like the dreaming stages of sleep, and they remain there until the Second Death is complete. Sometimes the dream-state of death is interrupted by unfinished business of various kinds, and it's in these situations that ghosts of our first two types—transitional ghosts and purposeful ghosts—appear to the living. These are normal phenomena of death, and most ghosts of this type move on to the Second Death without difficulty.

Under some circumstances, though, the dead can be trapped in the intermediate state between the two deaths for a longer period. There are various ways in which this can happen. The most common involves a sudden, violent death combined with strong negative emotions. A sudden death forces the dying person abruptly through the First Death with an etheric body at full strength; if the dying person is caught up in extreme pain, fear, or other powerful emotions, the energies of these emotions can forge an accidental link between the forces of the etheric body, on the one hand, and etherically receptive physical objects near the place of death. The same thing can happen, even without violent death, if the dying person remains fixated in a specific emotional state in the same place for an extended period.

The activities of the dead between the First and Second Deaths, whether this stage proceeds normally or not, thus give rise to ghost phenomena of three of the types we've discussed earlier, the first two types—transitional and purposeful ghosts—and the fourth—entity-based hauntings. The second type, the graveyard specter, has a related origin. According to magical lore, graveyard specters are simply the discarded etheric bodies of the recently buried dead. Like the physical body, the etheric body decays gradually after it has been abandoned. It may drift aimlessly about the vicinity of the corpse for as much as several months before it finally disintegrates. Larvae—low-grade entities that feed on discarded etheric substances—may also be seen around cemeteries, but these are covered in a different section of this book (see Spirits, pp. 131–144).

The fifth type of ghost phenomena discussed above, the replay haunting, is not actually a ghost-related phenomenon at all, but it has enough in common with ghosts that it's reasonable to include it under the same general heading. Just as strong emotions can bind a spirit to a place and create an entity haunting, they can also act on their own—without the benefit of a ghost—to leave an imprint on the area that sensitive individuals will be able to read for years, decades, or centuries thereafter. Many "haunted houses" and other places where human tragedies have played out are haunted, not by a trapped soul, but simply by the ghastly emotional patterns that were projected into the etheric and physical substance of the place. The same process in reverse can be seen (and felt) in holy places, where the spiritual experiences of generations of pilgrims have left an overwhelming imprint on the atmosphere of the area.

## Identifying Ghosts

As mentioned above, ghosts are among the most common of all monstrous beings, with up to one-third of the population reporting at least one encounter with a ghost. It's worth remembering, though, that this means that a majority of people never encounter one. Equally, some fraction of the "ghosts" in the surveys are the result of misperceptions, successful hoaxes, psychological problems, and the like. In dealing with an apparent ghost sighting, it's important to go through the details carefully, and make sure that they add up to an actual ghost rather than something else.

Of the five kinds of ghost phenomena discussed above, the last two—the entity haunting and the replay haunting—are most likely to repeat themselves, and so provide the widest range of possibilities for investigation. Graveyard specters are a good deal less predictable, but a cemetery where bodies are being buried on a regular basis is likely to have a good many of them around to be seen. Transitional and purposeful ghosts, on the other hand, normally vanish as soon as they have taken care of whatever business draws them back to Earth. They can rarely be investigated in any real sense, unless they pass on information that can be confirmed later on.

## Other Beings and Phenomena that Can Be Mistaken for a Ghost Include These:

### Nonhuman Spirits

It's important to remember that there are many kinds of beings without physical bodies, and only a certain percentage of them were once living human beings. A pale shape that goes drifting through the air on a moonlit night may be a ghost, but equally well it may be some other sort of spirit. Ghosts play so large a role in surviving folklore traditions that almost any nonphysical entity is likely to be identified as a ghost, whether it has any connection to the human world or not. In outdoor settings or places where ritual magic has been practiced, in particular, the possibility of a nonhuman spirit should always be kept in mind.

### Misinterpreted Natural Phenomena

For similar reasons, many completely natural phenomena may be misinterpreted as the activities of a ghost. This is especially common when the "ghost" is never seen, and makes its presence known entirely by way of sound. Loose window frames can rattle and bang at night, rats or other animals can get inside the walls and scurry about, aged plumbing systems can thump, gurgle, or moan, damage to buildings or inept repairs can produce settling noises, and so on—any of which can create a very good imitation of a ghost when nothing out of the ordinary is involved.

### Living Human Beings

It also happens surprisingly often that an apparent "ghost" is simply a living human being seen in an unexpected place. Living "ghosts" of this sort include burglars and other trespassers, but they can also include people who have every right to be where they are. If you're looking into an apparent ghost sighting, it's almost always a good idea to make a careful examination of the area over which the ghost passed, and look for footprints and other signs that a solid human body passed by.

## *Psychological or Medical Problems*

Our culture's confused attitudes toward the natural processes of death and dying have produced a bumper crop of psycho-pathologies, and one place where these show up is in the realm of ghost research. Some people who claim to see ghosts of dead lovers, parents, children, and the like are simply fantasizing, on one level or another, as a way to avoid dealing with the reality of death. Others may be suffering from delusions caused by various kinds of mental illness or by drug abuse. Such cases can normally be sorted out with a little research and some care in the interview process, but it's important to be aware of the possibility.

## *Deliberate Hoaxing*

It's also relatively common for "ghosts" to be the product of intentional hoaxing. Even outside of the world of professional spiritu-alism, where systematic fraud is quite com-mon, there are a good many people who find reasons to fake the presence of the dead, and the level of ingenuity that has sometimes gone into this sort of project is astonishing. The methods involved range all the way from fishing lines and old sheets to sophisticated projection equipment and computers. The motives for hoaxes range equally widely. If you are examining a pos-sible haunting, keep your eyes open for the possibility of fraud, especially if the "ghost"

appears on cue whenever spectators are in a particular place, if there is obviously a money motive, or if attempts to investigate the situation more closely are blocked by the people involved.

## The Signs that Point to an Actual Haunting Are These:

- A humanlike apparition is seen by one or more witnesses;

- The apparition has no apparent weight, leaves no footprints or other marks, and passes through physical objects without difficulty;

- Research into the history of the place turns up records of previous sightings, or of a situation (such as violent death) that makes the presence of a ghost or replay haunting plausible;

- The clothes, hairstyle, jewelry, and other details of the apparition are con-sistent with each other—they all come from the same historical period and might reasonably have been worn by the same person at the same time;

- Alternatively, the apparent ghost is of someone recently dead, is seen by a family member or friend, and is either dressed as the person in question nor-mally was in life, or is wearing the clothes in which he or she was buried;

- Other psychological, criminological, and medical explanations have been effectively ruled out.

Only if all the applicable points on this list are met should a tentative diagnosis of an actual ghost sighting be made. In particular, it's rarely safe to assume that a ghost is involved if the only factors involved are sounds, atmospheres, or poltergeist effects, since so many different monstrous beings can cause these. An actual ghost will normally produce an apparition sighting sooner or later, and this can often be used as a touchstone for the presence of a ghost as such.

## Dealing with Ghosts

The different classes of ghost mentioned above need to be dealt with in different ways. In most cases, ghosts of the first two classes—transitional ghosts and purposeful ghosts—need no particular response, unless they themselves ask for one. Once they accomplish their business, they normally leave the human world for good. If you encounter a ghost who makes a request of you, it's normally wise to carry it out if you reasonably and ethically can do so.

If you can't, or if you choose not to, you may need to make use of some of the protective methods covered in the final part of this book, since the ghost may try to haunt you until you give in, or even attempt violence. Methods of natural magic that pre-vent etheric forces from coalescing are wise in such cases; so are ritual techniques to banish the ghost and protect yourself. The details are in Part IV of this book.

Graveyard specters, even on those rare occasions when they do appear nowadays, are unlikely to be a problem unless you happen to live close to a cemetery. They may scare the bejesus out of you, but they can't actually harm you. If you do happen to live next door to a cemetery and don't like the thought of etheric corpses bobbing about in your yard, plant protective plants in your garden or put up a hawthorn hedge along the side of your house facing the graveyard.

Replay hauntings are a good deal more complex. With a haunting of this type, the amount of work involved in dispelling the effect can range from the simple to the enormously complex and expensive. Magical methods of blessing and purification are a good place to start, and it's also often useful simply to spread rock salt all over the area to be cleansed, let it sit there for several days, and then sweep it up and dispose of it. Methods of eliminating etheric patterns are important tools in cases of this sort. Depending on the nature of the event that set the haunting in motion, though, it may not be possible to dispel the energies thoroughly enough to bring the phenomena to an end. In extreme cases, moving out can be the only option.

Entity hauntings are an equally complex matter, and much depends on the circumstances and the level of difficulty you're willing to face. Some hauntings can be dispelled quickly and effectively by leaving a bowl of vinegar on the mantelpiece and keeping it filled for a week or so; acid vapors prevent etheric forces from condensing, and in the case of a ghost who is relatively weakly bound to the physical world, this can bring on the Second Death in short order.

Other hauntings take much more work, and the more traumatic the events that gave rise to the haunting, the more difficult it usually is to send the ghost on its way. The full range of natural and ritual magic can be used for this purpose, and it's often wise to make use of religious rituals and artifacts as well. Another approach, one that has been used with a good deal of success, is to find an honest trance medium who has some experience freeing trapped souls.

Some special considerations arise when dealing with the more communicative type of ghost—especially those entities (who may or may not actually be deceased human beings) that communicate with the living by way of trance mediums, automatic writing, or similar methods. As New Age comic Swami Beyondananda has pointed out with some cogency, "Just because they're dead doesn't mean they're smart." Embarrassingly often, people who deal with

such entities take their pronouncements on blind faith. The result has been a good deal of silliness and a certain number of human tragedies. The moral here is simple: the mere lack of a body is no guarantee of superior knowledge—or good intentions, for that matter.

Some people prefer to keep ghosts around, instead of sending them on their way through the Second Death, but this can't be recommended. On the one hand, this sort of approach is cruel to the ghost, who is trapped between the worlds and unable to go on to another life; on the other hand, it can be unhealthy for the living people involved. Even when a ghost has no ill will toward the living, its presence tends to attract larvae, who will sometimes try to feed on the etheric bodies of the living; this can produce chronic illness and loss of vitality. Other spirits, not all of them friendly, may also try to make use of the connection between the worlds. Furthermore, ghosts created as a result of tragedy will often carry a strong emotional atmosphere with them, and in some cases—especially those involving murder or suicide—the atmosphere can have powerful negative effects on the living. Too often for comfort, those living in a place haunted by a suicide end up falling into severe depression and killing themselves in turn.

Under some circumstances, furthermore, ghosts can obsess or possess the living. (The processes that magicians call obsession and possession are covered in Demons, pp. 161–174.) Either one of these is a nasty situation, requiring religious or magical exorcism to resolve.

There are also certain types of ghost that are dangerous by their very nature. People who were violent, destructive, or insane in life are rarely improved much by death, and if they become trapped in the transition to the afterlife they can become sources of much evil. Partly this is an effect of the emotional atmosphere they generate, but they can also take a more active role in causing harm. If the probable source of a haunting is someone who would be considered dangerous if still alive, or if ghostly activities seem to be moving in the direction of violence, drastic measures should be taken immediately, either to bind or banish the ghost or to leave the area at once and get to a place of safety.

A final source of danger from ghosts comes from the spirits of those who die by drowning. Water, particularly cold and still or slow-moving water, absorbs and holds onto etheric patterns extremely well, and so the ghosts of the drowned typically have much more energy than those who die by most other means. In addition, the energies of water have complex and unsettling effects on the dead; it's part of folklore in most traditional cultures that the drowned seek company, and will draw other people to their deaths if they can. The increased level of etheric energy such ghosts have at their disposal gives them the power, in some cases, to cause lethal "accidents" of various sorts. Any place where a drowning has occurred should be avoided as much as possible for a year or more thereafter, and only competent magicians or religious personnel trained in exorcism should attempt to banish such entities.

# WEREWOLVES

The werewolf is another of the monsters that populate horror movies and Halloween parties throughout modern American society, and it shares the same heritage of folk tradition heavily obscured by media images. When modern people think about werewolves, the image that usually comes to mind is Lon Chaney in the classic horror movie *The Wolf Man*—a human form in half-shredded clothing, with a snarling half-animal face and shaggy fur covering every visible inch of skin. This somewhat furry reworking of Dr. Jekyll and Mr. Hyde, though, is largely a product of the special effects technology that was available in the early years of horror films. In folklore sources, by contrast, a werewolf was a man or woman who changed entirely into a wolf.

The idea seems preposterous at first glance. The process of physically transforming a human being into a wolf would require massive reshaping of bones, muscles, and internal organs—a task far beyond the reach of the most advanced medical techniques. If some weird genetic fluke allowed it to take place at all, it would require months, not the minutes allowed by folklore accounts. It's easy to see, therefore, why tales of werewolves and other shapeshifters were labeled nonsense by scientists hundreds of years ago.

Still, that rejection is based on a misunderstanding. The accounts of werewolves in folklore and magical tradition do not require a *physical* transformation of human into wolf. In fact, when these accounts are read with a careful eye, it's obvious that something very different is going on.

## Shifting Shapes

The critical point that needs to be grasped here is that shapeshifting is not a matter of physical transformation. This is anything but a new discovery. Nearly everyone who wrote about werewolves in the Middle Ages and the Renaissance, for example, held that a physical transformation of man into wolf was impossible, and discussed in fine detail whether lycanthropy was pure hallucination or whether something more complex was going on. The first significant textbook of the modern magical revival, Eliphas Lévi's *Transcendental Magic*, includes a discussion of shapeshifting in terms not far different from the ones we'll be using here.

The same point can also be found throughout the actual records of lycanthropy. In many cases, the human body of the werewolf was found lying asleep in bed, or curled up under a bush in the forest, while the werewolf prowled the night. In other cases, the animal form seems to have surrounded the human body of the werewolf like a garment. That garment was not always complete. Medieval records are full of accounts like that of Benoist Bidel, fatally wounded while trying to defend his sister from a werewolf, who reported before he died that the wolf who attacked him had

forefeet like a man's hands covered with hair; this particular account is from Henri Boquet's *Discours des Sorciers* of 1590 (Summers, 1966, p. 122).

Accounts of the method of transformation vary widely in the records, changing form nearly as readily as werewolves themselves. The idea that the transformation happens by itself at the full of the moon—a notion made famous by any number of horror films—can be found in werewolf folklore all over Europe, but it's not the only explanation. Norse werewolves, according to the sixteenth-century historian Olaus Magnus, murmured a charm over a cup of ale and then drank it. In Western Europe and among the Slavic peoples of the same period, the process involved rubbing a magical ointment all over the body, and then donning a wolf's pelt or a belt made of wolfskin. Many records of lycanthropy suggest that a charm was sung or spoken aloud by the werewolf as part of the shapeshifting process.

The ointment mentioned in many werewolf accounts is an interesting point. There are some hints that hallucinogenic drugs played an important part in the werewolf tradition, and certainly the few recorded recipes for werewolf ointments contain powerful hallucinogenic herbs such as belladonna, monkshood, henbane, and the like—herbs that also had a place in the "flying ointments" used by medieval witches.

(Be aware, though, that all these plants are extremely poisonous and can cause cardiac arrest and sudden death. If you plan on taking up lycanthropy yourself, there are much safer ways to go about it.)

The process used to change back from wolf-shape to human-shape also takes different forms in the lore. Many of those traditions that speak of a wolfskin belt indicate that the werewolf has only to unfasten this to return to human form. A large number of sources suggest that the werewolf has to bathe in running water in order to take on a human shape. In other traditions, by contrast, the transformation back to human form can be done at will by the shapeshifter.

The ways people defended themselves against werewolves are also relevant. The monster-movie cliché that werewolves can only be harmed by a weapon made of silver appears in some sources, but others suggest that any metal weapon can injure or kill a werewolf, and some claim that the animal form is as vulnerable as an ordinary wolf. A claim of particular importance, found in French and Eastern European sources, is that cold iron will cause the wolf-form of a werewolf to instantly disappear.

## The Ancient Wolf-Magic

The dimension of time is critical in understanding lycanthropy. The classic European werewolf has a pedigree as illustrious as any monster, with roots that reach far back into prehistory and equivalents found over most of the planet.

Tracing the lore and legends back, it's possible to make out the dim outlines of an ancient tradition of wolf-magic among the first Indo-Europeans in their ancient homeland, in what is now southern Russia. When the great Indo-European migrations began more than three thousand years ago, the tribes took their wolf wisdom with them to Europe—where they gradually separated and evolved into Celtic, Germanic, Italic, Greek, Slavic, and Baltic peoples—and to Asia, where Indo-European tribes settled in Persia and most of northern India, spread across the Asiatic steppes, and founded the Hittite empire in what is now Turkey.

The original form of this ancient tradition is barely more than a guess nowadays. It's been suggested that young warriors seeking initiation into wolf magic went into the wilderness and lived as wolves, wearing wolfskins and eating only raw flesh, while they passed tests of strength and courage and then learned the secrets of the tradition from tribal elders.

Even at the time, the wolf warriors apparently had a mixed reputation. The closely related tradition of bear magic that gave the English language the word "berserk" may suggest why; records of shapeshifting warriors of later times suggest that they too often lost control of their animal aspect in fits of terrifying violence. The ancient Indo-European root *vark-*, "wolf," left echoes in many of the daughter tongues of the Indo-European family—Sanskrit *vrikas*, Old Persian *varka*, German *warg*, Old Norse *vargr*, Old Common Slavic *velku*, Hittite *hirkas*—all of which mean both "wolf" and "outlaw."

Traces of the ancient wolf magic show up in a wide range of historical sources. Quite a few tribal groups among the Indo-Europeans had names that translate into English as "wolf people." The Greek historian Herodotus mentions a nomadic tribe called the Neuri, each member of which turned into a wolf for several days each year. Another tribe found in old Iranian records is called the Haumavarka—literally *soma*-wolf; *soma* is a ritual drug mentioned many times in ancient Sanskrit and Persian texts, another hint of the connection between shapeshifting and ritual drug use.

It's in the records of the Norse, though, that the Indo-European wolf magic comes into the full light of history. Most of this material comes from Iceland, where monks shortly after the coming of Christianity were still proud enough of their native culture and traditions to write down the old sagas intact. Some very old material appears in these epic poems—the *Volsunga saga*, for example, is partly based on historical events that took place well before the fall of Rome.

The practice of shapeshifting appears over and over again in these tales. Many of the greatest warriors of the sagas were shapeshifters as well, and their adventures in animal form make up a common theme. Wolf and bear were the most usual animal forms, but swans, otters, salmon, and other creatures also appear in the Norse repertoire of transformations.

The activities of these shapeshifting warriors are worth mentioning. Of the great berserker Bodvar Biarki, one of the warriors of Hrolf Kraki, King of Denmark, it is recorded that in the king's final battle Bodvar was for a long time nowhere to be seen. During his absence, however, men in the front lines saw a great bear plunge into the battle before King Hrolf's men, slaying the men and horses of the enemy. One of Bodvar's friends finally found him sitting motionless in his tent and roused him; at that moment, the bear suddenly vanished.

More often the berserkers and wolf-warriors were physically present on the field of battle, but still had much the same impact as Bodvar's phantasmal bear-shape. The thirteenth-century Icelandic poet Snorri Sturluson commented in *Ynglinga saga*: "These men (the berserkers) went without their mailcoats and were mad as hounds or wolves, bit their shields and were as strong as bears or bulls. They slew men, but neither fire nor iron had effect upon them. This is called 'going berserk.'"

The *berserkrgang*, the "way of the bear-shirt," as well as its wolfish equivalent, seem to have fallen out of common practice as Christianity rose to dominance in Europe. As the Middle Ages gave way to the Renaissance, pockets of the old tradition seem to have lingered on in Western Europe only in isolated rural areas. There are a good many accounts from mountainous areas of Germany and southern France as late as the 1500s, but in more recent years werewolf activity seems to have become a good deal more sporadic. Eastern Europe was another story, for a variety of historical reasons. In some parts of the Balkans, the ancient wolf magic was apparently preserved into quite recent times—and may survive there still.

## Native American Shapeshifting

The ancient Indo-Europeans were far from the only people to master the trick of taking on animal shapes, however. The magical disciplines necessary to accomplish shapeshifting are known, at least to a limited degree, in most magical traditions that survive from before the Scientific Revolution. In North America, and west of the Mississippi in particular, many Native cultures preserve a great deal of the old lore, and shapeshifting magic is still practiced by a number of First Nations.

Among the Navajos, for example, *yenaaldlooshi* or "skinwalkers" are sorcerers who change into dogs or coyotes as part of a much-feared tradition of evil magic. Skinwalkers are believed to practice cannibalism and to use a magical powder made from corpses—two traits that may link them with the Anasazi (Navajo for "the ancient enemy"), a long-extinct Southwestern culture to whom Navajos as well as some anthropologists attribute the same nasty habits. Skinwalkers themselves are anything but legendary beings in Navajo country. Even today, both native and white people see them, interact with them, and seek protection from their destructive powers by a variety of magical means.

Much less malignant are the *nahuales*, the shapeshifters of central Mexico. Nahuales can turn themselves into several types of animals, including dogs, donkeys, and wild turkeys. The nahual art of shapeshifting, along with allied powers of hypnotism and magic, is passed on from master to apprentice in a period of training that can last up to two years. All these powers are put to use in the service of ordinary greed, for it's held that nahuales are basically lazy people who use their gifts to get by without working. They steal valuables, commit rape, and play nasty pranks on people whom they dislike, but their powers don't allow them to kill or even to cause serious physical injury. It's worth noting that nahuales are said to become frightened and lose control of their powers if they touch metal.

Certain Northwest Coast First Nations, in turn, have preserved a system of lycanthropy as part of a rich heritage of ceremonial initiations and magical secret societies. Initiates of this wolf tradition are taken into the deep forest, in much the same way as the ancient Indo-European wolf warriors, and there learn the songs, dances, and inner disciplines of the shapeshifting art. Very little is known about their traditions and activities; it is not a subject discussed with white people, except in very special circumstances.

These Native American traditions, and others much like them, remain living realities today. Nor are werewolf sightings entirely unheard of, even in present-day America; most reports are concentrated in the Southwest and Midwest, but there seem to be few areas of the continent that have not seen the mark of the werewolf's paw.

## The Animal Body of Transformation

With werewolves and other shapeshifters, as with many of the other important monsters of traditional lore, it's clear that we're considering a specific and consistent phenomenon. In the case of shapeshifting, the key to that phenomenon is to be found in the etheric level of being, and specifically in

what magicians call the *body of transformation*.

Along with the material body, as we've seen, magical philosophy teaches that there are a series of other, subtler bodies: the etheric body, the astral body, the mental body, and the spiritual body. Under some conditions, the three higher bodies of a human being can either leave behind the two lower ones, traveling out of the body, or split the etheric body, leaving part in the physical body and using part as a vehicle for out-of-body travel. The first of these is called astral projection, the second etheric projection.

In most cases of etheric projection, the etheric vehicle still retains the shape of the human body, just as it does after death. By certain techniques, though, the etheric vehicle can be reshaped into an animal form, and charged with etheric substance drawn from sources outside the body. If this is done in the right way, much of the animal's power and perceptions will infuse the etheric vehicle as well.

The result is an *animal body of transformation*, an almost physical animal shape in which the shapeshifter can travel about at will. The lore of animal bodies of transformation can be found in many of the world's surviving magical systems, since these etheric structures are a very useful part of the magician's toolkit, for two main reasons.

First of all, because the animal body of transformation will have many of the characteristics of the animal on which it is modeled, those who take on such a body will have abilities and senses possessed by animals but not, under normal conditions, by human beings. A hawk's exceptional sight, a wolf's tireless pace, or a bear's overwhelming strength can thus be drawn on by the shapeshifter who takes on the form of these animals.

Second, a properly constructed body of transformation is far more robust than the "body of light" used in astral projection and similar forms of out-of-body experience. Since it draws on etheric material from outside the shapeshifter's own etheric body, it isn't limited to the amount of etheric substance the shapeshifter can afford to divert from the work of keeping his or her physical body alive. The result is a far more intense (and far more useful) body of transformation, one that can accomplish many tasks that ordinary etheric or astral projection cannot.

To judge by the old lore, there are two different ways in which an animal body of transformation can be used. The first is a variant of etheric projection, used for a more robust variety of out-of-body experience. Using this method, the shapeshifter leaves his or her physical body in a state of deep trance, and formulates the animal body of transformation as a vehicle for the astral, mental, and spiritual parts of himself or herself. This is the easier and more common of the two methods.

In the second method, the shapeshifter formulates an animal body of transformation while remaining awake and active in his or her physical body. The body of transformation becomes a shell of etheric substance around the shapeshifter's human form, adding its animal powers to the human capabilities of the shapeshifter. This is the method that was apparently used by most of the werewolves of the Middle Ages, and most of the Norse berserkers; it seems to be the only method that allows shapeshifters to cause direct physical injuries to people and animals—although the story of Bodvar Biarki mentioned above suggests that things might once have been different.

Once the etheric basis of shapeshifting is understood, most of the puzzling features of the old lore make sense at once. For example, since the moon governs the etheric tides on Earth, and the full moon marks the peak of those tides, it's not surprising that in many areas shapeshifters carry out their art when the moon is full. Etheric energies in the *spiritus mundi* or subtle body of the Earth are at their peak when the moon is full, and the task of formulating a body of transformation is much easier.

Magical teachings about the etheric body also make sense out of the lore surrounding methods of wounding or killing werewolves.

Dense etheric patterns are more or less invulnerable to most ordinary physical objects, but can be damaged by metals, especially highly conductive ones like silver. Since the shapeshifter's own etheric body provides at least some of the substance of the body of transformation, and since the etheric body forms the framework on which the dense matter of the physical body is arranged, any damage to the animal form will be mirrored in the shapeshifter's human body as well. This is known as *repercussion* among magicians, and forms one of the potential hazards of any sort of out-of-body experience.

More drastic results are caused by a conductive metal object that passes through the core of the body of transformation. If the shapeshifter is projecting the animal body at some distance from his or her physical body, the result is usually sudden death. The body of transformation implodes, and the shapeshifter—with no way to reconnect to the physical body—passes through the Second Death instantly.

If the shapeshifter is physically present within the body of transformation, on the other hand, the results are less immediately fatal, but the shapeshifter is likely to be pretty dazed from etheric rebound, and may slip into a life-threatening state of shock. Either way, the werewolf's traditional dread of silver makes a great deal of sense in magical terms.

## Identifying Werewolves

The classic European werewolf is not a common monster in the present age, and unless you spend time in isolated corners of Eastern Europe or in areas heavily settled by immigrants from Slavic countries, your chance of encountering one is fairly low. Matters are far different with the shapeshifting traditions that were here long before Columbus blundered his way to American shores. All through the western half of the continent, in particular, shapeshifters of various kinds remain an active presence. If you live in the right part of the country, it's not impossible that you may find yourself dealing with shapeshifters at some point.

## Other Beings and Phenomena that Can Be Mistaken for a True Werewolf (or Other Shapeshifter) Include These:

### Faeries and Nature Spirits

According to traditional folklore, it's quite common for faeries and other nonhuman spirits to take on any of a wide range of animal forms for their own purposes. The process involved is very similar to the one used by human shapeshifters, although faeries typically manage it with a great deal more flair and competence, since they live and function primarily on the etheric level rather than the physical one, and know its ways much better than we do. See Creatures of Faery, pp. 83–107.

### *Ordinary Animals*

This is the most common and most likely source of mistaken shapeshifter sightings. A wolflike creature seen padding through the streets of a modern city is most likely nothing more than a stray mongrel with a good deal of German Shepherd in its pedigree. Similarly, a coyote seen trotting through the desert—even if the particular piece of desert is inside the borders of the Navajo reservation—is probably just what it seems.

There is an additional potential for trouble here, since one of the more common elements of shapeshifter reports is an animal that is acting strangely, out of character for its species. While this might be a sign that a shapeshifter is at work, nowadays it's more likely to mean that the animal is seriously ill, and some of the potential illnesses (such as rabies and bubonic plague) can be a serious problem for human beings as well. If you sight such an animal, it's usually wisest to give it a wide berth and call the local Animal Control authorities as soon as possible.

## The Signs that Point to a Case of Actual Shapeshifting Are These:

- One or more animals are sighted behaving in ways out of character for the species in question, or in an area in which that species is definitely known to be extinct;

- The area of the sighting is one in which magical shapeshifting traditions are known or very strongly suspected to have survived;

- The type, behavior, and activities of the animal in question correspond closely to these specific traditions;

- The animal is seen to act in ways that suggest very high intelligence, unusual physical abilities (such as the ability to keep pace with a car driving at highway speeds), and/or an interest in things (such as money or other valuables) that animals of that species normally neglect;

- If the animal is struck with a non-metallic object, this has no apparent effect on it;

- Other psychological, criminological, and medical explanations have been effectively ruled out.

The great majority of these signs should be present in order to justify a tentative diagnosis of shapeshifting. Because different cultures have very different traditions of shapeshifting magic, it's of central importance to check the details of the sighting against the lore concerning local shapeshifting traditions, as this offers the best way of testing for the presence of an actual shapeshifter. If you are in a region where there are nahuales, check for the characteristic behaviors of the nahual; if your sighting happens in an area with a large concentration of immigrants from southeastern Europe, read up on Slavic werewolf lore, and check the phase of the moon on the date of your sighting.

## Dealing with Werewolves

In the great majority of cases, the best option when dealing with a suspected shapeshifter is to do nothing at all, beyond the actions appropriate when facing a normal animal of the same kind. Shapeshifters in animal form will normally be busy with their own affairs—which are not necessarily yours—and there's often no good reason for you to get involved.

It's entirely sensible, on the other hand, to learn about local shapeshifting traditions and to pay attention to accounts or rumors of shapeshifters in action. If you know what the local variety tends to do and how their actions can be countered, you're in a much better position to respond intelligently if you have to deal with one face to face.

Still, some shapeshifting traditions have deep ties to various kinds of destructive magic, to criminal activities, or to violence, and it's just possible that if you live in an area where such connections exist, you may

find yourself running the risk of magical or physical attack. If the attack in question is magical, the information in this book's section on magical self-defense can be used to provide effective protection.

If physical attack is a serious possibility, a three-foot-long hardwood walking stick topped with silver (get the top made by a jeweler) is a useful self-defense item, and as of this writing it's legal to carry in all US jurisdictions. Classes in self-defense or saber fencing will give you enough knowledge to use it effectively; you can also find a book on stick fighting, and practice until you know what you're doing. Of course, this needs to be done *before* you have to put the skills into practice. Like all self-defense tools, it also needs to be used with intelligence, prudence, and common sense. You're going to look extremely stupid, to use no stronger word, if your attempts to defend yourself from a supposed werewolf cause you to beat someone's pet Alsatian to death.

Other kinds of weaponry tend to involve even more serious legal and safety issues, and can't be recommended except in the most extreme circumstances. If you own a handgun, can legally carry it with you, and know how to make and load your own ammunition, silver bullets of the classic type are not out of the question. This is a drastic approach, however, and it should not even be considered except in situations of the gravest danger.

If you are actually attacked by a werewolf (or any other type of shapeshifter), remember that there may or may not be a human body inside the body of transformation, and that in the former case the human body may be carrying a weapon of some kind. Either way, the animal form is your best point of attack. If you can hit it near the center with a highly conductive metal such as silver, it will almost certainly implode, leaving you facing either a dazed and disoriented shapeshifter, or empty air.

In the former case, keep in mind that laws about assault apply to lycanthropes as much as to anybody else, and that you're unlikely to get far with the judge by claiming that your actions were justified because your attacker was a werewolf. In the latter, be aware that severe etheric rebound is usually fatal to projecting shapeshifters, and that a corpse may turn up in some unexpected place the next morning. Either way, you may end up in serious legal trouble.

The lesson here is simply that with werewolves, as with any other potential opponent, it's best to avoid a direct physical confrontation unless you have no other choice, and it's absolutely essential to know the legal, ethical, and practical issues involved before you put yourself in a situation where violence may result. A word to the wise is sufficient.

# CREATURES
# OF FAERY

The entities covered in this section are perhaps the most interesting, and certainly among the strangest, of all the monstrous beings we'll be examining. It's hard to sense this from the images and accounts in current popular culture, though. The beings known nowadays as fairies have suffered more at the hands of the "Halloween consciousness" of modern commercialism than any other of those diverse creatures we have called "monsters."

The confusion begins with the very terms we use. The word "fairy" or "faery" comes from the Latin verb *fatare*, "to enchant," and actually means a state, condition, or realm of enchantment. The word "fay," in turn, comes from the same root, and means an enchanted or enchanting being; this is the term that will be used here for a creature of faery. Both "fay" and "faery" entered the English language with the Normans, and came to be used as synonyms for two older English words, "elf" and "elfhame."

The same degree of confusion appears in our culture's standard image of fays—or, rather, images, for even in their modern forms, the folk of faery change shape easily and are unnervingly hard to pin down. The most common modern image of a "fairy" is a tiny human figure, usually female, with wings borrowed from one of the cuter flying insects. Pointed ears, and sometimes little antennae curving up from the forehead, serve as identifying markers; clothing tends toward the fluffily medieval; sometimes a "magic wand" tipped with a star completes the kit.

Another version shows up at a different time of the year, as fays are among the few uncanny beings to break out of the late October monster ghetto. Dressed in a bright green version of Victorian working-class Sunday best, the leprechaun puffs his pipe, brandishes shamrocks, or cools his heels near an improbable-looking pot of gold coins every March. Spin the year's wheel most of another turn, and yet another version appears, manufacturing toys at the North Pole under the watchful eye of Santa Claus.

Other than small size, outdated clothing, and a bad case of excess cuteness, it's hard to see anything that connects the butterfly-winged girl in the gauzy dress with the chubby Irish sprite and the Christmas toy-maker. Nor do we get much enlightenment by going from these to the other common images of faery in modern culture, those introduced to the modern mind by the imagination of J. R. R. Tolkien and copied endlessly ever since by the modern fantasy fiction industry.

Middle Earth's wise and magical elves, sturdy dwarves, strong but stupid trolls, and savage orcs were all products of Tolkien's own intensely personal vision, not of traditional faery lore. Since Tolkien's time, though, they have become the inspi-

ration for hundreds of similar species in the linked worlds of fantasy fiction and role-playing games. Given the substantial overlap between fantasy fandom and the various alternative subcultures in our present society, Tolkien's creations have become part of the mental furniture of the latter, and far too many of the people who are actually interested in faery lore have wildly inaccurate ideas about what fays are, how they behave, and how they relate to the human world.

The result has been a remarkably dense fog of confusion surrounding the realm of Faery—appropriately enough, as vanishing in a fog is a typical faery trick. To navigate through that fog to a clearer understanding of the faery realm is no mean trick itself. Fortunately, the lore of the Western magical tradition casts some useful light on the subject.

## Different Forms, Similar Tales

The fog of confusion that surrounds current understandings of the faery folk is no new thing, and it becomes steadily worse as we try to trace the silver thread of faery into the past. It's sometimes all but impossible to untangle fays from other beings, particularly gods, demons, animal spirits, and the ghosts of the human dead. The perception that fays are something distinct from these other categories is a relatively recent one, and it's by no means universal even now.

Three examples will show something of the difficulties that arise from this point. Most of the Celtic countries of northwestern Europe are full of faery legends. In Brittany—the Celtic region of western France, where most people speak a language closely related to Welsh—these same stories appear; in the Breton versions, though, the role of the fays is filled by ghosts, and in place of the faery monarchs of Irish lore one hears of Ankou, the King of the Dead. The dead of Brittany and the sidhe or faery folk of Ireland have the same characteristics, do the same things, and populate the same stories; it's just that one branch of the Celts identifies them as nonhuman beings, while another identifies them as human ghosts.

More than halfway around the world, in Japan, many of the same stories appear; to the Japanese, though, the beings who act out these stories are neither ghosts nor fays, but foxes. Many centuries ago, Japanese folklore absorbed Chinese legends of magical, shapeshifting white foxes, and these beings play exactly the same role in folktale and legend that the sidhe play in Ireland and the ghosts of the dead play in Brittany.

At the same time, the classic European fay is by no means a culturally specific entity. Beings all but indistinguishable from fays can be found in the folklore of many places far from the northern European home of the old faery-faith. Here in the Puget Sound country of Washington State, for example, the native Coast Salish people tell of beings called *swawtix^w ted*, "Little Earths," who dwell in low mounds in the forest. Little Earths appear to be the size of human children, and have magical powers; they can be helpful to humans—especially to shamans, who seek their assistance on journeys to the other world to retrieve lost souls—but they can be very dangerous if treated disrespectfully. It would be hard to find anything more like traditional European faery lore, yet Little Earths were part of Coast Salish tradition long before the first white traders arrived in Puget Sound.

We can make sense of this baffling mix of wide divergences and consistent similarities only by paying close attention to the contexts in which each of these tends to happen. While there are exceptions, it's very often the case that different cultures agree, down to points of fine detail, about what fays or faerylike beings *do*; the disagreements come in when they start speculating about what fays or faerylike beings *are*. When the same behaviors and habits are credited to fays in Ireland, ghosts in Brittany, fox spirits in Japan, Little Earths in the Puget Sound area, and so on, it may not be clear exactly what is behind all the legends, but it seems likely that something specific is responsible—something with the behaviors and habits recorded in each of these folklore traditions.

That "something" has been put into many different categories over the course of human history. In ancient times, beings of the faery type were often lumped together with gods and goddesses, producing complex pagan pantheons in which vast cosmic powers rub shoulders with minor entities whose authority extends to a few square miles of territory or a single medium-sized lake. This was certainly the case in Europe before the arrival of Christianity, where most deities seem to have been intensely local, with a single temple or shrine. Some of these minor deities show up in later faery lore—a point that has much to teach about the origins and nature of the fays.

## The Rise and Fall of Faery

The coming of Christianity put an end to this comfortable vagueness, at least in a formal sense. As the countries of early medieval Europe converted to Christianity, the word "god" and its equivalents in other languages was restricted to the deity of the new faith, and other terms had to be found for the minor powers of the old. Those other terms—*elf* and *fay* in English, *fee* in French, *sidhe* in Gaelic, *alf* in Norse, and so on—provide us with our first clear markers for the existence of the faery folk. In regions that embraced the other major monotheistic religion of the Piscean age, Islam, similar terms—*jinn* in Arabic, *peri* in Persian—were found for similar beings.

It's in the Middle Ages, then, that the faery folk become clearly visible in the historical record. Medieval monks and chroniclers include much in their writings that parallels later lore. The seventh-century scholar Isidore of Seville identified the *dusii*, or faery folk of Gaul, with the god Pan, but described them in terms any modern folklorist would recognize. Writing in the thirteenth century, Gervase of Tilbury discussed *portunes*, who are identical to the brownies or house fays of modern folklore, and recounted stories that still have living equivalents. Dozens of other writers added to the stock of written faery lore during the medieval period.

A curious note, however, enters the picture at this same time. While most of the medieval writers treat fays as a familiar presence, some speak of them in the past tense, as beings who were once common but could no longer be found. In Geoffrey Chaucer's *Canterbury Tales*, the Wife of Bath explains that faeries were common hundreds of years ago, but had been driven away by the prayers and blessings of Christian friars:

> For now the mighty charity and prayers
> Of limitours and other holy friars,
> That search through every land and
>    every stream,
> As thick as dust-motes in a bright
>    sunbeam,
> Blessing halls, chambers, kitchens and
>    fair bowers,

Towns and cities, castles and high
    towers,
Farmsteads and barns and stables,
    mews and dairies,
This is the reason there are now no
    faeries.

This first note of retreat was nearly drowned out in the busy clamor of medieval faery lore, but appeared more often as the Middle Ages drew to a close. Belief in fays became restricted to rural folk, and then to rural folk in isolated areas; literary images began to drown out traditional lore.

The fading away of faery did not go on unnoticed, and Chaucer's theory was far from the only one advanced. Some suggested that the fays had departed for reasons of their own, while others claimed that fays were dependent on the existence of unfarmed and unsettled land, and the spread of human towns and agriculture drove them away.

An account published in 1841 reported that one Sunday morning, nearly sixty years before, two children watched a long procession of dwarfish figures on small, shaggy ponies ride up a hillside past a small village near Glend Eathie, Scotland. One of the children finally asked the last of the riders, "What are ye, little mannie? And where are ye going?" The rider was said to have answered: "Not of the race of Adam. The People of Peace shall never more be seen in Scotland." Whether this story is authentic folklore or a literary creation—and it's worth noting that the "People of Peace" have indeed been seen since that time, in Scotland and elsewhere—it does a good job of capturing the flavor of faery's slow retreat.

With the birth of modern scientific thought came another theory, one claiming that fays had never existed in the first place. This last suggestion faced a hard road on the way to its present dominance, however. Through what historians awkwardly call the "early modern period" (from about 1550 to 1750), the reality of fays, like that of ghosts and other nonphysical beings, was a subject of fierce debate. Thoughtful people from many different viewpoints realized that the rise of the new scientific ideology threatened the elimination of every form of spiritual approach to the universe. They also saw that the best line of defense lay in evidence that nonphysical beings existed and had definite effects on the human world. The resulting struggle saw the unlikely spectacle of devout Christian theologians arguing for the reality of Faery, and amassing thick volumes of evidence for its existence.

Once scientific ideology had finished its rise to dominance, on the other hand, all such accounts were assigned to the category of ignorant superstition, and those who encountered fays and had the poor judgment to mention it were normally ridiculed into silence. Until the last half century or so, the exceptions to this rule took place in isolated areas such as rural Ireland and Scotland, where the new ways of thinking faced considerable resistance from a well-established folk culture. There, people continued to encounter fays (and other monstrous beings, of course), as people did elsewhere, but they went on to discuss the experience with their neighbors, as people in less isolated regions did not. There, in turn, collectors of folklore traveled to collect the beliefs and stories of "primitive" and "backwards" peoples, secure in the confidence that the scientific view of reality was the only one that mattered.

This is still the situation with regard to traditional fays, although the areas where classic faery lore remains a living current are even smaller now. Even in these areas, the encroachments of mass media and official education have forced it into a defensive attitude, and few people in such areas will discuss the subject with outsiders for fear of ridicule. At the same time, however, the entire subject has been profoundly reshaped by the emergence of a new manifestation of faery: one which is closely akin to the older traditions, but which has been recognized as a faery manifestation at all by very few.

## Fays and Aliens

This new manifestation is the UFO phenomenon—or, more precisely, certain parts of the complex social phenomenon that has grown up around the UFO sightings of the late 1940s and 1950s and their later equivalents. Many other things have contributed to that phenomenon, among them psychopathology, blatant fraud, the social impact of science fiction, and the poorly understood side effects of hypnosis. Furthermore, as we saw in the case of Val's "flying saucer sighting" discussed in the first part of this book, the assumptions and beliefs that have built up around UFOs can easily be a hindrance rather than a help to clarity.

One particular assumption has been a fruitful source of confusion: that the UFO phenomenon relates to beings from other planets. It's a very common assumption, of course, and the only problem with it is that it's not actually backed up by any real evidence. It was simply assumed by a few influential figures in the wake of the first UFO sightings, and has been too rarely questioned since that time.

Nor, it bears pointing out, is there any need to postulate travelers from other worlds in order to explain UFOs. One of the more important pieces of the puzzle, after all, is the fact that entities very similar to UFO "aliens" have been described in folklore since ancient times. These entities have been called fays, elves, and many other names, but they share certain critical characteristics with the occupants of modern UFOs:

## Appearance

While both fays and "aliens" apparently come in a wide array of sizes, shapes, and species, the most common forms of each are small (two to four feet tall) and humanoid, with large heads and eyes, small and thin bodies, and grayish or brownish skin. Several of the other common types of fays and aliens are closely similar as well; for example, the tall, blond, blue-eyed "Nordics" described by many witnesses bear a striking resemblance to the sidhe of Irish legend and the *lios-alfar* of the Norse sagas.

## Mental Powers

Fays and "aliens" alike have remarkable powers over the human mind; both seem to paralyze, confuse, delude, and mislead human beings more or less at will. People who report close encounters with "aliens" also describe distortions of consciousness, especially consciousness of time, that have very close parallels in faery folklore.

## Relation to an "Otherworld" of Uncertain Location

The location of Faery was a matter of much dispute in the Middle Ages, and it's worth noting that the locations proposed then have exact equivalents in modern UFO lore. The idea that fays come from another world entirely has its echo in modern UFO lore, although modern thought defines "other worlds" purely in terms of physical planets somewhere in space. Similarly, the subterranean bases of modern UFO lore are in some sense simply a reworking of the hollow hills and underworld kingdoms of faery tradition. Even the undersea kingdoms of Irish faery lore have their equivalent in the ideas of UFO researchers such as Ivan Sanderson, who pointed to accounts of UFOs coming out of or going into the sea, and proposed that some unknown group of intelligent beings has secret bases on the ocean floor.

## Relation to Human Reproduction

Some of the most surprising connections between fays and "aliens" fall under this heading. To judge from the alien-abduction accounts of the last two decades or so, UFO occupants seem to be obsessed with human reproduction; it's alleged that they are engaged in some sort of inter-species breeding program to improve their race. This has an extraordinary similarity to the changeling theme in faery lore—a consistent body of tales from many parts of the world, alleging that faeries kidnap human infants to strengthen their own faltering bloodlines. Faery lore also includes many accounts of adult humans who are abducted by fays or simply visited at night for what amount to breeding purposes.

### Relation to Flying Craft and Lights

Several different traditions within faery lore speak of "flying craft" in which fays can travel from place to place. The Tuatha de Danaan, the most important branch of the Irish faery folk, are said to have come to Ireland in flying ships, and the faery people of Magonia—an otherworld realm mentioned in records from early medieval France—had similar vehicles. Other accounts claim that many fays themselves can fly. Certain faery beings, in fact, are described in the lore as taking on the appearance of luminous flying spheres.

### Relation to Human Cultural Patterns

This is in many ways the strangest of the connections, and it has given rise to an enormous amount of dispute and some complicated theories. It's a common feature of faery lore and UFO lore alike that the entities under discussion seem to echo human ideas and cultural fashions to a remarkable degree. We've seen already that fays seem to take on the shape of whatever the local human culture expects, so that the same reality expresses itself as sidhe in Ireland, ghosts in Brittany, magical foxes in Japan, and so on. It's been noted more than once, on the "alien" side of the riddle, that disk-shaped spacecraft appeared first on the covers of science fiction pulp magazines in the mid-1930s, roughly a decade before Kenneth Arnold's epochal 1947 sighting, and that the technology used by UFO occupants in any given era bears a suspicious resemblance to that era's human ideas about what "advanced technology" would be like.

An awareness of points such as these has forced UFO researchers such as John Keel and Jacques Vallee to the conclusion that medieval fays and modern "aliens" are two expressions of the same underlying reality. Keel, Vallee, and other students of the UFO phenomenon have also pointed out that this reality seems to have been present here on Earth since the beginning of recorded history, and there is very little evidence supporting the idea that it comes from another planet. It seems likely, therefore, that the same entities that appear as elves in Europe, magical white foxes in Japan, and Little Earths around Puget Sound have taken on yet another guise to deal with the modern industrial world.

It deserves to be noted, though, that whatever the relation between fays and the UFO phenomenon, fays of the classic type are also seen in the modern world. At least one capably researched book (*Fairies: Real Encounters with Little People* by Janet Bord) has been devoted to eyewitness accounts of fays, many of them from the twentieth century. Most of the standard elements of faery folklore are well represented in these recent accounts. It seems clear that whatever reality is behind the traditional folklore of faery remains a living presence today.

## Making Sense (?) of Faery

The long history of interactions between fays and humans has given rise to an enormous amount of lore regarding fays and faylike beings. If the phenomena of faery were relatively straightforward, the sheer volume and complexity of this lore would long since have reduced every detail of faery to a matter of detailed knowledge. The phenomena of faery, however, are anything but straightforward, and as a result the amount that we actually know about these beings is quite limited.

Every statement one can make about faery risks falling afoul of what is, in many ways, the defining characteristic of the faery realm: the role of illusion, or (to give it its traditional name) *glamour*. In the words of Sir Walter Scott, glamour:

Could make a ladye seem a knight
A nutshell seem a gilded barge
A sheeling seem a palace large

And youth seem age and age seem youth
All was delusion, nought was truth.

In faery, as a rule, nothing is *ever* what it seems. Fays are masters of illusion; they appear to have an inborn power to distort human consciousness, and they use this power frequently, ruthlessly, and capriciously, in ways that usually do not make sense by the rules of human logic.

The power of glamour to confuse and delude the human mind is nearly limitless. "Nearly," however, is the relevant word. One consistent detail of faery lore from around the world is that no matter how convincing the illusion cast by glamour may be at first sight, there is always at least one telltale flaw in it, and if this can be spotted the whole illusion unravels.

The traditional lore of glamour actually makes a good deal of sense when approached from the standpoint of magical philosophy. From more common human perspectives, by contrast, it makes no sense at all, and this points to a central point about much that we know or think we know about fays. Dealings with the faery realm are always hedged about with complicated taboos, odd rituals, unexplained requirements, and equally unexplained prohibitions. What all this suggests is that in the creatures of faery we are actually dealing with entities who are not human, whose actions do not follow human logic or respond to human concerns. To encounter faery, even distantly, is to brush against the absolutely Other.

Within the limits imposed by faery glamour and the sheer incomprehensibility of the faery realm, though, there are some things that can be said. It seems clear, for example, that there are several different types of fay, and one way to begin sorting through the lore of faery is to look first of all at these.

## Archfays

Archfays such as the *daoine sidhe* of Ireland, the *peri* of Iran, and the "blonds" or "Nordics" of current UFO lore are sometimes pictured as the aristocracy of the faery realm, with a position of authority over other fays. In northwestern Europe, and in several other parts of the world, archfays are believed to inhabit certain hills and artificial mounds, and local folklore in some areas records the name of the ruling fay in any given hill and the extent of his or her realm. (In Ireland, where the fays appear to have a much more complex social structure than elsewhere, Fionn Bheara of the hill of Knockma in Galway is still said to reign as High King of the Irish faery folk.) Tradition has it that archfays belong to a complex, deeply hierarchical society with its own ancient customs and lore. Many are apparently literate—Robert Kirk, whose *Secret Commonwealth* is among our

best sources for Scottish faery lore, records that the archfays of Scotland possessed "pleasant toyish books," others "of involved abstruse sense, much like the Rosicrucian style," as well as "collected parcels of charms and counter-charms" in written form, which are used as a resource for magical practice. In Celtic countries, they have (or at least once had) their own breeds of horses, cattle, and hounds, and they themselves are usually described as tall, beautiful, and luminous beings dressed in rich garments.

Archfays seem to be active in only a few parts of the world nowadays—even their appearances in UFO-related contexts tend to be geographically limited—and records from the Middle Ages suggest that even then the period of their greatest power and activity was a matter of folk memory from the more or less distant past. Nor is it entirely certain that their pomp and panoply is more than a play of faery glamour, and they themselves may simply be fays of a more ordinary kind, playing an extended practical joke on us.

## Communal Fays

Communal fays such as the Cornish pigsies, Hawaiian *menehune*, Norwegian *huldrefolk*, and UFO "grays" sometimes seem to relate to the aristocratic archfays roughly as commoners do to the ruling classes in human societies, but are also found in regions where no trace of archfays appears in traditional folklore. These are the "generic" fays, elves, goblins, and dwarfs of countless legends, and the most common type of "aliens" in modern UFO accounts. In traditional faery lore, they are often to be found dwelling in low hills or mounds; it's an intriguing coincidence, if nothing more, that the classic "fairy hills" of Ireland and other European countries are often shaped like grounded flying saucers.

Communal fays seem to be responsible for a large proportion of those faery activities that affect human beings most directly. When a traveler at night is faery-led into a bog, when a child is stolen and replaced with a changeling, when a household is cursed or blessed as a result of some accidental interaction with the faery realm, it is most likely to be the work of communal fays.

The appearance of communal fays is familiar to most people nowadays. Smaller than human beings and much more delicately built, they tend to have comparatively large and often hairless heads, grayish or brownish skin, and large eyes. (The huge, featureless black eyes reported by a few modern UFO-related bestsellers are actually not that common even in UFO contacts, and unknown in faery lore; if they are more than an effect of glamour, they may represent anything from a variant type of entity to the faery equivalent of sunglasses.) Their clothing varies widely from one description

to another, but tends to imitate local human types closely.

## House Fays

House fays such as the British brownie, the Russian *domovoi*, and the Norwegian *nisse* have adapted to the presence of human beings much more thoroughly than most other types. The typical house fay of folklore either lives inside a human dwelling or spends the daylight hours sleeping in the wilderness nearby. It shares to some extent in the fortunes of the human residents, and not uncommonly helps out with the housekeeping like a sort of benevolent poltergeist, in return for regular offerings of food and drink. Like most fays, house fays have no tolerance for laziness and dishonesty, and will annoy those who fail to live up to their standards in various ways—pounding on walls at night, making messes in the house, or pinching the offenders black and blue when they try to sleep. Those who earn their respect, though, can count not only on chores done by night, but also on good luck of all kinds.

In many cases, house fays are heard rather than seen, and the knocking, bumping, and tapping noises they tend to make as they go about their business have much to do with the old description of monsters as "things that go bump in the night." Those that are seen by human beings are usually described as small, brown (thus the term "brownie"), wrinkled figures; some traditions give them the large head and spindly body of communal fays, while others hold for something closer to human proportions. They are sometimes naked, sometimes clad in plain cloth garments. The naked sort should never be given clothes, for this is a traditional way to get rid of one; a bowl of milk left beside the hearth, on the other hand, is a common way to ensure good relations with a house fay.

Faery beings of the house-fay type can also apparently exist in other environments. In the days when ships were still crafted of wood and powered by the wind, shipborne fays such as the Baltic *klabautermann* ("knocking-man") played an important part in sailors' lore. The same sort of creature even made a brief appearance in an aerial setting, in the form of gremlins who were said to inhabit early airplanes. (Curiously, both klabautermannen and gremlins seem to have disappeared when their respective vehicles came to be made of metal rather than wood and natural fibers.)

House fays seem to have been very common in earlier times—certainly reports from rural Britain in the eighteenth century claim that in isolated areas, a good proportion of households had one—but the coming of modern mechanized agriculture seems to have driven them away. They apparently have no close equivalents in modern UFO folklore and experience.

## Solitary Fays

Solitary fays such as the Scottish *urisk* and the Manx *fenodyree* are similar to house fays, except that they lack the latter's defining habit of sharing space with humans. They live alone in wilderness settings, and some have a much less friendly attitude toward human beings than do house fays. Their dealings with lone travelers and other human beings who intrude on their territory are the subject of many legends.

In the old lore, solitary fays are often covered with a thick coat of hair. This and some of their other habits suggest a connection with another of the unexplained presences that haunt the shadowy places of the modern world.

The sasquatch, as mentioned earlier, is probably an undiscovered variety of primate, not a monster in the sense used in this book. The same is likely true of its close cousins across the Bering Straits in eastern Asia: the *yeti* or "abominable snowman" of the Himalayas, the *almas* of Mongolia, and similar creatures reported from western China and Siberia. On the other hand, there are many large, hairy, roughly humanoid entities reported by witnesses that seem to have nothing in common with the sasquatch and its kin. Members of the anomaly research community, whose sense of humor is among its greatest assets, have taken to calling these entities by the useful acronym BHM—"big hairy monster."

94

The differences between sasquatches and BHMs are easy to spot. First, Bigfoot and its kin are nearly always encountered in the wilderness, in a few specific geographical areas. BHMs, by contrast, routinely turn up in heavily settled areas that lack the resources to support a large primate. According to one tally, BHMs have been reported from every state in the Union except Rhode Island, and many reports come in from urban and suburban locations.

Second, the sasquatch is a fairly well-defined type of creature, an upright ape of roughly human proportions, averaging six to seven feet tall in adult specimens, with short brown or blackish hair covering all of its body except the face and palms, which are black. Its feet are a good deal larger and somewhat flatter than those of human beings, but have the same shape and structure, with five toes. BHMs, on the other hand, range from three to fifteen feet in height, with hair of any length and almost any color imaginable, and its tracks show anything from two to six toes. BHMs have been reported with long claws, no heads, webbed feet, protruding fangs, and other unlikely features. A significant number have eyes that glow red from within—not simply reflecting light, as a cat's eyes do, but shining even when there is no other light source.

Third, the sasquatch, like most wild animals, avoids human beings under most circumstances. BHMs do not; they routinely approach human beings, and are often reported peering in windows, banging on the walls of houses, and walking up to parked cars. While sasquatches have been reported to throw rocks and sticks at people and cars, BHMs are typically much more aggressive and will attack people, cars, and buildings in a variety of ways.

Fourth, both the sasquatch and the BHM have distinctive odors. There, however, the similarity ends. The sasquatch smells, reasonably enough, like a large, smelly, unwashed animal. The odor associated with BHM encounters is nothing so simple. It's astonishingly awful—one witness described it as smelling like "burning rubbish and the sweat of a hundred high-school football teams," while others have likened it to a rotting corpse. The sasquatch's odor departs when it does, while in many BHM cases the stench lingers afterwards for an unusually long time.

Last, sasquatches act like ordinary animals, if relatively intelligent ones. (Native traditions in the Pacific Northwest credit them with complex societies and magical powers, but also do the same with bears, salmon, and other living creatures.) BHMs, on the other hand, routinely behave like nonphysical beings. Examples could be listed by the page; a look through the literature on the subject will provide a dizzying array of cases. BHMs routinely appear and disappear suddenly, and show other signs of less-than-physical presence. BHM tracks often begin or end suddenly, as though the creature had materialized or dematerialized on the spot. Some are slightly transparent; most are invulnerable to bullets—although no one, to my knowledge, has tried silver bullets.

### Exotics

Beyond the basic types just mentioned, faery lore in many cultures describes what might best be called *exotics*—bizarre creatures that appear once, or in a very restricted region, and have no clear relation to any other type of fay. An example from the old lore is the *Nuckelavee*, a Scottish horror said to look like a centaur with one eye in the middle of its forehead. An added detail in the traditional accounts is that the Nuckelavee has no skin, so that its muscles, veins, and organs are visible to those who encounter it.

The burgeoning lore of the UFO phenomenon has plenty of similarly weird examples. What is one to make, for example, of the bizarre creature sighted in November of 1974 by several different witnesses in the vicinity of Bald Mountain, southeast of Tacoma, Washington? One such witness—Ernest Smith, a grocer from Seattle who was hunting in the area—reported that he was scanning a bluff with binoculars when the creature came into view. According to his description, it was roughly horse-shaped, but with four long tentacles in place of the legs, and a head shaped like a football with an antenna-like prong sticking up from the top end. It was surrounded by a greenish glow. Smith was carrying a rifle, but did not dare shoot at the creature for fear of attracting its attention. Several days previously, it may be worth noting, a flying object of unknown type had been seen to crash in the area.

It's all but impossible to tell how these baffling beings fit into the picture. They may simply be the illusory creations of faery glamour; they may be fays of variant types; they may be beings of some other sort altogether, classified with fays through the common human habit of putting everything incomprehensible together in a single pot. We simply don't know.

## The Nature of Faery

Of the behavior of all these various types of fays in their own natural context—whatever that may be—we know effectively nothing. Traditional folklore in the Middle Ages tended to describe faery society in the image of the human society of the time, with kings, feudal lords, and the like; modern UFO folklore does much the same thing in a different social setting, mapping various ideas about spaceship crews and galactic federations onto the inkblot patterns of faery glamour. None of this is likely to be anything more than a combination of human projections and faery illusion.

Equally uncertain, although just possibly concealing scraps of relevant information, are the many speculations about what fays are and how they relate to the universe as known by human beings. A good many of these have their roots in the attempt to fit fays in somehow to the accepted biblical ideas of creation; thus, for example, one reads in some sources that faery creatures were angels who remained neutral at the time of Satan's rebellion; too good for Hell but not good enough for Heaven, they were bound to dwell on the Earth until Judgment Day. This is ingenious but offers little of interest to anyone but a biblical literalist.

Equally detailed, although possibly worth more attention, are the descriptions and analyses of fays from the Renaissance, the last period in Western history when such things were taken seriously by scholars. *The Secret Commonwealth* by Robert Kirk, originally written around 1690, is one of the best examples of the type, but works by Jerome Cardan, Paracelsus, and other authors of the same period are also well worth consulting.

What these writers have to say is of some interest, and (as we'll see) relates closely to modern magical ideas about the faery realm. According to Kirk, for example, fays are another class of intelligent being inhab-

iting our world. Their bodies are formed of air or subtle vapors, and can be condensed to near-solidity or diffused into complete intangibility at will. They live underground, as their bodies can pass through solid matter, and are divided into different political and cultural groups. This same understanding of faery can be found in many other sources of the same period, though rarely in so detailed a form.

Some other, distinctly strange theories relate fays to tribal cultures displaced by later and more heavily armed peoples. In Scotland, for example, one common term for a fay was "Pecht," which is simply the Scots pronunciation of the word Pict, the name of the ancient "painted people" who inhabited Scotland before the Scots themselves arrived there. Similarly, the *menehune* of Hawaii—communal fays of the classic variety—are said by the native people to be descendants of an earlier wave of Polynesian settlers, displaced by the ancestors of the present Hawaiians and driven into the mountains and forests.

What truth there may be in these latter speculations is hard to say. An earlier generation of folklore scholars took the idea with great seriousness, and pointed out various ways in which traditional faery lore meshes with the realities that would be faced by small tribal groups surviving on such terms. It's certainly possible that faery lore includes memories of such groups, and just possible that something stranger and more complex is involved. As with so much of faery, it's all but impossible to be sure.

What we can speak of with a certain degree of sureness are the ways that faery activities have traditionally affected human beings. Human-fay interactions follow complex patterns, but there are common threads to be found throughout the world's faery lore, and some of these can be traced here.

One of the more interesting of these threads is the tradition of ordinary, neighborly relations between humans and fays. In Scottish folklore, for example, fays and humans living in close proximity would routinely borrow kettles and other large cooking utensils from each other, just as people in peasant societies do the world over. Fays were said to seek out human midwives to assist at faery births, while human farmers would sometimes hire fays to help with the reaping and threshing of grain at harvest time.

Such interactions always held the risk of danger. It's clear that even in societies that lived with fays on a daily basis, people were at least a little afraid of their faery neighbors. The habit of always referring to faery beings by a flattering nickname—"the Fair Folk," "the Gentry," "the People of Peace," and so on—has its roots in this fear.

Nonetheless, fays could be capable of a good deal of generosity as well, if folklore is to be believed. The image of the "fairy godmother" from childrens' stories is a distortion of a far older and more powerful figure, the guardian spirit, angel, or divinity; still, there are a good many accounts of fays providing unexpected help to human beings in need. Strange though their thinking patterns seem to us, fays (or at least some fays) do seem to have some sense of justice or rightness, and will act accordingly if the opportunity presents itself.

The moral notions of fays, on the other hand, apparently don't keep them from playing practical jokes on human beings whenever it strikes their fancy. Tales of such jokes make up a large percentage of faery lore in many societies.

Human-fay interactions attested in faery lore go in more intimate directions as well. Sexual relations between humans and fays are a universal feature of faery traditions, and also appear in current UFO-related accounts. Relationships of this sort span the full range, from brief encounters to lifelong pairings, and in a significant number of accounts, children are said to result from these liaisons. Under some circumstances, however, sexual contact with fays can apparently be dangerous for the human partner. Fays are capable of a form of sexual vampirism, and there are many accounts of people wasting away and dying as a result of such practices.

## Faery Abductions

A final, more hostile pattern of human-fay interactions has to do with the faery habit of abducting human beings. This is another constant theme in the old lore, and traditional magic in many countries includes ritual methods for preventing such abductions, as well as for forcing the fays to return a captive to the human world. Some humans went willingly into the faery realm—young men, in particular, might be lured there by the seductions of a beautiful fay—while others were taken by trickery, glamour, or force.

Once in the realm of Faery, escape was difficult at best. In many accounts the only way for a human captive to return to the ordinary world was for some other person to perform a specific set of ritual acts, which would force the fays to return their prisoner unharmed. If the ritual injunctions were not followed to the letter, any hope of rescue was lost. In other sources, the fays themselves decided to send one of their captives back, for reasons of their own.

According to lore from around the world, people who were taken by the fays and then returned often experienced drastic distortions in their relation to time—similar to the "missing time" phenomenon reported by many UFO contactees, but on a considerably larger scale. Some of the accounts sound uncomfortably close to the sort of relativistic time dilation associated with travel near the speed of light.

The targets for abduction vary somewhat in the folklore of different cultures, but there are common themes. Among the most frequent of these have to do with reproduction, as the fays were often said to be a dwindling and sickly race in need of new blood. Young men and women might be abducted for these reasons.

Human infants were considered to be at particularly high risk for abduction. Glamour, according to the accounts, would be used to make a wizened fay or a lump of wood resemble the stolen child; the replica might "die" and be buried after a short time, or it might remain in the human family as a changeling, dwarfish and sickly but always ravenously hungry. Meanwhile, the infant would be brought up among the fays and mate with them when it reached sexual maturity. Such children were often held to have become fays themselves, and in fact many of those abducted by fays were believed to lose their humanity in some sense, becoming part of the faery realm.

These legends, while ancient, have their exact equivalents in more current manifestations of faery. Much of the UFO furor of the last two and a half decades has revolved around claims that "aliens" are abducting human beings, performing painful medical procedures on them, and extracting semen and ova samples. Several abductees and authors have claimed that this last process is part of a breeding program intended to create human-alien hybrids, with the goal of bringing new genetic vigor into the bloodlines of a dying race.

There are a good many loose ends and unanswered questions in all of this modern UFO folklore, of course, and the careless use of hypnosis to retrieve "repressed memories" of alien abduction is also a major concern—"memories" brought out by means of hypnotic trance, however real they seem to the person experiencing them, have so poor a record as a way of recovering factual information that nowadays American courts will not admit them as testimony. The technology, if that is the right word for it, used by fays to abduct human children also differs sharply from the sort apparently used by modern "aliens." Still, the similarities between current alien-abduction claims and the lore surrounding changelings are unnerving, and it seems likely that both tie into the elusive reality underlying faery and UFO legends alike.

It's worth noting, finally, that at least in traditional faery lore, human beings are by no means powerless against the activities and illusions of fays. The most potent tool in the human arsenal is iron, which repels fays and can kill them if it is brought suddenly into contact with their bodies.

Another important protective method consists of the use of magical and religious rituals. It's worth noting that most religious traditions have or had effective ritual methods for controlling and banishing fays (as well as other paraphysical beings), but in many cases these have been allowed to fall into abeyance in modern times. There are few Christian clergy, certainly, who could match the fay-dispelling activities of Chaucer's "limitours and other holy friars" these days; it's just possible that the neglect of these once-potent formulae has something to do with the explosive modern reemergence of faery in the form of the UFO phenomenon.

Other protections exist as well, and were much used in earlier times. Most fays cannot cross running water, and they can be driven off by certain herbs and trees, especially those that magicians traditionally relate to the sun. Sunlight itself is a source of risk for many types of fay, and will either kill them or turn them to stone. Certain odd little tricks will also hamper their activities: turning a garment inside out, placing one's shoes with the toes pointing away from the bed, or fastening small bells to one's garments are all said to serve as effective protection.

## Inhabitants of the Etheric

Puzzling though fays may be, we are not entirely without ways of making sense of their actions and powers. We can begin making sense of faery by looking again at the etheric level of existence. While it's misleading to think of the etheric level as some sort of "other dimension" in science-fiction terms—it surrounds us constantly, and can be perceived directly by anyone willing to learn and practice relatively simple exercises—it is, to some extent, a realm of its own. It has its own "landscape," for example, made up of different densities and qualities of etheric substance, partly related to the physical landscape but partly independent of it.

It also has its own inhabitants: beings who exist on every level of reality except the physical one. Such beings have their consciousness focused on the etheric level, just as ours is normally focused on the physical one. There are many different kinds of etheric entity; the wild diversity of physical life on Earth is matched by an equal richness on the etheric level.

Of the inhabitants of the etheric level, the beings we've called fays fill roughly the same position that human beings hold in the physical world. They, like we, use languages and tools, are capable of abstract thought, and shape their behavior on the basis of learned cultural ideas rather than purely that of inherited instincts. On the other hand, all of these things are shaped by the etheric level rather than the physical one. Etheric tools are unlike physical ones;

languages expressed by projecting thought patterns through the ether differ in profound ways from languages expressed by sound vibrations in air or colored marks on solid paper; an environment of shifting etheric energies calls for different kinds of intelligence from an environment of physical solids, liquids, and gases.

The difference in levels has some odd consequences, which make sense only if the basic ideas of magic are kept in mind. Since we exist on the etheric level just as much as fays do, they can perceive our etheric bodies clearly, in much the same way that we perceive physical objects. Our feelings and thoughts also tend to show up clearly on the etheric level, as colors and patterns in the aura, and so their etheric perceptions allow fays to read human minds and hearts with a fair degree of accuracy. Since fays don't function on the physical level, though, they don't perceive our physical forms directly, and we normally don't perceive them at all.

The lopsided relation between human physical senses and faery etheric ones is at the root of glamour. Our minds are used to perceiving physical things, not etheric ones. When fays wish to interact with humans, they normally have to create the image of a physical form and project it onto what magicians call the Sphere of Sensation, the aspect of the etheric body that reflects perceptions and sensations up into the higher levels of the self. Since they have little knowledge of the physical world, their images typically come from the most readily available source: our own thoughts and imaginings, which are present in the Sphere of Sensation as well.

This is why human ideas about fays (or "aliens") are so often reflected back to us in the form of actual experiences; the fays are real, but the shapes they take when they appear to us are borrowed from our own imaginations. These forms are simply tools they use to interact with us, and have nothing to do with their actual forms; in their own realm, seen with the etheric senses, they resemble shimmering spheres or ovoids of multicolored light.

On the other hand, if we develop our etheric senses and our self-mastery of awareness through magical training, we can learn to meet them directly on their own level, and perceive them as clearly as they perceive us. To a very real sense, the power of glamour is a function of human weakness rather than faery strength. It is because we are so easily confused and distracted by everything around us that fays find it so easy to do a little confusing and distracting of their own.

The leprechaun, according to legend, can be forced to yield up its treasure if you can keep watching it without letting your attention wander for so much as a moment. This has so much in common with experiences in meditation that Zen masters in America use it as a metaphor for meditative practice. There's an important lesson here: glamour is hardly limited to the realm of faery. Most human beings live most of their lives under its spell, chasing after treasures that—like the golden coins in countless faery tales— turn to dried leaves the moment one looks away.

The etheric nature of faery creatures also goes a long way to explain why folklore traditions about fays and ghosts have so often become deeply tangled, since fays and ghosts are both etheric entities. It's quite possible that in earlier times, human souls who failed to pass through the Second Death might have become part of the complex ecosystem of etheric entities that formed the faery realm.

Certainly the role of the human etheric body in the death process explains a great many of the features of legends about faery abductions. The difference between those abductees who were able to return and those who could not was simply that the latter were dead, in human terms; their physical bodies had been taken from them. (Some legends claim that food offered by faeries was often poisonous toadstools under a glamour; this suggests one way in which this could have been managed.) Stolen infants, similarly, could be extracted not only from their cribs but from their physical bodies as well; while the abandoned body would normally have died after a short time, it might also be taken over by another entity—perhaps a fay, perhaps some other astral or etheric being—and turned into a fair approximation of the changelings of legend.

Equally, the traditions of sexual contact between humans and fays can be understood from an etheric perspective; as magicians have been pointing out for a long time, sex is much more an etheric phenomenon than a physical one. A being able to stimulate the etheric channels of sexual energy in the human body directly, instead of having to rely on the indirect means of friction and nerve stimulation, could easily create the sort of feverish eroticism one finds in the faery lore. Reproduction is a more complex matter—it seems unlikely that fay-human intercourse could ever have produced physical pregnancies and births, at least—but in the absence of clearer knowledge, it's hard to be sure.

Traditional means of protection against faery beings, finally, also have a clear etheric basis. Those human beings who have not awakened their inner senses and powers can do very little to affect a fay directly or indirectly, except by using the etheric effects of certain kinds of physical matter. Iron, which causes the explosive collapse of etheric patterns, and certain volatile plant compounds, which disperse or erase them, are among the few available options.

Human beings who know how to perceive and shape the etheric realm, on the other hand, can interact with fays directly on their own ground.

Unfortunately, human beings have had at least one powerful influence on the faery realm, and it has not been for the better. Modern approaches to agriculture, industry, and community design have had more impacts on the environment than most human beings ever perceive. Our civilization has defaced the countryside and the wilderness, not only in a physical sense, but on the etheric level as well. Human visionaries for more than two hundred years have been reporting with a good deal of horror on the etheric miasma that surrounds the sprawling, smoky cities of the industrial world.

It's not surprising, then, that the old, almost friendly relations between humans and fays described in folklore have fallen into abeyance over nearly all of the world. If our cultures can bring themselves into a wiser relationship with the natural world, it's possible that better relations can be restored, but that remains to be seen.

## Identifying Fays

The likelihood of encountering faery activity may vary widely depending on a dizzying assortment of factors—the location, the time of day and year, the presence of herbs and trees that are believed to attract or repel faery creatures, and so on. The fays of different areas and types also have habits and customs of their own, which can and should be studied in books on faery and UFO lore. Researchers studying the UFO phenomenon have long noted the existence of "flaps" or "waves," in which many sightings occur close together in a particular area; there are also "windows," regions where many sightings and waves tend to occur, while other regions nearby may report none for years on end. It's a complex situation, and in the absence of detailed information about the habits and intentions of the entities involved, it's unlikely to get simpler anytime soon.

There have nonetheless been plenty of faery sightings, both of the modern UFO-related type and of more traditional forms, in the developed world in recent years. The student of monster lore should always be aware of the possibility that fays are active whenever people begin reporting the presence and actions of entities that seem to violate our assumptions about the laws of nature.

## Other Beings and Phenomena that Can Be Mistaken for a Fay Include These:

### Ghosts

As mentioned above, fays and ghosts share a basis on the etheric level, and it's often hard to tell them apart. See Ghosts, pp. 53–69.

### Spirits

While there are clear differences between spirits as such, which are entities of the lower astral, and fays, which are etheric, it sometimes takes careful attention to detail to tell them apart. It's also worth remembering that entities contacted by trance mediumship, channeling, automatic writing, and similar methods are normally spirits, whether they call themselves angels, elves, seventh-density enlightened masters, or starship captains from Zeta Reticuli. See Spirits, pp. 131–144.

### Human Beings

The legendary connections between some types of fays and human tribes forced into a secretive existence through invasion and conquest should remind us that human beings can take on many of the traditional attributes of fays. These days, a half-seen figure moving noiselessly through the woods is more likely to be a forest-dwelling eccentric or a skilled outdoorsman than a fay. There is currently an entire subculture of people who have taken the back-to-the-land movement to its logical extreme, and live a neoprimitive lifestyle in wilderness areas all over North America, supporting themselves by hunting, gathering, and cultivating small, hard-to-notice patches of native food crops. Like fays, they have little interest in dealing with members of the dominant human culture. Sites of apparent faery activity should always be carefully examined for signs that ordinary, incarnate human beings are involved.

## *Artifacts of Hypnosis*

Any claim that fays (or "aliens") have interacted with human beings should be regarded with grave suspicion if the only evidence for the claim is a set of "repressed memories" brought out under hypnosis. As mentioned above, hypnotic regression is an extremely uncertain method of getting at facts, and there's good evidence suggesting that "memories" brought into awareness by this means tend to include large doses of fantasy, media imagery, and dream content, to say nothing of the results of leading questions and distortions introduced by incompetent or unscrupulous hypnotherapists. Until further research has sorted out the degree of reliance that can be placed on hypnotically recovered information, it's probably best to advise witnesses to monstrous phenomena not to be hypnotized, and to treat the testimony of anyone who has been hypnotized about a monster-related incident as unreliable unless it can be substantiated by some other means.

## *Human Fakery*

There is also, as with monster reports of every kind, a certain fraction of reported "fairy" or "alien" contacts that are simple (or not so simple) fakes. The popularity of UFO imagery over the last several decades has given rise to a particularly robust crop of hoaxes, ranging all the way from tall tales and poorly faked saucer photos to sophisticated attempts (like the bizarre UMMO hoax of the 1980s) to produce the illusion of an alien presence in Earth's skies.

The crop circle phenomenon of the last decade or so is an example of just how complex and many-layered this can become. Whatever the sources of the first circles—a question that may never be settled at this point—the crop circles of southwest England have become the center of an astonishing three-ring circus of self-proclaimed experts, New Age prophets, and promoters with an eye for the main chance. Behind it all lies several different groups of people for whom creating circles has become a form of performance art and a protest against the drabness of modern life. Aiding and abetting the circle-makers are local farmers, who have long since learned that a modest entrance fee from each visitor will earn them many times the value of the damaged crops. Fueling the whole frenzy is a steady flow of tourists with money to spend. It's quite a scene, and even though the details of the hoax have long since seen print, it's unlikely to die down very soon.

Few fay-related hoaxes reach this level of complexity, of course, but the canny monster investigator should remember that matters can sometimes go this far, given favorable circumstances and a strong financial incentive.

## The Signs that Point to an Actual Case of Faery Activity Are These:

- One or more entities corresponding either to local faery lore or to modern UFO lore are encountered by human beings;

- The entity behaves in ways that do not correspond with the normal capabilities of incarnate human beings or of physical matter (for example, it changes shape or vanishes into thin air), but relate closely to the powers attributed to fays in folklore;

- The entity can pass readily through solid matter, and if it is struck with a nonmetallic object, or a metal (such as lead) that does not absorb etheric charges effectively, this has no apparent effect on it;

- However, the entity avoids iron, running water, and other etheric barriers.

- Other psychological, criminological, and medical explanations have been effectively ruled out.

All of these signs, or as many of them as can be safely put to the test, should be pres-ent in order to justify a tentative diagnosis of faery activity.

## Dealing with Faery

By all accounts, most types of fay have become extremely shy of human beings in recent centuries, and even those that do deal with us regularly seem to have become far more cautious than in former times. The wary nocturnal visits of the communal fays responsible for most UFO-related encounters are worlds away from the proud pageantry of the "trooping faeries" of past centuries, who were said to ride through the countryside at night with hawks at their wrists and hounds at their sides. This shyness seems quite reasonable, all things considered, but it makes human interactions with faery folk much more complex—and often much briefer—than the folklore of the past would suggest.

If you are already in the midst of an interaction with fays, these points may seem rather academic. Still, the traditional methods of protection against faery creatures are readily available, and may be supplemented with the techniques included in Part IV of this book. I have not myself had the opportunity to test out the effect of a knife under the pillow, or a spray of St. John's Wort over the window, on a case of "alien" abduction; the results of such an experiment would be well worth knowing.

The various modern reinterpretations of faery entities, by turns sticky-sweet and idealized, have given rise to a whole range of false expectations about faery, and these are a potential source of trouble as well. There are books on the occult and New Age market today that treat fays as though they were sugar-plum fairies from a children's book, eager to cater to the whims and selfish demands of human beings. Nothing could be further from the truth. The people of Faery have no particular reason to love us or wish us well, and many good reasons to fear us, to mistrust us, and even to hate us.

Any direct dealing with faery entities thus risks serious dangers. The arrogant, the ignorant, and the greedy are most likely to come to grief when dealing with the faery realm, but even the best intentions are no guarantee of safety. The unpredictability of fays is legendary all over the world.

For this reason, although there are traditional magical methods for making contact with the faery realm and its inhabitants, none of them will be given here. If you wish to deal with fays directly, you will need to do the necessary research yourself. It's wise to remember, even so, that there will always be a price for such contacts—and they, not you, will decide what the price will be.

Much of the world's faery lore, on the other hand, takes a much safer tack, and deals with these beings in an indirect way. The country housewife who leaves milk and bread for the brownies, the farmer who leaves a corner of one field unharvested as an offering to the Fair Folk, or the landowner who plants a hawthorn tree in the hope of receiving good luck from the elves, are all following this approach. Those who live in North America should recall that a twist or small bag of tobacco is a traditional offering to such beings; local folklore, which can be researched in the anthropology section of libraries or learned by way of respectful contacts with local native peoples, can be of great help in learning the terms on which mutually helpful dealings with faery creatures can be carried out.

Whatever their attitudes toward human beings in general, the faery folk will help those who help them, and if they are treated with respect and honesty they have powerful blessings to offer. There are various magical techniques that can be used to foster this sort of productive relationship, but an attitude of caring for the natural world—one that expresses itself in action, not merely in words—will do at least as much in this direction as any more obviously magical process.

# MERMAIDS

Perhaps no uncanny creature deserves the title "monster" less, at least in the modern sense of the word, than the mermaid. Except for a traditional habit of raising storms with her singing, and occasional claims that she seduces and drowns hapless sailors, she seems to be among the most harmless of beings, and by all accounts she is among the loveliest as well. Only in the older sense of the word can the mermaid be called a monster at all—but in that sense the word fits well: the mermaid has much to reveal.

This chapter might more accurately be titled Merfolk, since both folklore and the surprisingly frequent eyewitness accounts of these creatures include mermen as well as mermaids. Still, since at least the Middle Ages, the female of the species has always been the more prominent, and male merfolk play only a limited role in the legends. At the risk of being accused of sexism, then, this chapter will principally discuss mermaids, bringing in mermen or merfolk in general only when the sources require it.

Like most other monstrous beings, mermaids and mermen have a generic image in modern culture, although for a change this actually isn't too far from eyewitness descriptions. Like most other monstrous beings, equally, they have been the subject of some very questionable claims on the part of would-be debunkers since the Scientific Revolution. For well over a century now, the standard scientific explanation for mermaid sightings—repeated in countless books and articles—has been that a manatee or dugong has been seen and mistaken for a mermaid.

There are few better examples of an "explanation" that actually explains nothing. Dugongs and manatees, marine mammals also known as "sea cows," are blubbery, whiskered creatures with walrus-like faces and paddle-shaped flippers. Anyone who could mistake the upper half of one for a human female would have to be dead drunk, to say the least, and neither species of sea cow sings or climbs onto rocks near the shore—two things mermaids are consistently reported as doing.

There is also a small problem with geography. Dugongs inhabit shallow waters along the coasts of the Indian Ocean; manatees are found around the Gulf of Mexico and in the Congo River; a (probably) extinct species, Steller's sea cow, lived in the North Pacific around the Aleutian Islands. None of them are found in the waters of the North Atlantic, where the majority of mermaid sightings have been recorded in the last few centuries.

It may come as a surprise to learn that the mermaid, one of those creatures that seems most obviously imaginary, has been sighted many times by sober observers familiar with the sea and its inhabitants. Still, even a quick glance over the history of mermaid lore turns up plenty of examples. On October 29, 1811, for example, one

John McIsaac gave sworn testimony to Duncan Campbell, Sheriff-Substitute of the Kintyre district, that he had seen a mermaid while walking along the beach near Campbeltown, Scotland. He gave a detailed description of the mermaid, who had red hair, skin white above the waist and brindled reddish-gray below, and who was sitting on a rock above the water. McIsaac had watched the mermaid for some time, then seen her dive into the water. Two clergymen and a justice of the peace testified that McIsaac was considered to be a sober, steady man and a reliable witness. Three days later, Sheriff-Substitute Campbell received a deposition from another witness, one Katherine Loynachan, who had seen an identical mermaid sunning herself on the rocks in the same area one week before.

These Scottish mermaid accounts can be multiplied almost endlessly. In 1809, one William Munro, a schoolteacher from Thurso in Caithness, reported sighting a mermaid on a rock near Sandside Head; in 1814, two fishermen in a small boat off Port Gordon encountered two, merman and mermaid; in 1949, fishermen reported seeing merfolk several times off Cape More, and the list goes on.

And what are we to make of the entry in the log of Henry Hudson's second voyage, dated June 15, 1608? The entry starts out as any other on that voyage: clear sunshine, wind from the east, latitude at noon 75 degrees 7 minutes, distance traveled 13 leagues. Then:

> This morning, one of our companie looking over boord saw a Mermaid, and calling up some of the companie to see her, one more came up, and by that time shee was come close to the ship's side, looking earnestly on the men: a little after, a Sea [i.e., a large wave] came and overturned her: From the Navill upward, her backe and breasts were like a womans (as they say that saw her) her body as big as one of us; her skin very white; and long haire hanging down behinde, of colour blacke; in her going downe they saw her tayle, which was like the tayle of a Porposse, and speckled like a Macrell. Their names that saw her were Thomas Hilles and Robert Raynar (Benwell and Waugh, p. 95).

Whatever Hilles and Raynar saw, it was not a dugong or a manatee, for Hudson's voyage was in the North Atlantic, in search of the Northwest Passage. Suggesting that it was a seal or a walrus strains the imagination just as far; Hudson's crew was made up of experienced mariners familiar with the North Atlantic and all its moods, men about as likely to mistake a walrus for a mermaid as to mistake a seagull for a fire-breathing dragon. Was the entire account a deliberate lie made up by the two men? Possibly, but few sailors are fool enough to risk their jobs and their reputations by telling lies about things seen on watch. If Hilles and Rayner had reported any other kind of marine life, it's worth noting, their report would be accepted as valid evidence by modern scholars without a second thought.

## Mermaid Legendry and Lore

The traditional lore concerning mermaids and mermen is fairly straightforward. By all accounts, merfolk live in the sea much as fishes do, with no particular need to return to land, although they are able to spend short periods out of the water. Most credit them with the fishtail standard in modern depictions; merfolk who have a tail usually have tailfins extending from side to side—like those of dolphins, whales, and other marine mammals—rather than up and down, like those of fish. Not all merfolk correspond to this classic image, though; a significant minority look exactly like human beings but live in the sea.

A common theme in mermaid lore is the connection between mermaids and storms. According to many accounts, mermaids either cause storms or predict them by singing—in fact, there was a spirited debate among scholars in the Middle Ages concerning whether mermaids actually had the power to raise storms, or whether their singing before a storm was simply a result of keen perception of oncoming weather. The debate was never conclusively settled, but certainly mariners all over the North Atlantic knew that if any member of the crew heard a mermaid singing, it was time to put into port as soon as possible.

Human interactions with merfolk, according to folklore, tend to be brief and at a distance. Some mermaid legends speak of sexual relations between humans and merfolk, parallel to the legends of matings between humans and fays, and these provide an important clue to the nature of merfolk generally.

There are few risks in dealing with merfolk. As monsters go, mermaids are fairly harmless. In a few parts of the world, folklore suggests otherwise—for example, in the Hebrides, local mermen have a nasty reputation as shipwreckers—but this is rare, and seems to relate to a history of soured relations between merfolk and the local human community.

Some dispute surrounds the legends, found in some sources and not in others, that sailors who hear a mermaid's song will throw themselves into the water and drown. There's good reason to believe that this detail entered the lore by way of a confusion between mermaids and the sirens of classical legend, originally an entirely different category of monster. On the other hand, the phenomenon itself is apparently

a real one. In 1973, after a number of cases of this kind, captains of the fishing fleet working the seas south of Spitzbergen brought an English exorcist to the area to banish the entities responsible. There is no particular reason to think, though, that mermaids were involved.

Accounts concur, though, that trying to harm a mermaid or merman can be a very dangerous habit. The connection between mermaids and storms is relevant here, for violence against a mermaid is said to bring on a storm of terrible intensity, strong enough to sink ships and wreck seaside buildings.

The great Norwegian historian Olaus Magnus, speaking of mermaids, comments as follows:

> Yea, this I adde from the faithfull assertions of the Norway fishers, that when such [merfolk] are taken, if they be not presently let go again, there ariseth such a fierce tempest [ . . . ] that a man would thinke the verie heavens were falling, and the vaulted roofe of the world running to ruine; insomuch that the fishermen have much ado to escape with their lives; whereupon they confirmed it as a law amongst them that if any chanced to hang such a fish upon his hook he should suddenly cut the line and let him go (Benwell and Waugh, p. 98).

## The Mermaid in History

Mermaids were never among the most important of monsters, in terms of their impact on human culture. Figures of the classic mermaid type can be found, though, from very ancient times, often as goddesses or semi-divine beings. The Syrian moon goddess Derceto and the Greek tritons and tritonids—companions and servants of the ocean gods—are good examples, and often appear in art with the classic mermaid fishtail. So does Ea, Lord of Time and Measurer of the Great Deep, one of the mightiest of the Babylonian gods.

By the Middle Ages, mermaids (along with all other spirits and powers of nature) had come down in the world, but had an important place in the bestiaries and natural histories of the time. Monkish writers tended to demonize them, as they did anything connected with women—celibacy has its built-in biases, after all—and also managed to confuse them with the sirens of Greek mythology.

Ireland, typically, had a less negative attitude. Irish annals record that in 558 a mermaid was drawn ashore in a fisherman's net, was baptized, and then died; she was afterwards honored as a holy virgin, and miracles were recorded at her shrine at Teo-da-Beoc. Another baptized member of the Irish merfolk—apparently of the tailless variety—was Fintan, who was converted to Christianity by Saint Patrick and later became an important saint in his own right.

Outside of Ireland, the last traces of the mermaid's divine status had more or less dropped from folk awareness by the High Middle Ages. The thirteenth-century writer Bartholomaeus Anglicus describes mermaids as "sea beasts wonderfully shapen" and "fishes of the sea in likeness of women"; the former goddess had become nothing more than an oddly shaped fish. Still, it is in this period that detailed, circumstantial accounts of mermaids and mermen become very common all over those parts of Europe close to the sea. Gervase of Tilbury, writing around 1211, commented in passing that mermaids and mermen dwelt in the seas around Britain in large numbers, and many of the chronicles of the time make note of merfolk seen or captured—the merman who was caught in fishing nets at Oreford in Suffolk in 1197, the mermaid who was stranded in the mud when the dikes near Edam in Holland broke in 1403, and many more.

Such sightings continued through the Renaissance up to the threshold of modern times. The North Atlantic in particular was the scene of a great many reports. These continued without a break into the nineteenth century, despite the increasing ridicule heaped on those who claimed to see such "imaginary creatures."

Scotland in particular was the scene of highly credible mermaid reports all through the nineteenth and early twentieth centuries. Only with the coming of propeller-driven ships at the very end of the nineteenth century did mermaid sightings drop off worldwide—a detail that makes perfect sense, since many other creatures of the ocean avoid the noise, the pollution, and the dangerously sharp, fast-spinning propellers of modern vessels. Even so, a handful of mermaid sightings have been reported in the second half of the twentieth century. There may well have been many other sightings that went unreported; given the current climate of opinion, it would hardly be surprising if most people who saw mermaids kept their mouths tightly shut about the experience.

## Mermaids as Aquatic Fays

The traditional lore of Western magic includes little on the subject of merfolk specifically, and there is a certain amount of confusion in the lore between mermaids and undines, the elemental spirits of water. Still, it's not hard to untangle the two, and the broader context of magical lore allows mermaids of the classic type to be understood fairly readily. From this standpoint, mermaids are aquatic fays, with all the capacities and limitations possessed by the faery folk. Their variations in shape, their

apparent magical powers over weather, their sexual interest in human beings, and many other features of mermaid legendry make perfect sense in this context. The exact relationship between mermaids and the other types of faery folk is anyone's guess, like so many details concerning the faery realm, but it seems most likely that the relationship is a close one.

## Identifying Mermaids

Generally speaking, mermaids (of the fish-tailed kind, at least) are fairly easy to identify when they are seen at all; there are few other things in the world that look like human beings above the waist and fish or dolphins below. A few other possibilities do need to be considered, however, in assessing a potential mermaid sighting.

### Other Beings and Phenomena that Can Be Mistaken for a True Mermaid Include These:

#### Seals and Other Aquatic Mammals

The standard "explanation" for mermaid sightings in modern times has generally been the claim that a seal, a sea lion, or some other aquatic mammal has been misidentified. While it's hard to credit this sort of claim in many cases—sailors and seaside villagers normally know perfectly well what a seal looks like—such confusions may have happened now and then, especially when the person reporting a mermaid is not familiar with seals, and this possibility should certainly be considered in investigating a mermaid sighting.

### Human Swimmers and Hoaxers

Obviously, the most likely source for an apparent "mermaid sighting" near the coastline is an ordinary human being swimming in the ocean. Since some merfolk apparently have a fully human form, this can be hard to rule out in some cases. If a definite fishtail is seen, this possibility is a good deal less likely, although there are records of hoaxers who have dressed up as fishtailed merfolk and splashed around in the water for various reasons.

## The Signs that Point to an Actual Mermaid Sighting Are These:

- The sighting occurs at the seashore, on the open ocean, or in another very large body of water, in a location far from major population centers or shipping lanes;

- The mermaid moves smoothly and efficiently in the water, although she may be somewhat clumsy on land, and she can swim quickly, dive deep, and stay below the surface indefinitely;

- If more than one person is present, the mermaid is visible to all, not merely to one or a few;

- If the apparent mermaid is heard to sing, bad weather follows within twenty-four hours;

- Other possible explanations have been effectively ruled out.

All these signs should be present in order to justify the tentative identification of a mermaid. In particular, human swimmers and hoaxers should be ruled out by careful investigation.

## Dealing with Mermaids

Unlike many of the other monsters discussed in this book, mermaids and mermen rarely have dealings with human beings, and are only a source of potential danger if bothered. Should you be fortunate enough to come across a mermaid, the one rule to follow is simple enough: do nothing that might possibly harm or harass her. This is partly for the mermaid's protection, but partly for yours, since the traditional lore holds that the one way to get hurt in a mermaid encounter is to do something stupid. As when dealing with any other rare, shy, and lovely creature, your best move is to stay still, try not to attract attention to yourself, and make detailed notes on the experience as soon as you possibly can. If the mermaid sings, make preparations for stormy weather, and head for port as quickly as possible if you are on a boat.

# DRAGONS

If a competition were to be held for the greatest monster of all time, the dragon would unquestionably win it hands (or claws) down. No other monster is more widespread in folklore, more important in legend and symbolism, or more popular in literature. Equally, however, few other monsters seem more likely to belong entirely to the world of legend and story.

Unlike most of the other monsters examined in this book—but like such wholly fictional monsters as the unicorn and the gryphon—the dragon seems to be manufactured out of spare parts from a selection of real animals: bat's wings, lizard's body, serpent's tail, and so on. In most cases, this sort of piecemeal design is a good sign of nonexistence. In the case of the dragon, on the other hand, what has happened is more complex.

To get behind the clouds of confusion surrounding the dragon, it's necessary to sort out the different elements of the construct, to discard several of the more common assumptions about what dragons are and what they do, and to consider evidence from sources that have rarely been linked to dragons and dragon lore at all.

Partly, the issue is simply a matter of deciding what qualifies as a dragon. The dragon lore of different parts of the world tends to vary dramatically in some details, although other elements remain quite surprisingly stable over space and time. The dragon has a reputation as a shapeshifter, and many stories describe its habit of taking on other forms to trick human beings—often to the humans' undoing.

For the time being, we'll classify as a dragon any entity, not currently known to science, that combines great size, serpent-like or reptilian form, and a special relationship to magic or supernatural power. Later on, we'll refine this definition somewhat, as we close in on the nature of the dragon itself.

## What Is a Dragon?

Trying to build up a more precise definition on the basis of any one traditional image of the dragon is not likely to help much. The differences between the types are too great. Our range of choices includes the classical Western dragon, belching flames as it faces the charge of an armor-clad knight; the sinuous Chinese *lung* chasing a flaming moon-pearl across the heavens; the coiling vision-serpent of the Mayas, with its quetzal-bird feathers and human face; the two-headed *aya'hos* of the Puget Sound Salish tribes, coiled around its rock by the sea; and many more. All these are dragons of one sort or another, but common ground between them is not necessarily easy to find.

Let's examine a few of the most common types in more detail. The standard dragon of Western legend usually has four legs, two batlike wings, a long neck and tail, and a thick coat of scales proof against weapons—although there is always one vulnerable patch, usually somewhere on the creature's belly. Many accounts and illustrations give it horns, although this doesn't seem to be a consistent part of the legend. Its body also had the curious property of melting away to nothing soon after death.

Its usual habitat was in mountain caves or in burial mounds, where it guarded stolen treasure against all comers. It was well equipped for such duties, as its fiery breath was only one of a range of deadly natural weapons attested in the literature. It also spat poison, its teeth and claws were sharp as knives and backed by powerful muscles, and it was also known to coil around its prey like a python and crush it to death. All in all, it's hard to find a more fearsome opponent for a hero to vanquish. Equally, though, it's hard to imagine anything quite as biologically improbable.

The Chinese dragon, or lung, is a somewhat different beast. According to the classical sources, it can be described by nine different likenesses—it has the horns of a stag, the head of a camel, the eyes of a demon, the neck of a snake, the belly of a clam, the scales of a carp, the claws of an eagle, the feet of a tiger, and the ears of a cow. Its classic image can be seen chasing the blazing moon-pearl across the sky in any number of ancient and modern artworks from all across eastern Asia. Five-clawed dragons were the most exalted grade, with four-clawed and three-clawed ones ranking progressively further down the social scale—but here we are dealing with the symbolism of an intensely class-ridden society, rather than anything more useful to the student of monsters.

The Chinese dragon was primarily a creature of water rather than of fire, and had a deep connection to underground waters and the life-giving rains. Chinese dragons could now and again be seen chasing clouds across the sky. Now and again one fell dead to earth; accounts from times as recent as the nineteenth century describe how the bodies would be respectfully covered with straw mats by the local villagers, and would vanish after a short time.

It's commonly stated in modern books of dragon lore that Chinese dragons are as benevolent as the Western variety are destructive, but this is a half-truth at best. While official accounts of Chinese dragons insist on their beneficence, there is a whole genre of Chinese folktales in which the lung is a devouring monster who must be slain by the local equivalent of Saint George. (It's possible, of course, that these stories started out as roundabout ways of criticizing the former imperial government—the Chinese dragon, like some of its Western equivalents, has its political dimension.)

Other cultures around the world have dragons of their own. To judge from native lore, for example, North America was once swarming with dragons of a very specific type. From the *aya'hos* of the Salish people of Puget Sound clear across to the *kitchi-at'husis* of the Micmac by the shores of the Gulf of Saint Lawrence, tribal traditions tell of great serpents with horns who dwell in deep waters but emerge and are seen now and then. Some of the white explorers of the continent recorded their encounters with the same type of creature. Curiously, like dragons elsewhere, some Native American dragons were believed to melt away to nothing if they were slain.

It would be possible to go on almost endlessly listing the different types of dragons recorded in the lore of cultures around the world and throughout time. Entities that fit our first definition of the dragon, after all, can be found all over the world as far back as records go. The ancient Egyptians had their demon-serpent Apep, who strove to swallow the sun and had to be fended off by the actions of various solar gods, as well as a variety of other serpent-like monsters who played roles in their legends and folklore. The Chinese dragon can be found, in something close to its modern form, at an astonishingly early date. Greek and Roman legends and zoological lore alike discuss dragonish beasts of various kinds. The Celts had their dragon lore, as did the Germanic tribes who settled what is now Germany, Scandinavia, and England.

121

It's no accident that the oldest surviving major work of English literature, *Beowulf,* includes a dragon as one of its major characters.

That dragon was essentially a literary creation, born of a fusion of Celtic and Germanic dragon lore with accounts from surviving classical literature. Still, accounts of dragons as actual beings are not all that hard to find, and these less literary dragons often had little in common with the imagery from epics and romances. These accounts appear mostly in parish records, monastic chronicles, and other local sources, and have received nothing like the attention they deserve. Similarly, the Chinese omen records include a good many accounts of dragon appearances.

## Modern Dragon Sightings

All this may seem to have the telltale air of faraway and long ago. Modern dragon sightings, however, are not impossible to find. One specific type of dragon, a winged snake several feet in length, is surprisingly well attested in recent times.

According to Marie Trevelyan's *Folk-Lore and Folk Stories of Wales* (1909), people still alive at the beginning of the twentieth century recalled that, when children, they had seen shimmering winged dragons in the forests around Penllin Castle and Penmark, in Glamorgan in southern Wales. One old man recalled that the dragons looked as if they were covered with jewels of all kinds; when they were disturbed, they would fly out of their dens and soar over people's heads, with their outspread wings sparkling. The same witness recalled that his father and uncle used to kill them because they were "as bad as foxes for the poultry."

Such dragons, according to folklore, were once common in the southwest of England, where they could be seen sunning themselves on rocks in Dartmoor and Bodmin. To judge from a pamphlet of 1669, the same sort of creature was seen in Henham in May of that year, and was chased away by villagers armed with pitchforks and stones. It was described as a flying serpent eight or nine feet long, as thick as a man's leg, with eyes as big as a sheep's, small wings, and sharp teeth. It's almost impossible to guess what this creature might actually have been.

Equally strange is the dragon of the little village of Fittleworth, in Sussex. As late as 1867, according to one report, villagers were afraid to pass the site of its den, insisting that it would rush out hissing at anyone who went by. What it was is anyone's guess at this point.

Still, a different kind of dragon makes up the bulk of modern reports. Given the dragon's penchant for varying its shape, it may come as no surprise that this last type isn't generally recognized as a dragon at all. Those who hunt it, using cameras, sonar equipment, and submarines in place of Saint George's spear, argue endlessly about what it is—a plesiosaur, a primitive whale, an unknown species of long-necked seal, a prehistoric invertebrate—but suggestions that it might best be described as a dragon are few and far between.

The dragon in question, of course, is the Loch Ness monster and its many equivalents in deepwater lakes around the world. Since ancient times, people have been seeing dragonlike creatures in and around the water, most commonly in deep, cold lakes of the sort dredged out by glaciers in the last Ice Age. The creatures typically have heads like horses, small hornlike projections above their eyes, long necks, massive bodies, and snakelike tails; they are seen as dark moving shapes in the water, as heads and necks suddenly rising from the surface, or in their full and frightening reality as dark shapes basking on the shore. A few photographs have been taken, especially at Loch Ness itself, but conclusive evidence of the monsters' existence continues to elude investigators.

It's possible, as most of the monster hunters who camp around Loch Ness each summer firmly believe, that "Nessie" and others of her ilk are actually living animals of a sort unknown to official science. On the other hand, there are some good reasons to question this assumption. In particular, such creatures are routinely reported from lakes too small and too poorly stocked with fish and other edibles to support a single large animal, much less a breeding population. (It's been argued that Loch Ness itself, which is only twenty-four miles long and averages a mile across, may fall into this category.) Small Irish loughs where "great wurrums" have been frequently sighted have been dragged from end to end with nets, without any result. At least one monster-infested lake—Lake Elsinore in California—actually dries up now and then, which would seem to be a problem for a flesh-and-blood animal!

Folklore, which as we've seen is often a useful guide in such matters, is not ambiguous on the subject: the lake monsters of Scotland, Ireland, and many other countries are at the center of a rich folklore of magic, portent, and prophecy, and are treated in traditional folk cultures as strictly supernatural creatures, in the same broad category as fays and ghosts, rather than in the category of ordinary animals. While it's possible that the cryptozoologists will have the last word here, then, it seems likely that Nessie and her ilk are indeed monsters in the sense used in this book.

## Untangling Dragon Lore

With dragons, as with several other traditional monsters, we are clearly dealing with a composite creature, put together in the folk imagination from many different sources. Some of those sources were non-physical beings; others were living animals of one kind or another; still others were travelers' tales, which may or may not have been based on real beings but which underwent various mutations on their way back from various far-off places. Mixed in with all of these is a level of spiritual, magical, and visionary material, deeply important in its own context but with little bearing on the subject of this book. To understand dragons, it's necessary to tease apart these tangled threads of legend and separate out the different beings and phenomena that have become part of the dragon's traditional image.

One important contribution to that image was made by living animals well known to science. There is, for example, the dragon of Wormingford in England. This dragon had no wings, a thick body, short legs with "grete Nayles," and a long, curved tail. According to an old account, it had been brought back from the Crusades by King Richard the Lionheart, and kept at the Tower of London, but had escaped and made its way through Essex to the vicinity of Wormingford, where it was finally slain in fierce combat by a local knight named Sir George de la Haye. In the same old record, the dragon is also called a "cock-adrille"—that is, a crocodile—an identification that makes perfect sense of the whole story.

No doubt the dragon of Wormingford is not the only one of these large, fierce reptiles to have contributed to dragon legendry. Equally, many of the "dragons" in the old bestiaries, described as serpents who wrap themselves around their prey, are pretty obviously based on travelers' tales of big snakes such as pythons and boa constrictors—an identification made even more likely by the fact that the Greek word *drako*, the origin of our word "dragon," is also the word for "snake."

Beyond these known animals, there is at least a good case to be made that one or more species of animal still unknown to science contributed something to the growth of dragon lore. Sea serpents, which have strong connections to dragons in the old lore, have a long and very detailed history on their own, and cryptozoologists have long argued that at least some of these are based on sightings of living animals. Surviving zeuglodons—long, serpentlike animals, ancestral to modern whales, which were very common a few tens of millions of years ago—form one possible source of these accounts; another proposed source is a hypothetical marine mammal related to seals and sea lions, with seal-like flippers, a blubbery body like that of a walrus (accounting for the variety of lumps seen breaking the water's surface), and a long neck. If either of these creatures exists, or existed recently enough to leave traces in folk memory, it's easy to see how they might have contributed a great deal to several branches of monster lore.

Back in 1886, too, folklorist Charles Gould speculated that behind the image of the legendary dragon might lurk memories of a large carnivorous lizard. It was twenty-six years later that the giant monitor or Komodo dragon, which fits Gould's description down to the fine details, was discovered in Indonesia, and subsequent research has shown that it once had a much wider range. Cryptozoologist Roy Mackal has unearthed evidence that similar large lizards may have survived into historic times in southeast Asia, and these could easily have become a source (by way of travelers' tales) of later dragon legends.

Mixed in with all of this material is a vast assemblage of magical, religious, and visionary symbolism in which dragons, serpents with and without wings, and similar creatures coil about one another in dizzying profusion. According to the Tantric traditions of India, for example, the energy that awakens the subtle-energy centers or chakras of the human body is coiled up at the base of the spine; the term for "coiled up" in Sanskrit is *kundala*, and the energy in question is named *kundalini*, "the coiled one." Tantric imagery pictures this energy as a tightly coiled serpent; awakened, it climbs up the central energy channel of the subtle body to the center at the crown of the head, awakening the chakras one by one as it rises.

This symbolism has a very straightforward origin. According to many of those who have experienced it, the process of energy flow up the central channel feels unnervingly like a snake slithering up the inside of one's spine. The effects of the process include spectacular energy discharges, sensations of heat and brilliant light, and dramatic expansions of consciousness. Most kinds of mystical practice can set off the process of awakening kundalini, and many traditions of mystical spirituality (including some with roots far from India) have this as their principal goal; it's therefore no wonder that images of fiery or luminous serpents climbing up tall, straight trees, coiled around poles, or flying up into the heavens play such an important part in traditional legend and lore.

At first glance, then, the array of possible sources for dragon lore already covered may well look sufficient to explain the whole tradition. Setting aside known animals such as crocodiles and pythons, unknown animals such as zeuglodons and long-necked seals, and symbolic creatures such as kundalini serpents, what remains?

In point of fact, there's more than enough to justify placing the dragon in the category of real monsters. The Loch Ness monster, the "great wurrums" of Irish lakes, and many other shadowy beasts of the same sort may not seem much like the fire-breathing dragons of modern fairy tales and fantasy fiction, but they do have definite links with older dragon lore.

Like the lung and other creatures from the older dragon lore, these dragons are associated with water more than fire, and have equally deep connections with the subtle currents of earth energy—the *lung-mei* or "dragon paths" of Chinese geomantic lore. They share the serpentlike body, the horns, and the long necks and small heads of traditional dragons.

They also have the disquieting habit of melting away to nothing, producing a prodigious stench in the process, shortly after death. This has been reported, for example, in western Ireland, where one such "wurrum" managed to get itself stuck in a culvert early in this century. It died there, and its body—which appeared to be a jellylike substance—dissolved away in a short time. In an age before mass media, no one thought of bringing the event to the attention of the outside world; researchers investigating more recent sightings in the same area turned up the story in the late 1960s and spoke to a number of people who saw (and smelled) the object.

One of those researchers, F. W. Holiday, ended up becoming convinced by his experiences at Loch Ness and elsewhere that lake monsters were not physical beings. He ended up hypothesizing that they were dragons in a sense that medieval people would have understood—shapeshifting, serpentine, evil entities. He thus took part in the attempted exorcism of Loch Ness by Anglican exorcist Dr. Donald Omand on June 2, 1973. According to Holiday (and other participants), the exorcism was followed by several days of bizarre and frightening paranormal events.

From a magical perspective, certainly, all this makes a certain definite degree of sense. It's not hard to see common patterns in the lore we've examined and trace out a possible explanation. Like so many of the monsters we've studied so far, the dragon seems to be an etheric entity. The deep waters of the lakes where so many "lake monsters" have been sighted would be an excellent place for such beings to take form, since cold, still water holds etheric charges extremely well. The character and probable behavior of such creatures is a harder matter to guess. The magical dimension of the dragon is not limited to the creature's origins and nature. There is some evidence—modern as well as ancient—suggesting that these entities will also respond to magical summonings. A group of witches attempted to call the Cornish sea serpent Morgawr in 1976 and 1977, in a series of public ceremonies that attracted a fair amount of media attention—largely because the witches performed their rites skyclad. While they themselves apparently didn't see anything out of the ordinary, each of these ceremonies was followed by a flurry of sightings.

Furthermore—and more unnervingly—it has been noted by more than one Loch Ness researcher that the modern era of Nessie appearances, which began with several celebrated sightings in 1933, started a few years after the celebrated (or infamous) magician Aleister Crowley rented a house at Boleskine, on the shores of the loch, and carried out an intensive series of magical rituals there. While it's by no means certain that these rituals and the monster's appearance are cause and effect, it may be unwise to rule out the possibility.

## Identifying Dragons

The task of sorting out dragons from other entities is in one sense fairly easy, as there isn't much else in the universe of our experience that looks or behaves like a dragon. On the other hand, since the nature of these entities remains a puzzle—it's at least possible, for example, that some such cases do relate to actual flesh-and-blood animals not yet officially recognized by science—hard and fast lines are difficult to draw. Utterly baffling creatures like the winged serpents of Wales add confusions of their own to the picture. Still, we can attempt to make sense of the data at hand.

## Other Beings and Phenomena that Can Be Mistaken for a True Dragon Include These:

### Large Fish

A certain number of lake monsters have actually turned out to be fish of certain large types. In Lake Washington, just east of Seattle, a lake monster was sighted a number of times by credible observers over a fifty-year period. Witnesses reported seeing something like a greenish-brown floating log eight to ten feet long, moving independently of winds and currents. Scientists scoffed at the reports, while anomaly researchers added them to the catalog of lake monster sightings. Recently, however, the corpse of the "monster" drifted ashore, and proved to be a huge, 900-pound female sturgeon—a large, slow-moving fish that does in fact look rather like a greenish-brown log when on the surface. From its size and growth pattern, marine biologists estimated that it was well over a century old.

### Inanimate Objects

A certain number of lake monster reports are the result of sightings of floating logs, pieces of driftwood, and other debris misinterpreted by inexperienced or overexcitable observers. Attention to wind and current patterns can rule these out fairly easily, but this takes a certain degree of calmness and common sense—two things that are often in short supply in the midst of an apparent monster sighting.

*Hoaxes*

It's also by no means unknown for people to fake "lake monster" sightings, either for the simple thrill of getting away with the hoax, or for more straightforwardly commercial reasons. For example, the "monster" of Silver Lake, New York, an inflated sea serpent of rubberized canvas, was manufactured by local businessmen and hauled about the lake by means of concealed ropes in order to attract attention and business to a declining resort town. Signs that someone is too obviously involved in the monster's appearances, or that someone is too clearly profiting by them, should be carefully watched.

## The Signs that Point to the Presence of an Actual Dragon Are These:

- One or more witnesses sight a relatively large serpentlike or dragonlike creature in or on the shore of the sea or a deep-water lake;

- The creature's movements have the effects on its surroundings that a physical object of comparable size would have—for example, waves or a wake in the water, or a trail of some sort on land;

- If more than one witness is present and looking in the right direction, the creature is seen by all, and if pictures are taken, the creature appears on them;

- If records of local folklore and legendry can be located, a dragonlike creature appears therein;

- Other zoological, psychological, and criminological explanations have been effectively ruled out.

All these signs should be present in order to justify the tentative diagnosis of the presence of a dragon.

## Dealing with Dragons

Few people are fortunate enough to have to deal with dragons in any concrete sense. It's a rare monster hunter, even in the most dragon-infested areas, who manages more than a handful of sightings in the course of a lifetime. Many people never do see one, despite hours spent scanning the surface of Loch Ness or some other dragon-haunted lake with binoculars.

Should you happen to beat the odds, your actions should be guided by the same principles you would keep in mind when sighting any other rare and shy creature—remain still, make as little noise as possible, and try to take a photograph if you possibly can. Noise is a particular issue; dragons are known to have keen hearing, and sudden noises will normally make them dive beneath the water at once. If there's any way you can alert other witnesses without making noise, do so.

Despite the legends, you're unlikely to need much in the way of dragon-slaying skill to come away from a dragon encounter unharmed. In the present, certainly, dragons seem more concerned with avoiding human beings than with taking any more active role in our lives. Still, F. W. Holiday's unnerving account of his adventures at Loch Ness is a reminder that the "ancient serpent" may not be entirely safe to encounter even yet.

# SPIRITS

Up to this point, we've dealt with monstrous beings that are familiar to most people in modern industrial society. However little attention gets paid to actual sightings of these beings, however debased or distorted their images have become, they do still maintain a presence of sorts in modern collective consciousness. With the next class of entities we'll be discussing, this is not the case at all. For complex reasons rooted in an equally complex history, the entities we're about to examine are all but unknown outside the still rather secretive community where Western magical traditions are taught and practiced.

These entities are traditionally called spirits, and they have played a long and curious role in the intellectual history of the Western world, especially during the last two thousand years. To a remarkable degree, indeed, the track of spirits through the historical record is made of attempts to deny that they exist at all, or to lump them together with some other type of monstrous being.

The absence of spirits as such—distinct from ghosts, demons, angels, and so on—from today's Halloween decorations and horror movies is simply the latest chapter in the history of their exclusion. As we'll see, there are reasons for that exclusion. Yet there are also reasons, stronger and far more relevant ones, why these particular inhabitants of the realm of monstrous beings deserve a name and a category of their own.

It's worth mentioning in advance that the realm of spirits is extraordinarily diverse and complicated—more so, in fact, than any other type of monster. The comment in "Concerning the Microcosms of Macrocosm," one of the classic knowledge lectures in the Golden Dawn magical tradition, is relevant:

> Besides these classes of life [the animal, vegetable, and mineral kingdoms] there be multitudinous existences representing Forces of the Macrocosm, each with its own microcosm. Such are Elemental Spirits, Planetary Spirits, Olympic Spirits, Fays, Arch-Fays, Genii, and many other potencies which cannot be classed under these forms.
>
> Thus the Macrocosmic Universe is one vast and infinite sphere containing so many and diverse infinite microcosmic forms, of which the perfect knowledge is only known to the advanced Adept (reprinted in Regardie 1971, pp. 109–110).

It may be worth commenting that adepts of this level of advancement are few and far between!

Certainly most works of magical lore have contented themselves with a few broad classifications, and this is probably wise, since finer details have an uncomfortable habit of varying sharply between different accounts, and there's reason to think that the realm of spirits itself may change radically over time. Some of the better magical handbooks of the Renaissance, in fact, state that any account of the world of spirits more than forty years old is no longer valid.

For this reason, as well as for reasons of sheer space, this section will content itself with a broad survey of spirits in history, and a very general account of the types and classes of spirits known to Western magical tradition. For most practical uses, this is more than enough. Just as very few people outside of the healing professions actually need to know the names of all the different bones and muscles in the human body, very few people other than practicing magicians need more than a general sense of the wide array of spirits that share the cosmos with us, and those interested in pursuing the point further can look up the finer details in textbooks of magic.

## The Exclusion of Spirits

Like fays, spirits have a presence that stretches back into prehistory, but just as with fays, the major difficulty in tracking that presence is one of drawing distinctions between spirits and the other denizens of the Unseen. Ancient cultures, like many modern non-Western ones, drew their lines of division at different points, and it's often hard to tell whether a particular entity should best be called a fay, a spirit, a demon, or a god. Still, it's clear that from a very early period, beings similar to those we now call spirits were known and named in the lore of all the ancient civilizations.

The spirit lore of ancient Greece is particularly useful here. When Greek civilization emerged from its own Dark Ages around 600 B.C.E., the worship of the great Olympian gods and goddesses—Zeus, Hera, Apollo, and other figures familiar to us from modern retellings—overlaid a complex religious and magical scene crowded with other entities. Among these were a class of beings known as *daimones*. Disembodied presences that brought good or evil to human beings, daimones were regarded with a mixture of veneration and fear, and sacrifices were made to them, less to win their cooperation than to encourage them to leave the human world alone. They were not, however, considered evil—simply unpredictable, like the weather.

As Greek culture absorbed influences from Egypt and Babylon, these vague but powerful entities took on more precise outlines. This was especially true in the magical traditions that coalesced in Egypt, in the five or six centuries after Alexander the Great's conquests brought that ancient land into the Greek cultural sphere. There, the term *daimon* came to be used generally for the wide range of bodiless entities that were neither gods, nature spirits, nor the ghosts of the human dead. When these magical traditions migrated west into lands where

Latin was the common tongue, the Latin word *spiritus* (originally a term for wind or breath, like so many spirit words around the world) was borrowed for the same purpose.

This habit of language was standard all through the Western world in the last centuries of the classical era, as the Roman Empire crumbled and Christianity rose to dominance. Followers of the new religion had deep doubts about any entity that was not part and parcel of their own theological structure, and treated the busy spiritual world of late classical paganism accordingly. It's from this period, therefore, that the term "daimon" lost its flavor of moral neutrality and took on the connotations of its English descendant "demon."

Many of the classical world's magical traditions made the transition to the new religious environment with ease. The transition was greatly helped out by attitudes, common even within the Christian church itself, that saw magic as harmless so long as it called on the right divine names and powers, stayed clear of dealings with evil spirits, and avoided doing harm to people. Magic involving spirits of any kind, however, remained highly suspect; the dualistic streak within Christianity encouraged many people to believe that any bodiless entity that was not a saint or an angel had to be a demon.

As a result, for more than a thousand years, the existence of morally neutral spirits

133

was a subject of constant debate. Some theologians made room in their discussions of "spiritual creatures" for beings who were neither angel nor demon, while others insisted that there could be no middle ground. Magicians generally fell into the first camp, but not always—and there were always some who were interested in demons as such, further confusing an already confused issue.

The long debate finally came to an end around the time of the Reformation. For a galaxy of reasons, the thinkers of that age were far more interested in drawing distinctions than in building bridges. More than ever before, the universe was seen as a cosmic battlefield in which there could be no middle ground. The warring fragments of the Christian church agreed on very little, but the nonexistence of morally neutral spirits was one point that nearly every side accepted.

During this same time, scholarly magicians such as Theophrastus von Hohenheim (better known by his pen name Paracelsus) and Jerome Cardan wrote important works on the nature and activities of spirits, laying the foundations for most current magical theory on the subject. Outside of the magical community of the time, though, no one was listening. When modern scientific thought emerged a little later, those who disagreed with its flat dismissal of everything beyond the physical

level argued on many different grounds, but the existence of spirits was rarely brought up by anyone.

By about 1700, therefore, the only people who paid any attention to the traditional lore about spirits were magicians of one sort or another, who continued their work in the face of nearly constant contempt and rejection from the society around them. A great deal of work went into the magical study of spirits in the years that followed; lore from the classical era, the Middle Ages, and the Renaissance was collected and compared, and the modern magical terminology of spirits was gradually developed.

Since then, very little has actually changed. The revival of popular interest in "mythical" creatures in the 1980s and 1990s, which spawned a flood of illustrated books and a plethora of would-be elves and vampires, missed the traditional lore of spirits entirely; somehow we managed to get by without a coffee-table book entitled *Elementals*. Even in the modern magical community itself, a good deal of confusion still exists about beings that were clearly understood by magicians of past centuries. Still, the texts and traditions remain, and many of them can be consulted by those who are willing to look.

## Sorting Out the Spirits

It would not be hard to fill an entire book with information on the different kinds of spirit known to Western magical lore. Still, such a book would be mostly of use to practicing magicians specializing in the evocation of spirits. Here, we will simply discuss the most general categories of spirits, and suggest something of the complexity within these broad types.

Four general terms have been used for these entities in magical circles: intelligences, spirits, elementals, and larvae. These form a descending scale of consciousness and power, and in older magical literature, much attention is given to the relation between certain members of the first two types.

### Intelligences

Intelligences, as the word suggests, are centers of consciousness with broad powers of understanding, knowledge, and insight. They can be difficult to describe, since they are primary beings of the mental level of reality. They are creatures of mind, and insofar as they can be said to have bodies at all, those "bodies" are made of patterns of consciousness, which we experience as ideas. In certain kinds of magical meditation, it's not uncommon to be contemplating some abstruse concept, and then to suddenly realize that there is an awareness within the "concept" that is looking back at you! When this happens, an intelligence has been contacted.

According to traditional lore and the experience of magicians alike, we are surrounded by intelligences at every moment. Many of the unexpected ideas, sudden hunches, and notions from "out of the blue" that occur throughout our lives are brought about by contact—unconscious, for the most part, but still real—with entities of this type.

Intelligences vary widely; some are minor entities, others vast and potent. A good many of the gods and goddesses worshipped in pagan religious traditions in the past seem to be powerful intelligences—although human beings are remarkably undiscriminating in their choice of things to worship, and angels, spirits, ghosts, elementals, living human beings, and demons have all been worshipped at different times and in different cultures. Whether or not it's appropriate to worship intelligences is a subject on which different people have widely different opinions, and it is not particularly relevant to the present book; it may be worth mentioning, though, that intelligences—even great ones—are far from the mightiest or the wisest of beings in the universe.

### Spirits

Spirits are to energy roughly what intelligences are to mind. Creatures of the astral realm, they are in some sense subordinate to intelligences. In magical lore, spirits are held to be "blind forces"—that is to say, patterns of energy with little connection to the spiritual levels of being.

As a result, they tend to act in unbalanced ways, especially when misdirected by ignorant or greedy human beings. Spirits as such have no sense of balance or proportion, and will typically do exactly what they are told to do, to the letter, whether or not what they have been told to do is what the magician who summoned them actually has in mind!

Some magical traditions, responding to this, have claimed that spirits are in some sense evil, while intelligences are good. Still, this is an oversimplification. Spirits are vessels of power, and any source of power can be lethally dangerous to the foolish; as a traditional magical saying puts it, "Power without wisdom is the name of death." Treated intelligently, honestly, and fairly, though, spirits can play an important part in magical work.

The manifestations of spirits are easier to recognize than to define. While they have bodies in a magical sense—astral, mental, and spiritual bodies, to be precise—they are not material beings, and have no fixed forms. Since their consciousness and actions are focused on the astral, they tend to appear most clearly to our minds and imaginations rather than to our senses. The experience of Val from Peckham with what

was most likely a planetary spirit of Venus, as described in the first part of this book, is not atypical.

The techniques of magical evocation—a ritual process by which human beings interact with nonhuman beings, including spirits—were thoroughly developed during the Middle Ages, when they represented the most important item in the magician's toolkit. They are still being practiced today, and detailed descriptions of the process can be looked up in any reasonably complete manual of ritual magic. Other branches of magical practice, including the consecration of talismans and certain kinds of divination, also involve interacting with spirits in various ways. Most places and objects associated with magical practice, as a result, have a fairly strong connection to the realm of spirits; in such places, even individuals with no particular magical training may suddenly find themselves face to face with entities of this sort.

### Elementals

Elementals are the inhabitants of the four magical elements: Earth, Water, Air, and Fire. These "elements" are not quite the same as the four substances that give them their names. Think of them as solid matter, liquid matter, gaseous matter, and energy, and you're most of the way to a clear understanding of the elements; remember that all of them are present in everything, all the time, and you know enough to make sense of most discussions of the elements in magical lore.

Each element has its own class of elementals. Gnomes are the elementals of Earth; undines, the elementals of Water; sylphs, the elementals of Air; and salamanders, the elementals of Fire. These terms can cause a certain amount of confusion. The word "gnome," of course, has been borrowed in several European languages for certain kinds of small earth-dwelling fay, and as such became the title of one of the coffee-table books mentioned a little earlier in this section; the account of "gnomes" in that book, it should probably be pointed out, has nothing whatever to do with gnomes in the magical sense. The word "salamander," in turn, is also used for small lizardlike animals related to frogs; they got the name centuries ago, because they live in decaying logs and have moist skins and so sometimes crawl unhurt out of a blazing fire.

The creatures of the elements, according to magical lore, are not so individualized as we are. They blend into one another both physically and at subtler levels, and form collective bodies from what most modern people call "inanimate" matter. They are present in greatest numbers and power where the forces of the elements are strongest—gnomes in mountains and caverns, undines in the ocean, sylphs in wind and storm, and salamanders in flames—but they surround us everywhere and at all times.

Individual elementals are said to have minds on roughly the same level as the more intelligent animals, but those of each type also share a much higher collective consciousness and intelligence, which is usually described in magical lore as the "king" of each elemental kingdom. These elemental kings are to elementals what intelligences are to spirits, and their roles in magical practice are similar.

This may seem reminiscent of fays, who are also said to have kings, and in fact there is a good deal of confusion between fays and elementals in the traditional lore. There seem to be definite similarities between elementals, on the one hand, and certain kinds of fays on the other— although how much of this is a product of faery glamour is anybody's guess. Some magical writings draw a useful distinction between elementals, who are creatures of a single element, and elementaries, who are composed of two or three elements (humans and other physical life forms are composed of four). As described in the old lore, elementaries have much in common with fays, and may be the same thing.

Handbooks of ritual magic relate that Ghob is the king of the gnomes, Nichsa the king of the undines, Paralda the king of the sylphs, and Djinn the king of the salamanders, and the collective minds of the elementals do seem to respond to these names in practice. The elemental kings, in turn, are overshadowed by the angels and archangels of the four elements, but the lore of the angelic kingdom belongs to a different section of this book and will not be covered here.

### Larvae

Larvae represent the lower end of the scale of spirits. Larvae are etheric beings, living entirely on the level of subtle energy. Just as the physical world has scavengers—worms, crows, fungi, and so on—that break down dead physical bodies and return their components to the ecosystem, so the etheric world has larvae, who serve the same function. The cast-off etheric shells of dead human beings and animals, the etheric patterns in feces and other waste products, and other stray bits of etheric substance serve as food to these entities. Slow, mindless, and persistent, larvae will occasionally seize on a damaged human etheric body, and in such cases can cause weakness, poor health, and wasting illnesses.

In the squalid etheric environments of modern cities, larvae are relatively common, and they can also be found in large numbers wherever deaths frequently happen—one of the reasons why hospitals and nursing homes can be very unhealthy places for the ill! They have been described as looking like pale, half-transparent bubbles or baglike shapes drifting through the air, or hovering around a food source. Fortunately, it's relatively easy to drive them away by magical means, and methods for doing so are discussed at the end of this chapter.

## Energies, Entities, and Spiritual Creatures

The student of monster lore has several important advantages when it comes to making sense of this particular branch of the traditional lore. For a good many centuries, magicians all over the Western world have put a great deal of time and effort into clarifying the nature, functions, and activities of spirits. While a certain amount of abstract curiosity has certainly been involved, much of this outpouring of energy has had entirely practical motives, and the results have been put to the test time and again in ritual workings. As a result, those who are willing to take magical traditions seriously will find a wealth of information on these otherwise puzzling entities.

Much of the basic information needed to understand spirits has already been covered in the section on spirit lore—another advantage of drawing on magical sources—and only a few additional comments will be needed here. Central to the magical understanding of spirits is the dictum "Every energy is an entity and every entity is an energy." In magical terms, any force in the cosmos can be understood and treated as a conscious being; when this is done, it becomes possible to relate to the force in ways that a purely impersonal relationship won't allow.

This concept has sometimes been taken to mean that all the forces of the universe *are* conscious beings, and indeed this is one possible interpretation. Still, in a very real sense we have no way of knowing the true nature of anything in the universe at all. It is quite possible to work magic on the basis of this awareness. As Aleister Crowley commented in one of his instructional papers:

> In this book it is spoken of the Sephiroth, and the Paths, of Spirits and Conjurations; of Gods, Spheres, Planes, and many other things which may or may not exist. It is immaterial whether they exist or not. By doing certain things certain results follow; students are most earnestly warned against attributing objective reality or philosophic validity to any of them (Crowley 1976, p. 375).

To put the same thing in a different way: we really have no way of knowing whether or not spirits exist; the point is that the universe appears to work as though they do.

## Identifying Spirits

The art of identifying spirits conclusively is among the more difficult branches of occult lore, and it demands a very extensive knowledge of symbolism and magical theory. Since all we will be trying to do here is tell spirits in general apart from other kinds of monstrous beings, however, the task is a good deal easier—though even so, it has its potential pitfalls.

The most important thing to remember when considering the possibility that a spirit was responsible for some particular occurrence, rather than some other type of monstrous entity, is this: spirits normally take no direct action on the material world. Even elementals, which are embodied in matter, have no more impact on the matter around them than a fish has on the ocean in which it swims. This point can sometimes be used to tell spirits apart from other denizens of the realm of monsters. Under certain very specific circumstances, this principle doesn't hold, but in nearly all such cases ritual magic is involved—and the traces of magical activity can themselves be an important diagnostic point.

It's important to remember, in trying to determine if a given entity is a spirit or something else, that the entity's own pronouncements should often be taken with at least a grain (and sometimes a bushel basket) of salt. As G. K. Chesterton commented after his own investigation of spiritualist phenomena, the one thing we know for sure about these entities is that they are capable of telling lies.

## Other Beings and Phenomena that Can Be Mistaken for a Spirit Include These:

### Ghosts

The term "spirit" has also been commonly used for nonphysical beings that were once human—i.e., for ghosts—and this piece of shared terminology marks a significant overlap in appearance and function. Some ghosts, like spirits, make themselves manifest primarily to the minds and imaginations of witnesses, and it's not unknown for ghosts to take on the same sort of dreamlike, shifting form common to many spirits. Larvae and graveyard specters are also often confused—not surprisingly, since they tend to occur together.

The best way to keep from confusing spirits and ghosts is to look for evidence that the entity you're researching was once a living human being, or is a replay haunting of some past event. Evidence that ritual magic has been practiced in a given area can also be useful evidence, as it makes it more likely that spirits may be active there. See Ghosts, pp. 53–69.

### Fays

Another important source of confusion comes from the blurry line between spirits and fays. While the two classes of entities are not quite the same—at least as far as we know!—their appearances and effects can be easy to confuse, especially when the influence of faery glamour is involved. The critical point to keep in mind here is that fays are repelled by things that do not bother spirits in the least. If an entity has crossed running water or ventured amid a thicket of St. John's Wort, for example, it is very unlikely to be a fay of any known kind. See Creatures of Faery, pp. 83–107.

### Demons

A third confusing factor consists of those malevolent and destructive entities traditionally called "demons." The line between demons and spirits has historically been drawn in many different places, resulting in almost endless confusion. This has been amplified by real similarities between the two classes of entity. Like spirits, demons interact with human beings on the astral level, and the forms they take are elusive and constantly changing. Like many types of spirits, too, demons are blind forces, with a weirdly mechanical approach to the universe and no sense whatever of balance or proportion—a lack which is at one and the same time a major source of danger to those who deal with them, and a major source of weakness that has been exploited by those who need to overcome them.

The primary difference between demons and spirits is one of character. Spirits have no comprehension of moral and ethical issues at all—to intelligences, for example, moral ideas are simply another set of abstract patterns—but they are not particularly malicious or destructive. Demons are both, and the actions of demonic entities typically show either a jeering and nasty sense of humor or a blind rage for destruction. See Demons, pp. 161–174.

## Psychological Conditions

Many of the forms of mental illness catalogued by modern psychologists include experiences that correspond closely with traditional accounts of contact with spirits. This similarity is a two-edged sword, of course; as magicians have been pointing out for some time, at least some of the people who go through life hearing disembodied voices inside their heads may be hearing the voices of real entities, however unpopular that idea may be just now. For such cases, exorcism may well be a more effective treatment than psychotherapy, although it's likely to be quite some time before any experiments along these lines are published in psychological journals.

Still, there are some mental and physical illnesses that can produce symptoms like those caused by spirits. Even if real spirits are involved, the possibility of a mental illness should be explored as soon as possible in any investigation.

## Human Fakery

A final source of confusion comes from "spirits" who are manufactured, for one reason or another, by human beings. The motives for this sort of fakery range from fairly harmless attempts to boost someone's sense of self-importance all the way up to thoroughly corrupt schemes in which messages from a "channeled entity" are used to obtain money, power, sexual favors, and similar ends. Sleight-of-hand tricks and amateur espionage have routinely been used to allow the "spirit" to show off knowledge that its human contacts supposedly wouldn't know, and thus produce the illusion of supernatural powers.

Since most spirits are seen only by one or a few people, there are few ways to conclusively show that a spirit is being faked. Still, if the spirit in question shows an undue interest in money or other material items, this is a fairly clear warning sign. Some investigators also make a habit of putting false information—for example, faked letters from a nonexistent family member—in a coat pocket, and then leaving the coat in a place where it can be searched by the spirit's human contact. If details from the faked information show up in the next round of spirit communication, it's a pretty good bet that nothing supernatural is going on.

## The Signs that Point to the Presence of an Actual Spirit Are These:

- An entity that seems to have no fixed shape, but shows definite signs of conscious activity and intention, and is encountered by one or more people;

- The entity's movements and activities are not hindered by most types of physical matter in any way;

- Conversely, the entity seems to be unable to affect physical matter directly;

- The entity may demonstrate knowledge that is not available to the human beings who encounter it;

- The entity's appearances and activities may correlate closely to the movements of the moon or some other celestial body;

- The entity's appearances may also correlate to signs that ritual magic has been practiced in the immediate area;

- The entity's activities do not demonstrate either a high degree of connection to positive spiritual forces, as do the sort displayed by angels, or deliberate malevolence of the sort displayed by demons;

- Other psychological, medical, and criminological explanations have been effectively ruled out.

A majority of these signs should be present before a tentative diagnosis of the presence of a spirit can be justified. A greater degree of certainty, or the identification of the spirit's specific type and name, often requires either ritual evocation or clairvoyant investigation by a trained magician.

## Dealing with Spirits

All contact with spirits should be carried on with the same mix of courtesy and caution one would use toward strangers in an unfamiliar city. Spirits are neither angels nor demons, but conscious individuals with their own motives and their own ways of understanding the universe; their behavior toward us can be as complex and as unpredictable as our behavior toward each other.

With the exception of larvae, who are effectively mindless, spirits communicate easily with human beings. It's generally a good idea to try communicating with a spirit during an encounter; whether its response is truthful or not, it can provide useful information. A spirit that appears more than once should be asked in detail about its purpose and its future plans. On the other hand, as mentioned above, not all spirits are honest, and lack of a physical body is by no means evidence of superior knowledge or good intentions.

If the spirit proves to be dishonest or aggressive, or if its presence becomes a source of problems, it may be banished using the methods given in Part IV of this book. Spirits are particularly vulnerable to ritual magic techniques, and these should be used by preference to remove unwanted spirits from an area. In an emergency, however, burning asafoetida (as described in Part IV of this book) will drive spirits away quite effectively, at least over the short term.

Elementals are in some ways a special case, and require somewhat different handling. Magical lore has it that contact with humans is important to the evolution of the elemental kingdoms; by interacting with us, they rise out of their collective state, taking on individuality, personality, and independent being. In a very real sense, we are the initiators of the elemental kingdom—although they also have initiations of great power to offer us—and all the responsibilities of an initiator rest on us in our dealings with the elemental realm.

Comments the Golden Dawn knowledge lecture already quoted, however:

> The Elemental Spirits and other of their kind are in organization not quite so complete as man. In spiritual consciousness more keen, and yet in some ways his spiritual superior although organically his inferior.

They are the formers of the primal Man, that is the Elementary Man, and they have other and greater offices, for in them are many ranks and worlds and spheres. They are as the younger man (i.e., child) and towards them also is Man responsible, and he hath wrought them much injustice.

Dealings with elementals have certain hidden dangers. These most commonly spring up when a human being interacts solely with elementals of a single type. As creatures of a single element, elementals will tend to strengthen their corresponding elemental force within the human microcosm, and this can lead to a wide range of physical, emotional, and mental imbalances. In extreme cases, according to the lore, a human being who becomes too deeply caught up in one of the elemental realms can be absorbed into it, losing his or her humanity (and physical body) in the process. The way to prevent this, sensibly enough, is to work with elementals of all four kinds, and to balance such interactions with normal involvements in the human sphere.

Larvae, finally, require somewhat different handling from other spirits. While they are useful and even necessary in their proper place, contact with larvae is unhealthy for human beings, and they should be driven away as soon as possible.

Small dishes of vinegar left to evaporate in a larva-infested area will clear them out, as will banishing incenses and the techniques of ritual magic. If larvae have fastened onto the etheric body of a living human being, a sharp iron or steel object (such as a dagger) should be moved in short, quick stabbing motions through an area three to five feet away from the victim's body in all directions. This will disrupt the etheric bodies of the larvae and detach them from their victim.

# ANGELS

Angels, the luminous messengers of the divine described in the scriptures of many faiths, may seem utterly out of place in a book like this one. The idea that angels might be classed with monsters is likely to sound blasphemous even to people whose opinions on the subject aren't shaped by any particular theology. As with so many of the beings we've examined in this book, though, appearances deceive, and the common habits of thinking in our culture—in or out of its more dogmatic religious movements—are a poor guide to the realities of the realm where monstrous beings walk.

Like most of the beings we've covered, angels have a generic form in the American popular imagination, one that has effectively nothing to do with the beings described in authentic folklore or reported from actual experience. In our current culture, an angel is imagined as an attractive woman with long hair and white feathered wings, dressed in a white robe loose enough to avoid any suggestion of sexuality. Now and again one also comes across "angels" who are depicted as naked toddlers with birds' wings—an old image from Renaissance art, this latter. In either case, halos are a fairly common accessory. Saccharine though it may be, it's hard to see anything particularly monstrous in such imagery.

The activities of angels, according to this same mindset, are equally nonthreatening. There's an entire literature nowadays of "I-was-saved-by-an-angel" books, full of accounts of angels doing good deeds and making people feel better, as well as a fair number of books on how to get angels to do various pleasant things for one's benefit. Many of these latter come close to treating angels as a sort of supernatural servant class devoted to the human beings under their care; it's rather reminiscent of Victorian stories about flower fairies, whose sole occupation is strewing rose petals on the garden walk before the children come out to play. Perhaps the furthest extent (so far) of this sort of thinking appeared in a popular bumper sticker of a few years ago: "Never drive faster than your angels can fly."

All this has been heightened in recent years as angels have become a hot property in the world of fashionable imagery, taking over much of the cultural territory once allotted to unicorns and large-eyed puppies. Mail-order catalogs aimed at the New Age market feature angel figurines, angel fortunetelling systems, angel T-shirts, and strap-to-the-back angel wings made of real feathers. One Minnesota couple whose love for their pets may exceed their sense of proportion have produced a website, a newsletter, and a book, all entitled "Angel Animals," treating pets as quasi-supernatural beings pouring out spiritual wisdom and unconditional love for their masters' benefit. Fifteen minutes spent cruising the Internet or scanning the bookshelves at a mass-market bookstore will turn up as many other examples as you wish—or can stomach.

It's instructive to compare such ideas with earlier accounts of angels. Here, for example, is a description of a group of angels, taken from the account of an actual sighting:

> Out of the middle of the fire came what appeared to be four living creatures. This was what they looked like: they had the appearance of human beings. Each one had four faces, and each one had four wings. Their legs were straight, and they had hooves like the hooves of calves, glittering like polished brass. Beneath their wings, they had human hands on all four sides, along with their four faces and four wings. . . . As for the appearance of their faces, each one had a human face, and a lion's face on the right side, and a bull's face on the left side, and an eagle's face . . . [Around them] were what looked like burning coals and lamps, going up and down among the living creatures. The fire was bright, and out of the fire came lightning.

It would be hard to mistake these terrifying "living creatures" for the angels of modern popular imagination. It's easier to see how such bizarre entities could be classed as monsters, in fact, than to find any connection between the "living creatures" and modern angel imagery. Yet the account just quoted is one of the sources from which current angel lore sprang. The witness was the prophet Ezekiel, and his encounter with the four "living creatures" on the bank of the river Chebar in 593 B.C.E., as described in the passage (Ezekiel 1:5–13) cited above, is among the few angelic visitations narrated in detail in the Bible.

Angels, in fact, have been more thoroughly debased by the popular imagination than any other type of entity covered in this book. Behind the well-behaved sweetness and light of the modern media image are older accounts of beings of shattering power and majesty, wielding physical and mental capacities we can scarcely imagine, obedient to purposes we cannot begin to comprehend. When we turn from current imagery to authentic angel lore, white-robed debutantes with pigeon wings give way with blinding suddenness to entities that are often terrifyingly unhuman.

These shapes are not simply a matter of mythology, either. Angels of the traditional sort are still encountered today, by visionaries and by ordinary people. As with the other impossible realities examined in this book, they represent a part of the universe that will not go away, however hard we try to pretend it isn't there.

## The Trace of Angel Wings

As with so many of the entities we've studied, angels can be traced far back in history, but become progressively harder to untangle from other spiritual beings the further

back one goes. The word "angel" itself is a borrowing from Greek *angelos*, "messenger," itself a translation of the Hebrew word for "messenger," *malak*. As this suggests, the concept of the angel in the Western world has deep roots in Jewish tradition, and indeed most Western ideas about angels come ultimately from Jewish sources.

Still, it's a common misconception that angels are purely a creation of the "Religions of the Book"—Judaism, Christianity, and Islam—or of Zoroastrianism, their more ancient equivalent. Pagan traditions from the classical world found room for beings of the same type.

Equally, angel-like beings can be found in a wide range of sources from points further east. Celestial messengers, guardians, and warriors can be found all through ancient Chinese and Indian sources. In early Buddhist art from the cave-temples of northern India, the heavenly beings who gather around the Buddha look so much like Western angels that many art historians simply use "angel" as the most convenient term for them.

More broadly, it's worth noting that the line between angels and gods can be a hard one to draw, and many of the entities that were called gods by the followers of pagan religions seem to have been called angels by later, monotheistic traditions. Between the archangel Michael, guardian power of the sun and slayer of the dragon, and the Greek god Apollo, deity of the sun and slayer of the giant serpent Pytho, it can be hard to find a relevant difference. The same is true of a good many other angels discussed in the traditional lore.

Be that as it may, for around a thousand years—from about 500 to about 1500—angels came to play a dominant role in the spiritual imagination of much of humankind. This was driven by the same forces that made fays (and their cross-cultural equivalents) so significant at the same time. The rise of new religions in East and West made it difficult to lump all the different powers of the Unseen together as gods, the way the older pagan faiths had done. New distinctions had to be drawn, new names devised, and as a result the lore of angels was created and developed in detail.

During this thousand-year period of angelic preeminence, an enormous amount of human energy and attention went into the task of learning as much about angels as possible. It's in this period, for example, that the question of how many angels could dance on the head of a pin was debated by scholars. (Granted that angels exist, this question actually touches on important points—whether angels take up physical space, for example.) Reports of angelic activities in the human world were collected and studied as never before or since, and used as raw material by students of angelol-

ogy; as a result, despite the doctrinal biases that tended to creep in, the angel theories produced by Christian, Jewish, Muslim, and Buddhist scholars all had definite resemblances to one another, and to the actual phenomena of angelic appearances.

As modern science rose to its current domination of the Western mind, by contrast, angels—like everything else that could not be weighed, measured, and dissected—were soon classed as irrelevant. The proponents of the new scientific ideology had to step cautiously at first, since angels had a place in Christian theology, and the Christian churches still held enough political power to make open flaunting of their teachings a risky proposition until well into the nineteenth century. Still, the writing was on the wall long before then, and the detailed systems of angel lore worked out with such care in the Middle Ages were largely forgotten by the time the Renaissance was over.

Swings in cultural fashion, then, made angels important topics of thought in the Middle Ages, and consigned them to the lunatic fringe in more recent years. Such shifts, though, do not seem to have had much impact on the frequency of human contact with angels. Now, as in earlier times, people encounter angels or angel-like beings—sometimes within the framework of religious tradition, sometimes outside of it. Like many of the other entities we've examined, they remain a living presence in the world of our experience.

## The Lore of Angels

So what is an angel? According to the traditional lore, angels are beings of pure consciousness who have no bodies in the ordinary sense of the word, but can take on bodily forms at will. They are neither male nor female; as the Zohar, a primary text of Jewish mystical thought, puts it: "Angels . . . turn themselves into different shapes, being sometimes female and sometimes male" (*Vayehi* 232b).

The forms they take are often those of human beings. Sometimes, though—as Ezekiel found out—angels get a good deal more creative in their appearance. The lore reports such remarkable forms as the Chalkydri, angels of the sun, who have twelve wings, heads like crocodiles, and serpent's bodies, or the Auphanim, who take the form of rapidly spinning wheels decked with countless eyes. Multiple faces are common—seraphim and cherubim alike are said to have four faces each—and wings, when they appear (and they often do not), may be of any number from two on up.

The consciousness of angels is utterly unlike ours. Human beings experience things with their senses and then understand them through reason, but the knowledge of angels was said to come through spiritual intuition. This faculty was called *intellectus* in medieval Latin, and it's one of the ironies of history that this word is the source of "intellect," which now means exactly the sort of reasoning angels *don't* have to do. By means of intellectus, angels know everything in the universe immediately and directly. They do not learn, forget, calculate, guess, or make mistakes; they simply *know*, instantly and without effort. There are certain limits to their knowledge—it's said, for example, that they do not actually know the future before it happens—but distance and all material factors are no obstacle to them.

These powers of awareness are matched by those of movement and action. They can travel from one end of the cosmos to another in an eyeblink, and pass with equal ease through solid matter and the vacuum of outer space. (So much for "Never drive faster than your angels can fly"!)

Though all angels share these powers, not all angels are equal; they are divided into different classes. Different accounts describe these differently. In the version standard in the medieval West, there are nine ranks of angels:

### Seraphim

The highest class, who are angels of radiant love, and contemplate the divine order and providence.

## Cherubim

Angels of absolute wisdom, who contemplate the divine essence and form.

## Thrones

Thrones also contemplate, though some proceed from contemplation to action.

## Dominations

Dominations are like architects, and plan what the lower orders carry out.

## Virtues

Virtues move the stars and planets, and serve as instruments of the divine in the working of miracles.

## Powers

Powers maintain the universe in harmony with the divine will; some descend to interact with human beings.

## Principalities

Principalities have nations and their rulers in their keeping.

## Archangels

Archangels have responsibility for religion and look after holy things;

## Angels

The lowest class, who take care of minor affairs and serve as guardian angels to individual human beings.

Other accounts give other classifications. In the Cabala—the Jewish tradition of spiritual philosophy that became the theoretical basis for most Western high magic—ten orders of angels are described, corresponding to the ten Spheres of the mystical Tree of Life:

## Chaioth ha-Qodesh

"Holy Living Creatures," the highest of the angels, who bear the throne of the Divine.

## Auphanim

"Wheels" or "Whirling Forces," angels of wisdom, described as "wheels within wheels" covered everywhere with eyes.

## Aralim

"Mighty Ones," angels of understanding.

## Chashmalim

"Shining Ones," angels of mercy and magnificence.

## Seraphim

"Burning Ones," angels of severity and justice.

## Malekim

"Kings," angels of beauty and harmony.

## Tarshishim

"Sparkling Ones," angels of victory.

## Beni Elohim

"Children of the Divine," angels of glory.

### Kerubim

"Strong Ones," angels of the foundation of the universe.

### Ishim

"Human beings," angels of the material world.

Many Cabalistic traditions make a distinction between these orders of angels, on the one hand, and archangels on the other. The archangels, according to these accounts, are a yet higher order of spiritual beings who govern and direct the orders of angels, and form the highest circle of spiralling powers around the infinite Divinity.

Thus, the word "archangel" can stand for the highest class of angels or the next-to-lowest rank, depending on the context. This sort of confusion is all too common in angel lore. It's not hard to find passages in old treatises of angelology assigning a given angel to different orders, or to different places in the complex geography of heaven. The study of angelology is rife with such confusions, which did not prevent scholars from working out accounts of the angelic kingdom in fine detail—like the four-teenth-century Cabalists who calculated the number of angels in the universe as exactly 301,655,722.

Equally precise claims based on equally murky foundations surround the question of the origin of angels. In Buddhism and many other Eastern traditions, angels are simply one of the various options for rein-carnation, and someone who is an angel in this cycle of time may be an ape, an amoeba, or a bodhisattva in the next, depending on their actions and state of awareness. In Christianity and many other Western traditions, angels are entirely separate from human beings, and came into being (according to a literal reading of Genesis) on a different day of Creation—although controversies raged all through the Middle Ages over which day it was. Somewhere in between was the Jewish approach, which argued that angels were, generally speaking, distinct from humanity, but held that at least two human beings—Enoch and Elijah—had become angels on their arrival in heaven, and suggested that virtuous human beings were the angels of the material world.

A list of such disputes could go on for many pages. If many of them seem pointless from a modern perspective, it's worth remembering that many of the hot intellectual disputes of the present will seem equally silly in a few centuries. The valuable core beneath all this husk lies in the efforts that were made, all through the great age of angelology, to relate the lore to actual experiences of angelic contact. It's here that the different systems of angel lore come closest to each other, and to modern accounts.

These latter are a very mixed bag indeed, and range all the way from narratives of profound experiences squarely in the great tradition of angel lore, through a wide variety of confused reports and honest misinterpretations, into a maze of crass stupidities and blatant frauds. Those who are interested in sampling the field may look in any of the current books on the subject. It's worth noting, though, that those accounts that seem more or less reliable (as well as a good many of those that don't, it must be admitted) describe angels carrying out much the same functions as the medieval lore relates.

Some angels guide, protect, and advise human beings; others seem to have functions related to the practices and holy things of the various religions. Less commonly encountered are angels set over nations and cultures and those who are involved in the performance of miracles. The angels of contemplation, whose work seems to underlie the fabric of existence itself, tend to be encountered only in profound visionary states.

## Understanding Angels

In most modern traditions of magic, angels are understood in ways that closely parallel the traditional ideas presented above. In particular, since the Cabala—originally a system of Jewish mysticism—has gone on to become the core theoretical structure of most systems of Western magic, magical teachings concerning the angelic realms are broadly the same as those of medieval Jewish angel lore. There are, however, a handful of important differences, mostly derived from the way the magical Cabala has evolved since it broke with strict Jewish orthodoxy and came into contact with the broader world of magical philosophy. In particular, the equation of angels with pagan deities, anathema to most Jewish thought, is a commonplace of the magical tradition.

It's worth mentioning that an alternative view of angels is held in some modern magical traditions. According to this view, which is rooted in Eastern mystical philosophies, angels represent the upper end of a process of evolution parallel to ours. Just as, in terms of biological evolution, single-celled organisms evolve into plants, animals, human beings, and eventually superhuman beings, so in this system elemental spirits evolve into elementaries, spirits, intelligences, and eventually angels and archangels. Which of these magical views of the angelic world is correct is anybody's guess; only the angels know for certain, and they're not telling.

In terms of the levels of being, angels are entities of the spiritual level, the timeless and spaceless realm that is the source of all things. Their powers seem to be effectively unlimited by human standards—a good sign of their connection with the spiritual realm of unlimited potential—and among those powers is the ability to take on temporary embodiments at any level of being. An angel, in other words, can appear at will on the mental, astral, etheric, or physical levels—which is to say that it can take shape as a pattern of abstract meaning, a thought or feeling, an energy, or a living being. It can also affect other beings directly or indirectly at any of the levels, or on all of them at once.

Further details on the magical lore of angels may be studied in books on the subject. Angels play a very important role in modern magical practice; it's been found through experience that angelic energies, invoked in a spirit of humility and profound respect, infuse magical workings with a degree of harmony and balance that reflects itself in the results obtained. The angelic energies can be invited, but never compelled, and so their presence or absence has also proven to be a good way to check on whether a given working is in harmony with the wider patterns and purposes of the cosmos.

## Identifying Angels

The art of distinguishing angels from other spiritual beings was once intensively studied and highly valued, but most religious means of doing so basically amount to checking the theological orthodoxy of the entity that presents itself. Since beings equally angelic seem to appear with equal frequency to Christians, Jews, Muslims, Buddhists, pagans, and people of no particular religious affiliation, this approach seems somewhat limited. Most magical approaches to the same task, in turn, require a thorough mastery of Cabalistic symbolism, and aren't really useable by the layperson.

A sensible approach, however, relies on the same principles of courtesy and caution discussed earlier as a guide to dealing with spirits of all kinds. No honest entity will resent reasonable questions or demand unthinking obedience, and any entity who does so—even if it takes the form of an angel of light—should be ignored and, if necessary, banished by the appropriate magical means.

## Other Beings and Phenomena that Can Be Mistaken for an Angel Include These:

### Other Nonphysical Beings

The current popularity of angels as a form of spiritual fashion statement, by bringing certain images of angels into new prominence, has had certain predictable consequences in the behavior of other inhabitants of the astral realm. Entities of the sort who presented themselves as the spirits of the dead during the spiritualist craze of the mid-nineteenth century, as Masters of the Great White Lodge during the heyday of Theosophy, and as enlightened beings from intergalactic civilizations during the era of

UFO contactees, are now presenting themselves to the innocent and the gullible as angels. In an embarrassing number of cases, despite the usual flurry of vacuous "spiritual teachings" and failed predictions of the future, such claims are being taken at face value.

It's worth remembering that not everything that calls itself an angel deserves the title. Fays, spirits, intelligences, and demonic entities, among others, are perfectly capable of putting on a vaguely angelic form and name if it suits their purposes. There are plenty of entities that will play such games.

This sort of charade is particularly common in the case of "channeled entities" who reveal themselves solely by way of a human channeler or medium. None of the traditional accounts of the angelic realm suggest that angels communicate in this way. While it's no doubt rash to claim that they can't— we simply don't know the limits, if there are any, on angelic power and activity—claims that a given channeled entity is actually an angel should be treated with a good deal of skepticism unless there is compelling evidence for the possibility.

### Human Fraud

Along similar lines, there are plenty of ordinary human beings who have made use of the same fad for angels in much the same way. To claim "angels talk to me" can be a useful tool for con artists, as well as for those who simply need to feel more privileged than other people. The point that it's very hard to disprove such claims makes them all the more convenient for these purposes.

### Misidentified Human Beings and Animals

The sheer sloppiness of much current talk about angels has enabled many people to see angelic interventions when some far more material being has actually been involved. When a stranger proves unexpectedly helpful in a difficult situation, or when a pet startles its owner with some display of intelligence or love, this should be taken as evidence of the potentials within human beings and animals, not as evidence of an angel's presence. These days, human vanity being what it is, this sort of perspective is too often lost—but it should always be kept in mind by the investigator.

## The Signs that Point to the Presence of an Actual Angel Are These:

- An entity interacts with one or more human beings in a wholly constructive and positive manner;

- The nature of the interaction corresponds broadly to those roles assigned to angels in the traditional lore;

- The entity either has no physical presence, or behaves in ways that ordinary physical beings cannot (for example, by appearing or disappearing suddenly without physical traces);

- The entity does not appear to be hindered by material objects in any way, but can manipulate such objects at will;

- If the entity makes any prediction about future events, it proves to be accurate in all details;

- Other magical, psychological, and criminological explanations have been effectively ruled out.

All of these symptoms should be present in order to justify a tentative diagnosis of angelic activity. Here, more than in other monster-related cases, the investigator may find his or her intuition a useful guide—although this should not be allowed to overrule the observed facts in any case.

There is, in particular, a curious "flavor" left behind in cases of actual angelic activity, difficult to describe but easy to recognize once felt. "A sense of clarity and peace" is perhaps the closest approximation in words to this effect, and it can generally be sensed in the person or people involved in the angelic activity, as well as in the place where the visitation occurred.

The presence of other types of spirits tends to produce a very different effect, a sense of murky, confused excitement in people and place alike. Most other spiritual beings, according to the lore, express various partial or unbalanced forces, and have a corresponding unbalancing effect on human beings and their surroundings. Angels, by contrast, are perfectly balanced in terms of the forces they express; human beings are potentially the same—although that potential is realized only in relatively rare cases.

## Dealing with Angels

Angels, as mentioned above, are entities of the spiritual level of being. One consequence of this is that when they act, they do so with the momentum of the entire cosmos, and no lesser power can hinder them. Angels cannot be summoned, commanded, bound, banished, or effectively interfered with in any way; interaction with them takes place on their terms. Our options for dealing with them in any meaningful sense are thus somewhat limited!

There are, however, traditions of magic that specifically focus on work with angels. Given the constraints just mentioned, angel magic may seem like a contradiction in terms, but this points up the differences between the realities of magic and the fantasies of unlimited power too often confused for magic in the modern world. The practitioner of angel magic learns to attune himself or herself to the angelic realm, becoming a conscious vehicle for angelic force and cooperating in the work that angels do in the world.

Outside of such specifically magical approaches, one thing that we can certainly do is to treat the interventions of angels in a sane and sensible manner. According to the lore, the visitations of angels are not a function of any special status or virtue on the part of the people visited. The fact that you may have encountered an angel, in other words, is no evidence that you are any better or more deserving than those who have not. This should be kept constantly in mind when dealing with angel apparitions, as it helps to prevent the vast inflation of the ego that sometimes happens in such cases.

A final note should be made about guardian angels. Angels, as mentioned above, do not experience the universe in the same way that human beings do, and this has practical consequences. Those who have human beings in their guardianship seem to have their own ideas about when human beings need to be protected and when they don't. If the traditional lore is to be relied upon, this may have to do with the differences between intellectus and the more limited and partial human modes of knowing. Most human beings treat pain, misery, and death as evils to be avoided at all costs; tradition and experience alike make it clear that angels see things differently. It's normally a poor bet to count on one's guardian angel to keep off the unpleasant consequences of one's own actions, or to help one dodge the limits of the human condition. Equally, there are times when the most fervent prayers and invocations won't turn aside the death of a child or the failure of a dream. The world's religions have pointed out that suffering has a necessary place in the universe of our experience, and important lessons to teach, and there's much to be said for this viewpoint.

# DEMONS

Of all monstrous beings, demons have kept the strongest hold on their ancient reputation. Their existence is an article of faith to people (for example, many conservative Christians) who would laugh at the idea that vampires or ghosts are real. Our culture has evolved a cartoon image of the demon to go along with its other Halloween-costume caricatures of the Unseen—red clothing, horns, barbed tail, pitchfork, and so on—but this image shares space in the zeitgeist with a vague but terrifying sense of cold, malignant, and disembodied presences watching us from just beyond the limits of our perception. Movies such as *The Exorcist* have kept the ideas of demonic possession and exorcism alive in the popular mind: so much so that Protestants and agnostics all over America routinely call up Catholic priests for help when they have had a frightening encounter with the supernatural.

At the same time, even mentioning the possibility that demons or evil spirits exist is enough to raise hackles in many circles—and not just those committed to the worldview of modern science. A surprising number of people, for example, are convinced that demons are a purely Christian concept, and reject the idea as part of their disagreements with Christianity. Another attitude common in alternative spirituality groups, from Gnostic times to the present, sees evil as a factor of the material level of existence alone. The idea seems to be that once one moves away from the world of matter, everything is well-behaved sweetness and light. A somewhat watered-down version of this attitude is found among people who, though they allow the existence of hostile or destructive spiritual beings, are uncomfortable with straightforward terms like "evil" and "demon" as descriptions for them, preferring to use various euphemisms instead.

These habits of thought, popular as they sometimes are, don't fit well with either common sense or experience. First of all, demon lore was around long before Christianity, and it plays an important role in nearly all of the world's spiritual traditions. There are good, logical reasons for the existence of demons, after all, once the possibility of spirits is admitted in the first place. It's clear enough that there are spirits who behave in a protective and loving fashion toward human beings, others whose actions toward us fall near the middle of the ethical spectrum, and still others who don't seem to be interested in us at all. It seems reasonable that there might be yet others whose behavior toward us is hostile, malicious, hurtful, or simply that of a predator toward its prey. Given that "demon" is a perfectly good English word for such entities, there seems little point in being mealy-mouthed; what we are talking about, after all, are entities that seek to hurt or kill human beings.

Certainly this is what a great many modern people have experienced firsthand. The Old Hag phenomenon mentioned previously should serve as a reminder that attack by disembodied beings is not exactly an unusual experience, even in our time. Certainly a good many haggings seem to be the work of ghosts or magical sendings, and (even in North America) some may well be the work of vampires, but there's reason to think that some are carried out by hostile or predatory nonhuman spirits—that is to say, by demons.

## Demons Through the Ages

Every culture in history has recognized that some spirits have malign intentions toward human beings, and most cultures have full-blown traditions of demonology that recount the nature, powers, character, and potential weaknesses of various kinds of demonic beings in lavish detail. We can't cover more than a tiny sample of these traditions, partly for sheer reasons of space—even a basic outline of, say, Babylonian or Chinese demonology would fill a fair-sized book all by itself—and partly because nearly all these accounts differ wildly from one another. The same sort of variation occurs within religious and magical traditions, and in modern experiences of demonic powers. The one thing that can be said for certain about demons is that they are a diverse lot.

In the earliest civilizations, demonology was already a well-developed branch of knowledge. The clay tablet libraries of Mesopotamia are full of rituals and charms to ward off demonic beings. Egypt and the ancient civilizations further east are equally rich in demon lore. The Roman Empire had its own demonological traditions, in turn, full of entities such as the lamia, a woman-headed serpent fond of shapeshifting and the taste of human flesh, and the strix, a birdlike horror that devoured human beings from the inside out, leaving straw in place of entrails.

A great deal of this material was absorbed into early Christian thought as the classical world tore itself apart. The strong dualistic strain in Christianity directed a good deal of attention toward the hosts of darkness, and much of the raw material for Christian demonology came from older classical sources. The traditional demon and monster lore of tribal peoples across northern Europe also played a role in enriching Christian demonology.

The Christian synthesis of the high Middle Ages included demonology as a branch of angelology, since official doctrine had it that demons were in fact fallen angels. The same attention and effort that enriched the lore of angels was lavished on describing the hosts of Hell. While the study of angels languished in the later Renaissance and the early modern period, however, that of demons thrived up until the final triumph of the scientific worldview.

The reasons for this are intensely human. To a society locked in turmoil, the forces of evil seemed far closer and more important than those of good, and the unreasoning brutality of the late Renaissance witch hunts show how many minds were fixated on "the Devil and all his works." The equally bloody religious wars between Catholics and Protestants also kept theologians on both sides busy explaining exactly how demons were responsible for the other side's activities.

All this ultimately had much to do with the general rejection of the supernatural during the Scientific Revolution. People all across Europe, sickened by the carnage of witch hunts and religious wars, backed away from spirituality of all kinds in the hope that a purely material approach to the universe would provide a framework on which all could agree. While they turned out to be wrong—a point that twentieth-century history has made with terrible force—the appeal of the idea is easy to understand.

All through the Middle Ages, the Renaissance, and the early modern period, though, another approach to demonology was taught and practiced in secretive circles all through the Western world. This was the approach of demonic, or to give it its proper name, goetic magic. Like the rest of the Western magical tradition, goetia has its roots in the classical world; the word *goetia* itself comes from ancient Greek, and originally denoted an ancient tradition of necromantic magic that evoked the spirits of the dead. By the Middle Ages, goetic traditions had shifted focus to more potent spirits, and evolved into full-scale magical systems based on the summoning of demons and other spiritual beings. By the late Middle Ages, there were dozens of grimoires—literally, "grammars" of magical practice—some of them teaching would-be sorcerers how to summon demons for a range of purposes.

Such approaches to magic were always limited to a minority, and the core Western magical traditions have generally warned students away from such activities—a point that hasn't stopped religious propagandists from treating goetia as typical of all magical practice. The popularity of the grimoires, though, and of related elements of folk culture such as the Faust legend, allowed a good deal of goetic lore to creep into wider circulation. Like the theological tradition of demonology, these scraps of goetia have fed into current ideas about demons, as exploited by horror writers, defended by religious conservatives, or recalled uneasily by ordinary people trying to convince themselves that they don't believe in the supernatural.

## Demon Lore

The lore of demons, like their history, is extraordinarily complex, and only a brief summary can be given here. The theologies of various religions have radically different accounts of the origin, nature, and purpose of demonic entities, which complicates matters a good deal; it seems clear, though, that these accounts were put together on the basis of doctrine rather than actual experience. Folklore, often a better guide, is just as murky here; many folk traditions identify demons with the ghosts of the evil dead, while others draw no definite lines between demons, fays, ghosts, spirits, and gods.

As with fays, the behavior of demons seems to be a good deal better understood than their nature. Three aspects of demonic behavior, in particular, can be outlined with a fair amount of clarity: their appearance, their actions toward human beings, and the things that repel or defeat them. This last point will be covered in the last part of this section, and in Part IV of this book; the first two, however, belong here.

When demonic beings interact with human beings, the forms they take are as diverse and confusing as demons themselves, but there is an important common factor. In nearly every culture, descriptions of demons stand out by their sheer weirdness. Reading the old grimoires, for example, one encounters such entities as Marchiosas, who takes the form of a wolf with gryphon's wings and a serpent's tail; Bael, who appears as a man with three heads—

one of a toad, one of a man, and one of a cat—and speaks with a hoarse voice; or Valefor, who has the body of a lion and the head of a thief. Cabalistic demon lore includes even weirder beings: the Tzelladimiron, who look like savage dogs, colored bronze and crimson, with triangular heads; the Neshimiron, who look like pallid and gleaming women starved to skeletal thinness, their bodies fused with those of serpents and fishes; or the Behemiron, who look like some huge animal—a hippopotamus or an elephant—crushed flat, but crawling over the ground with terrible strength.

The Japanese demons who have three eyes and infinitely extensible necks, or the Hindu *asuras* with their weird, composite animal forms, would fit right into the same crowd. The *bizarrerie* of demonic appearance is reminiscent, in a certain sense, of the always-flawed appearances of faery glamour; the difference is that while fays can never quite achieve a perfectly natural appearance, demons never even come close.

The behavior of demons is also relatively consistent from culture to culture, and their most famous habit—that of possession—has generated a substantial folklore of its own. Demons are not the only entities that possess human beings (a point we'll return to in more detail later on), but they are both the most well-known and the most destructive possessing entities.

Books and movies such as *The Exorcist* have caused a good deal of confusion about possession in recent years. Full-scale demonic possession, while it does occur, is actually one of the less common forms of assault by demons on human beings. Far more common is demonic obsession, which is different, a good deal subtler, but often every bit as destructive, and more common still are the less dangerous phenomena of demonic assault and demonic haunting.

### Demonic Assault

Demonic assault will be familiar to anyone who has read the introductory essay to this book. It is, in fact, the Old Hag phenomenon in its classic form. While many different types of entity can carry out a hagging, several of the most distinctive features—notably the sense of supernatural evil, commented on by so many victims of the experience—are characteristic of demonic activity.

### Demonic Haunting

Demonic haunting is closely related to haunting by ghosts, but tends to be a much more specific and localized phenomenon. Demonic hauntings happen in places that have been used for the regular practice of evil magic. Blood sacrifice, in particular, draws demons the way a dead sheep draws flies. Once the energies of a place have been corrupted by this sort of activity, it can take a good deal of very hard work to cleanse them again. Until the link is broken, demonic entities will tend to manifest in the area, and vulnerable people who spend any amount of time there will be at risk.

## Demonic Obsession

Demonic obsession is exactly what the term seems to imply. A victim of obsession is fixated on a specific idea or set of ideas, which are usually self-destructive in one sense or another. However rational he or she may be in any other sense, an obsessed person cannot think clearly about the subject of the obsession, and will attempt to follow the idea to its logical conclusions even when these are clearly disastrous or even suicidal.

All this sounds, in our modern psychoanalytic culture, very like the description of a mental illness. The magical lore concerning obsession would certainly support this idea, but suggests that a good many of the "mental illnesses" common in our society nowadays may be the result of obsession or similar factors. As magical theorist Dion Fortune pointed out some years ago, occultists and psychologists are in many ways talking about the same things in different languages, and in the case of certain members of each camp—C. G. Jung, in particular, on the psychological side, and Dion Fortune herself on the occult side—the languages themselves come close enough to allow easy translation.

Certainly there are mental illnesses that correspond precisely to the traditional picture of demonic obsession. The epidemic of anorexia nervosa—that disastrous amplification of our culture's dieting mania that causes several thousand deaths a year—is a fine example. In an uncomfortable number of cases, people suffering from anorexia have reported hearing voices in their heads encouraging them to starve themselves, or even described the presence of an entity "inside them" who is involved in the disease. Few medical or psychological treatments have been shown to work effectively with anorexia; exorcism, either religious or magical, may be an option worth trying—although such methods should always be used alongside competent medical care, never as a replacement for it.

It's worth noting that demons are not the only entities that can obsess a human being, according to traditional lore. Fays, ghosts, elementals, and (under very specific circumstances) incarnate human beings can obsess people, with similar results. The most notable difference between demonic obsession and other types is that, in most other cases, the obsession makes a certain degree of sense. An elemental obsession typically involves a fixation on one of the four elements; obsession by a ghost usually means that the interests of a dead person suddenly become the overpowering concerns of someone living; the results of obsession by a fay are harder to predict, and can sometimes betray a nearly diabolic sense of malicious humor, but even so there is normally some rhyme or reason to the obsession.

It is not so for demonic obsessions. In these cases, the pattern of obsessing thoughts (and their consequences, if the thoughts are followed out into action) are bizarre, nonsensical, and as often as not ghastly in their consequences. They do not make sense in any human way, and this sheer senselessness is in many ways their best diagnostic trait.

## Demonic Possession

Demonic possession is another matter entirely. The full syndrome of demonic possession has a range of behavioral and medical symptoms all its own. The list from Felicitas Goodman's valuable study *How About Demons?* is worth citing in full:

- insomnia;

- fever;

- agitation;

- roaming;

- compulsively eating strange or repulsive substances, or refusing all food, resulting in an anorexic condition;

- repulsive stench;

- copious foaming saliva;

- trembling, which may escalate into convulsions;

- rigidity of muscles up to a catatonic state;

- severe abdominal pain;

- screaming fits;

- grinding of teeth;

- uncontrollable weeping;

- superhuman strength;

- a near-total change in facial features;

- a number of different forms of aggression, especially autoaggression up to suicide and aggression against associates;

- the demons speak with a rasping, low voice completely unlike that of the natural voice of the speaker, often switching into

- coprolalia (uttering strings of insults and obscenities) in combination with copious divinatory or prophetic pronouncements.

In some ways, possession seems to have connections with multiple-personality disorder (MPD) and other mental illnesses of the same type (dissociative disorders, in psychological jargon). The victim of possession seems to take on a completely different personality, like the MPD patient, although the possessing entity in demonic possession is usually a much nastier customer than the "alters" (alternate personalities) seen in MPD. Cruelty and malice are the dominant factors in the demonic "personality," with an odd sort of self-pity breaking through now and again. As with obsession, possession may be the work of ghosts, fays, or spirits of various kinds, as well as demons; such possessions tend to be somewhat milder and less destructive than the full-scale syndrome of demonic possession outlined above.

Various other modes of attack have been noted. One thing that nearly all have in common is a tendency to assault the mind and emotions, rather than the body. (Even demonic assault, with its obvious etheric aspects, seems to terrify its victims rather than physically harm them—although the relation of hagging-type experiences to SUNDS is a reminder that this may not always be the case.) In certain ways, demons are oddly limited creatures, and it often seems as though they can only harm us to the extent that we let them. As we'll see, traditional lore suggests that this is indeed the case.

## Understanding Demons

The lore of Western magic has its own take on the origin and nature of demonic entities. According to the Cabala, the core philosophy of Western magic, the demonic powers are entities surviving from a universe that existed before this one. Of that earlier universe little is known, but it is said to have been a realm of unbalanced force that destroyed itself after a relatively short period of existence.

The demonic powers of the present cosmos, in Cabalistic lore, are called *Qlippoth*—Hebrew for "husks" or "shells." They are fragmentary and unbalanced powers of the older universe that have become part of the fabric of the universe we know, like stones from an ancient ruin in the structure of a new building. Their presence here is not accidental; their energies are in some sense necessary to the cosmos, and eventually those energies will be brought into a final synthesis.

"Eventually," however, is a very long time, measured in cosmic cycles of almost inconceivable length. In the meantime, although the Qlippoth have a place and a purpose in the universe, they are as alien and destructive to humanity as a black hole or the heart of a star. They interact with us at all, according to the lore, only because of certain major missteps in the early course of human evolution.

To some extent, this can be seen as another theoretical take on demons, like those of other mystical or religious traditions. Still, it has certain practical implications in the magical realms of experience, and it explains—perhaps better than any other account—the sheer bizarreness that is one of the chief hallmarks of the demonic.

In terms of other magical lore we've covered, the demonic realm represents the one area where the traditional system of the levels of being breaks down. This is for a curious reason. Demons are held to inhabit a level of being that is *beneath* matter as we experience it (using "beneath," again, in a metaphorical sense). Physical matter is to the substance of the demonic level what etheric substance is to matter; our physical bodies are said to be like phantoms to demonic perception, while their bodies are on a level we can't perceive at all. The connection between demons and humans (again, according to magical theory, formed due to mistakes in our evolutionary process) is on the astral level, and it's for this reason that our imaginations, thoughts, and feelings are the principal point of assault when demons seek to cause us harm.

Equally, this is a source of strength to us—if we choose to use it. It's a commonplace of the lore that demonic possession and obsession are both voluntary states. In order to become subject to one or the other, a link has to be formed between human awareness and the demonic plane, and that link must be formed from the human side. Demons, in other words, cannot force their way into the human mind or body uninvited, for despite all their powers and unnerving forms, we are stronger than they are—at least potentially. They must seduce, flatter, wheedle, and cajole their way in, for they can only enter with our permission.

Magical lore gives a good deal of information on the events that lead up to a case of obsession or possession, and attention to these details can allow one to be stopped before it becomes established. (Here, as elsewhere in magic, an ounce of prevention is worth a good deal more than a pound of cure.) The syndrome usually begins with brooding over thoughts or feelings of a destructive nature—anger, resentment, jealousy, selfish greed, or the like. This is followed by feelings of chill and drowsiness, which mark the entrance of the demonic entity.

At this point, a clairvoyant will often notice energy changes at the back of the head and neck, where the spine joins the base of the skull, and those who can perceive their own energy flows clearly often feel disruptions there. This is the major point of attack. Natural magic or energy healing focused there will often help substantially, but it's even more important to turn the mind forcibly away from the destructive broodings that admitted the demon in the first place, and to immediately use some way of making contact with the Higher—ritual, meditation, prayer, or what have you. If this is done and persevered in, the intruding entity will be quickly driven off.

Simple courage and perseverance can overcome demons all by themselves, and when these are united with effective magical or religious rituals, the Powers of the Abyss can be readily sent back where they belong. On the other hand, there is little that the magician or anyone else can do if a possessed or obsessed person keeps facing the universe in a passive way. As with so many other issues, the personal equation is the deciding factor.

A word should be added here, along the same lines, about the consequences of goetic magic. There are plenty of books in print that give the methods used to summon demons into manifestation. In the hands of a competent, experienced, and courageous magician, these techniques can be used with relative safety, and there are situations in which such a person may need to deal directly with the inhabitants of the Kingdom of Shells.

Used by the inept, the untrained, or the emotionally unprepared, on the other hand, such methods can be extremely dangerous, because they can form a potent link between the people who take part in such rituals and the demonic entities who are evoked. Admittedly, most such attempts at magic go precisely nowhere—the most common result of incompetently done magic is no result at all—but there is always the possibility of serious trouble. Dabbling in magic without knowledge and systematic training is like mixing together chemicals from a chemistry set at random; most of the mixtures will do nothing, but there's always the chance that one will blow your hand off.

## Identifying Demons

The task of precisely identifying demons can be a difficult one, since the potential for confusion between demons, certain kinds of spirits, and the more malicious sort of fay is fairly large, and the potential overlap between demons and mental illness is even larger. Certain advanced magical and divinatory methods can be used to make sure, but these aren't suited to a book of this type. Still, since nearly all protective measures used against demons will also function well against other spirits—and have been used to good effect in less obviously spirit-caused mental conditions as well—the practical implications aren't as drastic as they might otherwise be.

## Other Beings and Phenomena that Can Be Mistaken for a Demon Include These:

### Other Monstrous Beings

As mentioned above, there's a great deal of potential for confusion among monstrous beings, and there are many different classes of entities who, in some cases and circumstances, will attack human beings. A certain odd sort of vanity adds confusion here; being attacked by one of the Lords of the Abyss can be a good deal more gratifying to the ego than being pestered by an irritated house fay or haunted by a ghost. It's wise to test for the various other types of entity first, using the methods of banishing discussed elsewhere in this book, and conclude that a demon is present only if other possibilities have been ruled out.

### Mental Illness

This is the most important source of confusion in cases of demonic activity, and it's made even more difficult by the overlap between the work of demons and the ordinary (or extraordinary) malfunctions of the human mind. Even when an actual demon is present, there is often a certain degree of mental illness as well; in some cases, this is produced by the demon's activities, while in others, it provides the weakness that allows the demon to get a foothold in the first place. Since possessed or obsessed persons can become a danger to themselves or others, any person who may be possessed or obsessed should receive competent, professional psychological care at once. Rituals, protective measures, and exorcisms must be treated as a supplement to psychotherapy, never as a replacement for it. To do otherwise is potentially to put lives at risk.

### Fantasy and Fraud

There are also those whose sense of self-importance or need for attention expresses itself in fantasies that place them at the center of cosmic battles between good and evil. Most people who have been around awhile in the magical community have met the type. These people will happily talk by the hour about the persecutions inflicted upon them by various and sundry powers of evil; the pout you'll get if you allow a raised eyebrow to express your doubts is among the better signs that this is the sort of person you're dealing with.

It's by no means unknown for people engaged in this sort of behavior to imitate possession, writhe on the floor, cut or injure themselves, and so forth. Pay attention to whether such events have any relation to a lack of attention being paid to the "victim," or to expressions of doubt as to the genuineness of his or her symptoms; the results can be illuminating.

## The Signs that Point to a Case of Actual Demonic Activity Are These:

- One or more witnesses describes a series of events corresponding to the basic patterns of assault, haunting, obsession, or possession as outlined above;

- The apparent victims show no signs of having other personal or psychological motives for falsifying such an account;

- In the case of assault, signs that might identify the spectral assailant as a ghost, vampire, or fay are not present;

- In the case of haunting, evidence for the use of negative magic in the area of the haunting can be found, and evidence for ghosts or other potential causes is absent;

- In the case of obsession, the characteristic patterns of demonic obsession are present, and appear clearly to the investigator;

- In the case of possession, the great majority of the classic symptoms are present, and can be witnessed by the investigator;

- Protective and banishing measures bring at least short-term relief;

- Other medical, psychological, and criminological explanations have been effectively ruled out.

All the above factors that are relevant to the case should certainly be present in order to justify a tentative diagnosis of demonic activity. In any such case where obsession or possession is involved, prompt psychological help by a mental health professional should be arranged as soon as possible.

## Dealing with Demons

From ancient times, in most of the world's cultures, dealing with demons has been one of the occupational specialties of the priest, the shaman, or the magician. Just as the traditional Hmong relied on religious specialists to carry out the ceremonies that kept dab tsog at bay, and the Babylonian commoner made offerings at the local temple for protection against demonic planet-spirits, the European peasant once turned to the local parish priest (or, if he or she happened to be Jewish, to the chief rabbi of the local synagogue) for exorcisms, prayers, and blessings to ward off the forces of supernatural evil.

In a few parts of the Western world, this still holds true. Elsewhere, though, the Reformation and the rise of scientific ideology led the religions of the West to jettison traditions of religious magic that once served an important role in preserving the mental and spiritual health of their lay members. A few denominations still maintain the ancient protective rituals, although many of these have been watered down, or are so rarely practiced that a competent performance is hard to come by.

For the last three centuries, as a result, the only source of help for people in the Western world plagued by demonic powers has been the underground subculture of magical practitioners. Unfortunately, the magical community is a very mixed bag. Extremely competent magicians are to be found there, but so are poseurs, self-proclaimed adepts of negligible power and knowledge, and a wide array of swindlers and crooks. There are also, unfortunately, a good many kind and honest souls whose training and experience simply isn't up to the demands of dealing with demons one-on-one.

This is especially true when obsession or possession are involved. Exorcism is not a job for amateurs; it is difficult, dangerous work. Carrying out an effective exorcism requires unshakable courage and self-control, total mastery of the ritual forms that are to be used, a thorough knowledge of all one's own weaknesses and limitations, and access to the sources of spiritual power—an access that is gained only by systematic magical or spiritual practice backed up by a

life of complete commitment to the Higher. With anything less than these qualifications, the exorcist is likely to end up at the mercy of the forces he or she seeks to banish, and the possessed person may end up much worse off than he or she started.

If you're dealing with a full-blown case of possession or obsession, therefore, your options are fairly limited. Much depends on the attitude of the person affected, of course, and if he or she is willing to fight back the outlook is good. If you feel comfortable taking up the matter with a religious specialist, this is often a possibility, although you should make sure that the person in question has some experience in the subject. If you have connections in your local magical community and can get referred to someone with a solid reputation, that is also a route worth following. There are also psychotherapists who have added religious or shamanic practices into their professional toolkits, and some of these can handle cases of this sort effectively.

Another possibility, one that often has good results, is to make contact with a circle, coven, or other working group that does collective prayers or blessings. These should be repeated on a regular basis, at least once weekly if possible. The focused will of a trained group can often break even a strongly established link between a human soul and a demonic power. The possessed or obsessed person should not be physically present when the prayer or blessing is performed, as he or she will bring discordant energy into the space and may try to disrupt the working itself; such things are best done at a distance of at least one city block, if at all possible, to minimize interference.

If you find yourself facing an apparent demonic intrusion into your own psyche, you are on much stronger ground. Here the crucial point has already been made: you need to avoid a passive attitude to the phenomenon at all costs. Both ritual and natural magic, of the sort outlined in Part IV of this book, can be used effectively. So can any of the methods mentioned above.

There are also several simpler steps to take. If you find an idea obsessing you, force it out of your mind whenever you notice it, and put something else in its place. Arrange to spend as little time alone as possible while this is happening. Massage, energy-based healing work, and spiritual or religious rituals of blessing and healing are other resources you should not neglect, and some form of psychological counseling is a must, if only to help you keep your grip on the ordinary world while dealing with the problem. Faced with this sort of response, demonic entities quickly go off in search of easier prey.

In any event, it's a good idea to hinder and harass the demon as much as possible, and here the methods in Part IV of this book are a good place to start. Natural magic will do some good; although it normally can't break the link between the victim and the demon, it can at least make life harder for the entity. Ritual magic will do a great deal more, and can drive off a demon in short order if it's done competently. Any other form of spiritual practice, prayer, blessing, or positive working will also tend to make the environment hostile to demons. When these are combined with more robust methods of exorcism or banishing, and with psychological care (and ordinary kindness) for the victim, the results are usually good.

In the event that some lesser form of demonic manifestation is involved, your options are correspondingly greater. The basic protective rituals given in Part IV of this book, if memorized, carried out precisely as written, and repeated daily, will chase off demonic entities in short order. If the entities have become well established in a location, it may take some time for the link to be broken, but broken it will be.

Regular spiritual practices of any sort will tend to have similar effects. So, it deserves to be said, will the practice of ordinary human virtues such as courage, persistence, patience, and love. For all their nightmare forms and reputations, demons are inferior to us; limited and unbalanced, they have no power over us unless we give it to them.

*Part III*

# A GUIDE TO MONSTER INVESTIGATION

# THE COMPLEAT INVESTIGATOR

As we saw in Part I of this book, monsters are a pervasive factor in the universe of human experience, and the material covered in the Field Guide shows something of the diversity of monsters encountered by human beings. For most modern Americans, such information is the stuff of nightmares. Monster movies and monster-related horror fiction are popular precisely because people don't believe in the reality of monsters; the thrill of vicarious fear can be enjoyed because no one worries about being attacked by a vampire, a demon, or a vengeful ghost on the way home from the theater. Faced with the reality of monsters, most people nowadays would find them a good deal less entertaining.

For those people whose lives have already been affected by monsters, though, it can be hard to recover the comforts of disbelief, and potentially dangerous to try. Turning one's back on a troubling or traumatic experience, however "impossible" our culture may label the experience, is a good way to risk one's mental health. If the entity involved is dangerous or predatory, furthermore, convincing oneself that nothing really happened makes it hard to prevent a recurrence of the encounter—and the consequences of ignoring certain types of monstrous phenomena can be life-threatening. For those who are already dealing with monsters willy-nilly, then, it's imperative to face the reality of the impossible and to try to learn as much as possible about what is happening and why.

177

There are also people who are drawn to monstrous phenomena—those who seek out the unknown and the impossible. Despite the stereotypes, surveys have shown that most of these people are above average in intelligence and education, and are no crazier than the rest of the population; they simply find the cozy image of reality marketed by our culture's official information sources too stifling to tolerate. To such people, the reality of monsters is not a threat but a challenge, and the possibility of finding out more about monsters is a source of fascination rather than of fear.

Finally, there are those who have already abandoned our culture's limited approaches to reality in favor of the older and wider vistas of traditional magical philosophy and practice. For such people, the magical lore of monsters is one field of knowledge within a broader realm, and may be studied to a greater or lesser degree as part of the path of magical training.

For all three of these groups of people—those who have encountered monsters and need to understand the experience, those who seek to unravel the mysteries of monstrous phenomena, and those who come to monster lore from the standpoint of the practicing magician—the material we've already covered is a prologue to the real work. Beyond the insights of theory, the teachings of folklore and occult tradition, and the body of modern accounts of mon-ster activity, lies the task of identifying, understanding, and dealing with monstrous beings in the specific situations where they interact with the human world. To take on this task is to leave behind the generalities we've considered so far, and to face the realm of monsters from a new perspective—the perspective of the investigator.

## Requirements of the Art

The art of hunting monsters, to use a possibly flippant phrase for this difficult and demanding job, has rarely been handled well in modern times. In part, this is because most of those who have attempted it have been poorly trained and prepared for the hunt. This has a good deal to do with the very mixed motives that lead people into monster investigations. Debunkers of the dogmatic variety, who assume from the start that all monster reports must be some combination of delusion, misunderstanding, and fraud, are unlikely (to say the least) to have the sort of training that would enable them to detect and deal with real monsters. Their opposite numbers, those people who assume from the start that all monster reports must be produced by actual monsters, are just as unlikely to have the sort of detective skills that would warn them when the witnesses are in fact deluded, lying, or misinterpreting some perfectly natural phenomenon. The result has been far too many bungled monster investigations, and far too little useful information about monsters.

Assuming that you, the reader, hope to investigate apparent monster sightings (your own or someone else's) in a less inept manner, where do you start? There are no academies, professional associations, or licensing exams for the would-be monster hunter, nor will you find night classes in Monstrology 101 at your local community college. Monsters are so far outside the boundaries of our culture's definitions of reality that even groups on the cultural fringe shun them; most parapsychologists, for example, will have nothing to do with perspectives of the sort advanced in this book. As a result, even those who deal with other unexplained phenomena may be at a loss when dealing with monsters; a background in modern parapsychology, again, will be little help to the monster hunter (although a background in old-fashioned psychical research is another matter).

If you intend to start probing into the realm of the monstrous, then, you're largely on your own as far as education and training are concerned. Still, this doesn't mean that trial and error is your only option. While there's little information or training available that directly addresses the needs of a would-be monster hunter, the skills and personal qualities needed for this neg-

lected art are also central to various other hobbies and professions.

In a very real sense, a monster hunter is one part private detective, one part folklore researcher, and one part naturalist. To this, for those who are willing to meet monsters on their own ground, can be added an additional part: practitioner of magic.

These comparisons can be worked out in detail. Like a private eye, a monster researcher is in the business of finding things that are hidden. Both interview witnesses, ask questions, conduct surveillance, locate information sources, and piece together clues. Both are always alert to the potential for fraud and deception, and use many of the same techniques and strategies to get at the truth.

Like a folklore scholar, in turn, a monster researcher works with the wealth of knowledge held by ordinary people, some of it rejected and despised by our culture's official sources of information. Both are skilled listeners, good at putting people at their ease and encouraging them to talk about what they know. Both keep meticulous records, and both know how to search out connections between a local tale or an odd fact and the vast wealth of folklore gathered by other scholars around the world.

Like a naturalist, in addition, a monster researcher studies rare and elusive creatures that tend to avoid human beings. Both must be watchful, perceptive, and almost inhumanly patient, aware that their contacts with the creatures they study will almost always be carried out on the creature's terms, not their own. Both learn as much as possible about the subjects of their research in advance, so that the brief moments of direct interaction will not be wasted. Both can expect to venture into unfamiliar territory, and must know how to prepare for the trip.

Like a practitioner of magic, finally, a monster researcher deals with things that operate beyond the edges of our culture's ideological radar screens. Both must be comfortable with the reality of the impossible, able to work calmly and efficiently when unnerving events are going on all around them. Both study the traditional lore about the powers with which they deal, learning the nature and habits of those powers, the dangers involved in interacting with them, and the ways those dangers can be held in check. Both know that fear is the first enemy that has to be fought and mastered in any quest worth the name.

## Preparing for the Hunt

All this may sound like a tall order—and it is. To some extent, the above description is an ideal, not a practical job description, but it's an ideal toward which anyone seriously interested in investigating monsters can and should strive. All the things mentioned above, magic included, can be studied in books from your local bookstore or public library, and if you live in an urban area odds are good that you can find classes on some or all of them as well. Such resources may not seem very helpful if you're in the middle of a poltergeist outbreak or some other continuing monster experience, but in any encounter with a monster, the more you know, the better prepared you will be; even one afternoon spent at the public library, reading all the books you can find on the subject, may provide you with information of critical importance.

Books or classes, however, aren't going to be enough. No matter how much you read or how many classes you take, if you don't have personal experience in using the skills you learn, they are worthless. You can read thirty different books on private investigation, for example, and still be completely at a loss the first time you have to search a house for clues. The only way to develop the skills and practical knowledge you need is to put it to actual use.

There are various ways to do this, but they all add up to the same thing: practice. The skills you need to know in order to investigate a monster sighting can and must be practiced over and over again. As you read the following pages, and as you extend your studies into other books, keep an eye open for possible ways of putting the material into practice.

There is nothing like on-the-job training for the would-be monster hunter, and if you are in the middle of a series of monster encounters your best bet is to try to put skills to use as soon as you learn them. If you don't happen to have a monster handy to experiment on, though, there are other options. Perhaps the most effective is to conduct a practice monster hunt, a full-scale investigation in which everything is present except the monster. This can be as simple or as elaborate as you wish, and works particularly well if you are training together with other apprentice investigators. Come up with a scenario—a given type of monster, sighted in a given place under some specific set of conditions—and then carry out the investigation in as much detail as you can. A series of practice hunts, carried out with different scenarios in different places, can provide a solid foundation of skills for actual investigations—especially if the participants sit down afterward and discuss the strengths and weaknesses of the way each part of the exercise was handled.

Alternatively, it's possible (and often useful) to break the process of monster hunting down into different sets of skills, and then put one or more of them to use in some appropriate context. One very good way to practice interviewing skills, for example, is to ask your own friends and relatives about any strange experiences they may have had in the past—visits by dead relatives, attacks of the Old Hag type, or what have you. Given the percentage of people in our society who have had at least one such experience, you're likely to come up with several accounts to work with. Since most people like to talk about themselves, too, asking around for personal experiences is also a good way to announce your interest in monsters, and will make it more likely that you'll get a call if someone you know has a monster-related experience.

## Tools of the Trade

As you're learning the tricks of the monster-hunting trade, you'll need to start collecting the tools of the trade as well. Monsters vary widely in their effects and the traces they leave behind them, and the equipment and supplies you'll need will vary accordingly. Some basic tools, though, will see you through most monster investigations:

### Notebook and Pen

The first requirement in any monster investigation is to get down the facts in some form more durable than human memory. A notebook and pen may seem old-fashioned in today's high-tech environment, but they have some major advantages over electronic media: they don't need batteries, they can be used silently, and they aren't vulnerable to the weird electrical effects that accompany some types of monstrous phenomena. If your investigations are likely to take you outdoors and you live in a rainy climate, try to find notebooks of waterproof paper, which can be written on in pouring rain without becoming illegible; many camping-supply stores and stationers carry these. Several good ballpoint pens would also be a wise investment.

### Maps of the Area in Which You Will Be Working

Depending on where you live and how far afield you pursue your researches, this may be anything from a city map to a packet of USGS topographic maps of wilderness areas. You'll need these first to find your way to the monster sighting, second to provide clues about the way the monster relates to the local surroundings, and third to help you find your way to safety if you get lost while chasing the monster in unfamiliar territory.

### Graph Paper

This is used to make a sketch map of the area of a monster sighting, and to note down the exact location of the clues you may find. It's possible to buy graph paper printed on waterproof paper stock, and if you have outdoor monster hunting in mind this is often a good idea.

### Tape Measure

Exact measurements are of the highest importance in mapping a monster's activities, especially if tracks or other physical traces are involved. A carpenter's twenty-foot tape measure is normally enough.

### Compass

Directions are also important in mapping out the scene of a monster sighting, and a compass can also help you find your way to safety if you get lost during a monster hunt. The best compasses for this purpose are the sort mounted on clear plastic bases, which are meant to be used with maps. Don't hesitate to spend a few dollars extra here, since a cheaply made compass can be worse than useless in an emergency.

### Watch

What a map is to space, an accurate watch is to time. One that has mechanical works, even if it's battery-operated, will be less likely to jam up in the presence of monstrous phenomena than a digital electronic watch, and a good, hand-wound, spring-driven pocket watch in a metal case is worth its weight in wolfsbane to the monster hunter.

### Polaroid Camera with Flash

A picture, as the old saying has it, is worth a thousand words, and nowhere is this more true than in monster research. Not all monsters can be photographed, but some can, and photographs of any physical traces a monster leaves behind may be worth more than a close-up shot of the monster itself. Polaroid cameras are far and away the most useful, since you can see at once whether or not anything has interfered with the picture.

## Swiss Army Knife or Pocket Tool

Many tools are occasionally useful in monster hunting, but carrying around a pickup full of tools is not a very efficient response! Fortunately, there are now various brands of folding pocket tools available combining pliers, wire cutters, screwdrivers, files, knives, awls and so forth in a single easily carried device. Some types of Swiss Army knife also have a good selection of useful tools to offer. Plan on spending some money for a sturdy model that can stand up to wear and tear; many of the cheap models are made of soft metal and will break under any kind of serious use.

## Weather Thermometer

Several different kinds of monsters, including ghosts and vampires, produce a noticeable chill in the air around them as they pass through an area, and this can often be detected with a weather thermometer. A fairly large model, with an easy-to-read face, makes a good investment.

## Flashlight

A small flashlight or penlight is a necessity for nocturnal monster hunts; it's often wise to pocket two of them in case one fails in the middle of the night, and to have backup batteries and at least two spare light bulbs. A red filter, or a piece of red cellophane taped over the lens, makes it possible to read your watch and the weather thermometer without wrecking your night vision; it can also reveal fishing line, plastic transparencies, or holograms, all of which are sometimes used by hoaxers to fake a monster sighting. A large, bright flashlight of the sort carried by night watchmen can also be useful, since suddenly flooding an area with light is a good way to catch hoaxers, animals, and other material causes of apparent "monster activity."

## Candle Lantern, Candle in Open Candlestick, and Waterproof/ Windproof Matches

Electrical devices routinely misbehave in the presence of preternatural beings, and this is true of flashlights just as much as more complex devices. Camping-supply stores sell small lanterns that hold votive candles or tea lights, and allow them to burn free of wind, rain, and the danger of accidentally starting a fire. One of these can be a useful addition to a monster hunting kit if you expect to do any work during the hours of darkness. A burning candle can also serve as a early warning system for some kinds of monsters, since traditional lore insists that candles burn blue in the presence of ghosts, vampires, demons, and spirits. To detect subtle air movements that can cause false "cold spots," a candle burning in an ordinary candlestick is perhaps the most sensitive tool (watch the way the flame moves). With either or both, bring plenty of camper's waterproof/windproof matches so that you can be sure of striking a light even in adverse conditions.

### Tape Recorder

Since you're unlikely to be able to write as fast as witnesses can talk, a portable tape recorder of the sort used for taking dictation is useful for interviewing those present at a monster sighting. Bring extra batteries and at least two more cassettes than you think you'll possibly need.

### Hoax-Detection Equipment

Various simple, low-tech methods can be used to detect monster hoaxes, and an assortment of them should certainly find a place in your equipment. Especially useful is a length of dark thread that can be stretched across a doorway, a corridor, a space between trees, or any similar opening, and fastened on both ends with small balls of rubber cement; if anything more solid than a ghost passes through, the evidence will be clear in the morning. Other good

examples are masking tape to seal doors and windows (with your name signed across the opening to prevent easy replacement), and chalk powder or cornstarch to show footprints.

## Filling Out Your Kit

All these supplies can be kept in a shoulder bag or small backpack, so that you don't have to scramble around putting together a kit in a hurry before you can get to work investigating a monster sighting. Make sure there's additional room in the bag or pack, since there are other things you'll need to add on a case-by-case basis:

- If you expect to investigate monsters in rural or wilderness areas, *always* add the following ingredients to your kit before you start: food and water, appropriate clothing for the season and area, sunglasses and sunscreen, matches in a waterproof container, a pocketknife, a good outdoors-oriented first-aid kit, and a lightweight metallized-plastic survival blanket. If you become lost or stranded in the backcountry during your investigation, these things can quite literally save your life.

- In urban or suburban areas, change for phone calls and transit fare, food and water, additional warm clothing in anything but high summer, and a can of pepper spray for protection from hostile dogs or humans are nearly always worth taking along.

- If there is any chance that the monster may attack or negatively affect human beings in the area you will be visiting, or if it has already done so, bring the magical emergency kit (described in the section on Natural Magic, pp. 217–227) with you, and any protective magical devices you wish. If you have already made and consecrated it, the Trident of Paracelsus should certainly be included (see pp. 225–227). If you can identify the monster based on information you've already received, check Part II of this book for specific protective gear that you may want to bring along as well.

The same cardinal rule mentioned above for skills also goes for these, and all other tools of the trade: if you don't have personal experience in using them, they are worthless. Very few people nowadays, for example, have any clear idea of how to read a compass the right way, and if the first time you've ever tried to do so is on a dark night when you're trying to find your way back five miles through dense woods to your car, you may be in real trouble. Similarly, if you hope to use thread and rubber cement to trap a hoaxer, you need to have tried the process out yourself at home,

preferably more than once, so you know how to put the trap in place quickly and effectively, and how to read the clues left behind when something more solid than a ghost passes through it.

Here again, a few practice monster hunts of the sort described above can provide effective training for the real thing. If you're working with others, it can be an educational experience to have one or more apprentice monster hunters prepare a house or apartment with thread, rubber cement, tape, chalk powder, and similar hoax-detection gear, and then have someone else try his or her best to get in and move around at night without falling afoul of the various traps. The "ghost" can leave notes in each room he or she visits to prove that he or she was actually there, and "ghost" and hunters can go into the house in the morning together and examine the results.

Along the same lines, there's much to be learned from carrying out an all-night outdoor monster surveillance for the sake of practice. Choose a location where you will not attract attention, and where your presence won't put you on the wrong side of trespassing laws; take up a position around sunset, in a location with a clear view of the area you intend to watch; wear dark clothing, and bring thermos bottles of soup, coffee, tea, or something else hot, along with your ordinary monster-hunting kit. Keep watch, noting down whatever happens, until dawn. This can be particularly useful if you've arranged for someone to represent the monster by showing up one or more times in the middle of the night and walking through the area under surveillance. A monster costume for your nocturnal visitor is optional, though gorilla suits or Hollywood vampire attire can certainly add to the entertainment value of the exercise.

## Principles of Investigation

Each monster investigation is different. Just as there are skills and tools you will need for any monster hunt, though, there are basic principles that govern any investigation. As with any art—and monster hunting is certainly an art—there are various pointers that will help keep you on the right track as you go to work.

Certain principles need to be covered at the very beginning, as they govern everything that a monster hunter does from the start of an investigation to its end. These can be summed up in seven basic rules that should govern all investigations.

### Know Your Priorities

The competent and ethical monster hunter has three priorities in mind as he or she carries out any investigation. The first priority—and it must *always* come first—is to safeguard the physical and mental well-being of everyone involved, including the

investigator. The second is to deal with the monster, if it is still in the area or seems likely to return. The third, which should be considered only after the first two are taken care of, is to gather as much information as possible about the monster and the experiences of those people who encountered it. These priorities should govern everything you do in the course of an investigation; if the person who encountered the monster is hurt or in hysterics, for example, or if something less than physical is making noises in the house around you, you have no business sitting down to interview another witness or making a search of the yard unless someone else is already taking care of the immediate situation and your help is not needed.

### Know Your Limits

As a monster hunter, you are an amateur practitioner of a specific, rather unusual avocation, and—unless you've been doing it in all your spare moments for a couple of decades—there are sure to be many things even in that avocation that you don't yet know or can't do well. It's critically important that when you encounter a situation you can't or shouldn't handle, you should recognize this and get skilled help. In particular, unless you're a licensed health practitioner, your healing activities should be limited to providing first aid for serious injuries while the ambulance is on its way, or making a cup of herb tea for someone who has a stress headache or a mild case of nerves. Similarly, if you come across evidence that laws are being broken, you have a legal as well as an ethical duty to report it to law enforcement personnel, rather than trying to play Sherlock Holmes yourself.

## Work with Others Whenever Possible

For the same reasons that police officers work with partners and mountain climbers tackle peaks in parties, monster hunters should never work alone if there is any alternative. If the hunt takes you somewhere out of the reach of immediate help, a simple accident or injury (say, a broken bone) could put your life at risk if you are alone. There are also other issues. Whether you encounter an apparently real monster or evidence of a hoax, two witnesses are better than one; having at least two people present also helps insure that all the tasks that may be part of a monster investigation can be done quickly and efficiently.

## Always Use Caution and Common Sense

Monster hunting is not a risk-free occupation. Over and above the possible dangers from hostile or predatory monsters themselves, risks from human and animal attack, weather, and a wide range of accidents are all potential problems that the monster hunter may face. Most of these problems can be prevented or handled safely by the use of sensible caution and ordinary common sense. Similarly, attention to legal details (such as trespassing laws) will keep you out of a good deal of completely avoidable trouble.

## Maintain an Open Mind While Investigating a Case

Many people who investigate strange events of any sort start out with a set of assumptions and goals that make it impossible to study any individual case with an open mind. The debunker assumes that all such phenomena are nonsense, while the true believer assumes that all are real, both, however, tend (consciously or not) to see what they want to see, and to ask questions and pay attention to evidence that will support their preconceived ideas. To avoid this habit, not to mention the incompetent investigations that tend to result from it, it's critical that you investigate first and interpret the results afterward. Remember that any given monster sighting may be caused by a real monster, a misidentified natural phenomenon, a mental illness on the part of the witness, or a deliberate hoax on the part of either the witness or someone else. Above all else, remember that your job is to find out what actually happened, not to bolster the case for some particular pet theory.

## Always Use Tact, Courtesy, and Honesty

If there is one rule that all would-be monster hunters should burn onto their backsides with a branding iron, it is this: *You cannot expect help or respect from anyone unless you earn it by your behavior.* To most modern-day Americans, your interest in monsters—not to mention your willingness to think of them as possibly real—marks you as a potentially dangerous crackpot, and the only way you are going to change their minds is to behave in a polite, considerate, and strictly ethical fashion at all times. No matter how much you want to find additional witnesses to a monster sighting, pounding on doors at two o'clock in the morning is out, and so is continuing to pester people who have already said that they don't want to discuss the matter with you. If you are told something in confidence, then you must keep it in confidence, no matter how much you may want to publicize it; if a witness requests that her name and address not be made public, then you need to keep it private, and that is that. Word gets around, and earning a reputation for honesty, accuracy, and courtesy will get you much more cooperation (and, if you're seeking them, many more cases) than leaving behind a trail of angry and upset people whom you've hurt, embarrassed, or annoyed.

### Set Realistic Goals

Most apparent monster sightings are never conclusively solved one way or another, despite all the efforts and resources that investigators may bring to bear. (This is, after all, one of the major reasons why monstrous beings have remained outside our culture's official version of reality.) Odds are that the best you will be able to do, in most cases, is to come to a tentative identification of the cause of the event, and provide some helpful advice to the people affected by it. It's entirely appropriate to set out with high hopes, but if you judge your work by standards of perfection, you're bound to end up disappointed.

## Essential Skills: Interviewing

One of the most important skills you will need to develop is the skill of interviewing people who claim to have encountered a monster. Although many people who are drawn to monster lore like to imagine themselves in face-to-face contact with unearthly creatures, even the most common types of monsters are relatively rare, and odds are that unless you start out in the middle of a monster-related event, you'll spend much more time listening to the details of other peoples' monster experiences than having experiences of your own.

*Listening*, here, is the most important word. The point of an interview is to gather information, not to show off your own knowledge, argue with the witness, or get involved in any of the various self-defeating personality games that make up so much of ordinary human conversation. The more time you spend with your mouth closed and your ears wide open, the more effective a job you'll do and the more information you'll gather.

The information you need will vary from case to case, but some things always need to be learned if there is any possible way to do so. It's almost always best to let the witness tell his or her story from beginning to end first, but once this is done, you should start asking questions. Always try to get information about the following points in as much detail as possible:

### What is the name, age, gender, and occupation of the witness being interviewed?

If the witness doesn't want his or her full name used, stress that this (or any other) information can be kept confidential if the witness prefers; if this doesn't solve the problem, ask for a first name, pointing out that you would rather not have to call them "Hey you" all the time. Someone who doesn't want to give any identifying information may be honestly afraid of being treated like a lunatic—such treatment is all too often inflicted on people who experience "impossible" events—but this sort of behavior is also a common habit of the more casual sort of hoaxer, and should be treated as a warning sign.

### What was the date, time, and location of the encounter?

These should be determined as exactly as possible. A floor plan or a sketch map of the area, with locations of the witness, the monster or monsters, and other significant objects marked on it is invaluable.

### Where was the witness and what was he or she doing at the time that the encounter started?

Some monsters are associated with certain places, while others may be attracted or even summoned by certain activities on the part of witnesses. These possibilities should always be kept in mind. The location and activities of the witnesses are also of high importance for figuring out the exact movements and actions of the monster.

### What was the emotional state of the witness immediately before the encounter?

Like the last question, this helps determine how the state of the witness may have affected the experience.

### Was the witness using any sort of medication, drugs, or alcohol at the time of the encounter? Does he or she have any vision or hearing problems, or any medical conditions that might be relevant to the experience?

Again, this question is meant to sort out some of the variables rising from the state of the witness. You'll want to be careful in phrasing this question so that the witness doesn't think you're accusing him or her of being drunk or on drugs; it often works well to start off with "Just for the record . . ." or some similar phrase, to let the witness know that this is a standard question that everyone gets asked.

### How did the encounter begin?

Some monsters seem to materialize out of thin air, others move into view of the witness from some place out of sight, while still others may be discovered looming over the bedside of a suddenly awakened sleeper. All these details are of importance. The precise location of the monster at the time it was first sighted is especially important, and should be noted down with care in both the report and the floor plan or sketch map.

### What did the monster look like?

The size, color, shape, and other characteristics of the entity are of high importance. Be sure to note down (or to ask) whether it appeared to be solid, misty and diffuse, or near-transparent, and whether it had a visible aura (a zone around it containing a noticeably different color or level of light than the rest of the surroundings). If it was clothed, make note of the type, color, style, and apparent historical period of the clothing; if it seemed to be carrying anything, make note of what the item was and what the entity did with it.

### What did the monster do during the time when the witness observed it?

The movements and other actions of the monster should be noted down as exactly as possible. Important points are whether it passed through walls, furniture, or people; whether it made any noise; and whether it moved any objects in the surrounding space. Its movements should be noted in detail, and traced out on the floor plan or sketch map.

### Did the monster seem to have any particular personality, or show any emotions?

This is a judgment call on the part of the witnesses, of course, but it can include important information. One of the classic features of the Old Hag experience, for example, is the sense of malignant evil that normally accompanies it. Ghosts often have a specific emotional tone, and may also be observed behaving in ways that suggest grief, anger, depression, or other emotional states. Other monsters, by contrast, show no signs of emotion at all.

### Did the monster seem to notice or interact with the witness in any way? If so, how?

Interactions between monsters and witnesses vary from none at all—many preternatural beings seem not even to notice the human beings who see them—through glances, gestures, and spoken words, to attempts at sexual seduction or an all-out physical or psychic attack. Once again, note down the details.

### Did any sounds, visual effects, odors, or changes in temperature seem to be associated with the encounter?

Some monsters make noise, and some are accompanied by noises that they do not appear to make. Certain visual effects accompany certain preternatural beings; for example, candle flames changing suddenly bluish is a traditional sign of the presence of spirits. Scents, ranging from roses to rotting flesh, and sudden increases or decreases in temperature are also common in certain kinds of monster encounters.

### When and how did the witness first realize that the encounter involved something unusual?

Some monsters obviously violate our ordinary notions of what is real, but others may not—at least at first glance. A mermaid may look like a woman swimming in the sea until her fishtail comes into view, or a ghost may resemble an ordinary human being until it walks through a wall.

### What did the witness do during the time that the monster was visible?

The activities of the witness are important for figuring out the sequence of events during the encounter. If the witness' description of his or her actions differs sharply from other people's accounts or the evidence of the scene, on the other hand, the sighting may be a hoax.

### Did anything else unusual happen immediately before, during, or immediately after the encounter?

In dealing with monstrous beings—or, for that matter, with hoaxes—events surrounding the actual experience, no matter how minor they seem, can provide major clues.

### Were other people present, and did they seem to perceive anything?

Not all people perceive the same thing when a monstrous entity shows up. In the presence of the same ghost, for instance, one witness may see a human shape, another may see a blurry patch of dim light, and a third may see nothing at all. If more than one person saw the entity, or if only one saw it but others noticed details about the situation in which the encounter took place, each one may have something of importance to report.

### If there were other witnesses, what did they do immediately before, during, and immediately after the time when the monster was present?

This question allows you to check the different accounts you may get from different witnesses, and it also provides another way to detect possible human influences on the monster.

### Were any animals present during the encounter, and if so, how did they react?

Animals, since they have never been taught to ignore their own perceptions of the paranormal, are much more sensitive to the presence of monstrous phenomena than most human beings nowadays. The ability of dogs and cats, in particular, to see and react to spirits is well attested both in folklore and in parapsychological literature. Information about the reactions of pets, or other animals who happened to be nearby, can be a valuable clue to the nature of an apparent monster.

### How did the encounter come to an end?

Just as monster sightings begin in a variety of ways, their endings are equally diverse. The monster may vanish, suddenly or gradually, or it may simply move out of sight; the witness may black out and find the monster gone, or may suddenly realize that it is no longer there but have no idea what happened to it. The location of the monster at the time the witness stopped observing it should be carefully noted, and added to the floor plan or sketch map.

### Did the monster leave any physical traces behind?

Most monstrous beings leave few traces in the material world, but there are important exceptions, and any tracks or other marks of the monster's passage through the area should be located, photographed, measured, and mapped in detail. (Physical traces left by the witnesses, and any other people, animals, and beings involved in the sighting, are also important, but we'll be covering these elsewhere.)

### Before this encounter, had the witness ever experienced, or heard or read about, an entity anything like this?

### Does the witness know about any other unusual events in the area that occurred before the encounter? When did he or she learn about them?

### Has the witness ever experienced any other unusual or unexplained phenomena?

### Does the witness consider himself or herself psychic?

These four questions are intended to measure two things—first, the likelihood that the witness is a person who is sensitive to psychic phenomena; and second, the likelihood that the witness has been influenced by reading or hearing other accounts of preternatural phenomena, real or bogus.

### Does the witness know of anyone performing magical rituals, holding séances, using an Ouija board, or

*engaging in any other sort of occult practice in the area?*

### Did the witness do any of these things before the encounter?

Questions involving magic and other occult practices tend to get extreme responses in most parts of our culture; these two questions should probably be left to the end of the interview when you are taking down the statement of a witness, unless he or she brings the subject up earlier. Sometimes the first of these questions will produce a laundry list of groundless accusations, sometimes a shocked look and an insistence that nobody the witness knows does anything like that. Sometimes, though, it will turn up important clues. The second question is in some ways even more loaded, since our culture's ignorance about magic has created a situation in which many people perform magic without ever realizing that this is what they're doing. Still, the question needs to be asked, since some forms of monstrous phenomena have a good deal to do with occult practice.

### Finally, what does the witness think he or she saw?

Whether the witness' own identification of the entity turns out to be right or hopelessly wrong, it can contain valuable clues. This is especially likely if the identification the witness makes seems baffling or preposterous to the investigator. By saying "That's interesting; I'm not sure I follow you" and gently trying to get the witness to explain his or her reasoning, it's sometimes possible to uncover a series of details that earlier questions had missed.

Remember that it's *never* a good idea to argue with a witness about what he or she saw, or to insist that your own ideas about what it was are the correct ones. Even if you were there at the same time, you weren't looking through anyone's eyes but your own. No matter how silly the witness' ideas sound, save your smirks and chuckles for some other occasion. Your witness has most likely been frightened out of his or her wits by the experience itself, will probably still be badly shaken by a head-on collision with the reality of the impossible, and can also count on being pilloried as an idiot and a fraud by the media and by organizations such as CSICOP—the Committee for Scientific Investigation of Claims of the Paranormal, an organization founded by scientists and engineers to debunk claims of paranormal, supernatural, or unknown phenomena—if they get wind of the encounter. Courtesy, tact, and a little compassion on your part can go a long way to make his or her life easier in a very trying time; it can also mean the difference between sullen silence and active cooperation, and thus often between failure and success in your investigation.

## The Art of the Trap Question

These last comments assume, of course, that the witness is telling the truth about his or her experience. It would be nice if this were always the case; unfortunately, you can't count on that. If you are taking down an account by a witness, therefore, at least one additional question should be asked somewhere in the process of the interview. This is a trap question. It's designed to catch people who are making up a story and adding details as they go along, based on your questions and reactions. The trap question you use should vary from case to case to keep hoaxers from knowing when to say "No, there was nothing like that."

A classic example of a trap question was the one used in the famous 1991 Roper Organization poll on unusual experiences. Along with straight questions about seeing ghosts, having out-of-body experiences, undergoing periods of "missing time," and so on, subjects were asked whether they had ever heard or seen the word TRONDANT and known that it had a hidden meaning for them. The word TRONDANT was made up by the pollsters, and it means absolutely nothing. Anyone who answered "yes" to this question had their responses tossed out for "positive response bias," which is a polite way of saying "making things up."

Your trap questions should be ones that sound plausible, but that no one honest will answer positively. If you think you're dealing with a probable hoaxer, you can use facial expression, posture, and the tone of your voice to make it seem as though the trap question will reveal something really important about the alleged monster. For example, you might lean slightly toward the witness and ask, "One thing—did you notice any change in the weather about the time the entity appeared?" Lightly stress the words "change in the weather," and if the witness starts telling you about how it suddenly started to rain, nod slightly, rather slowly, as though this detail confirms everything. If your witness is a hoaxer, you'll probably get quite a lot of detail about the weird weather that accompanied the alleged monster's appearance and disappearance; you can then check this with the local weather bureau. (Please note that this is only an example, and probably not one you should actually use—after all, hoaxers sometimes read books like this one! You should use a different trap question in each investigation, and the way you ask them should change every time you use one.)

Trap questions are not the only line of defense you have against bogus witnesses. Less obvious but even more effective is the habit of always checking details for consistency. As a witness is first describing his or her experience, take note of a few of the very minor details, and later in the interview ask about those same points. A witness who is remembering an actual experience will usually repeat the same story, while one who is faking will often slip up on the minor points.

You can also compare the account of a witness with the reports of others, if more than one person was present at the encounter, or with any physical traces the monster or the witnesses left in the area where the encounter took place. This is one reason why interviews with witnesses should be done individually, with other witnesses out of earshot, and why a search of the area should be carried out as soon as possible.

If different witnesses confirm one another's accounts even when their statements are made out of the others' hearing, and if physical traces match the accounts— if you find cigarette ash on the ground where one witness said he stood and smoked, for example, or footprints in the mud heading the way another witness said she walked—you may well have a real sighting. If accounts differ from each other and from the physical evidence on significant details—if three witnesses point to three widely separated places as the spot where an entity clearly visible to all of them suddenly vanished, or if a fourth said he was out driving on back roads the previous night but his car shows no signs of

mud the next morning—you may well have a hoax.

## Essential Skills: Research

Living witnesses are only part of the resources you can draw on for information on a reported monster sighting. Another consists of written and electronic data. While these will rarely give you anything about the specific sighting you're investigating, they can provide background material—reports of similar sightings, historical events related to the monster's presence, folklore traditions involving the monster, and so on—that can be vital to the successful investigation of a case.

If your only exposure to research is the sort of simple-minded approach taught in most public schools, you have a lot to learn. Still, none of the skills involved are particularly difficult. In fact, if you can read this book, you already have the one essential tool you need to do effective monster research. To put that tool to work, all you need to know is what to read and how to find it.

Finding it, most of the time, is the problem. There's a vast amount of information available about monsters, but it's no more than a drop in the ocean of data that surges through our information society on a daily basis. The books, articles, and papers you need for any given case are almost certainly sitting on shelves right now at the local public library, the city or county records office, or the nearest university, but that does you no good unless you know how and where to look, and what to look for.

Information on monsters sometimes turns up in the strangest places, but certain sources usually yield the richest rewards to the monster hunter:

### *Newspapers*

Your most valuable resources for monster hunting are usually old newspapers from the area in which you're working. Newspaper access can be easy or hard, depending on the attitude of your local newspaper publisher and the resources of your local library. All newspapers keep a library of back issues, called the "morgue" in journalists' slang. Some newspapers allow the public access to the morgue, and some don't. If yours doesn't, head down to the central branch of the local public library, and ask the librarian whether there's a collection of back issues and a subject index for local stories. If this latter doesn't exist, look for approximate dates of monster-related events from other sources, and plan on spending a lot of time reading through decades-old news in the papers for a couple of days before and after any given event.

### *Magazines*

Local-interest and specialty magazines are another important resource. Finding these can be difficult, though the Internet is making this somewhat easier, and there are several book-length bibliographies of monster-related magazine articles—see especially Eberhart 1980 and Eberhart 1983 in the bibliography at the end of this book.

### *Books*

The vast majority of monster lore these days is found in book form. If you're starting research on a particular type of monster, especially, the bookshelves should always be your first stop. Books of monster lore fall into three broad categories: popular mass-market books, which are the easiest to find but are often not very accurate or useful; scholarly books, which are harder to find (unless you live within range of a good university library) but which tend to be scrupulously accurate and full of references you can follow further; and books from within the monster-hunting community itself, which are of wildly varying quality and availability.

For book access, your first stop should always be the public library. You'll want to learn your library's cataloging system well enough that you can find things quickly and effectively. If your library uses the Dewey decimal system for nonfiction books (most do), 001.9, 133, and 398 are the most common places, but every library has its own habits. If you keep a note of the call number and location of each monster book you find, you'll quickly figure out where to look.

Two other public library resources are worth checking into. Your library system may have a local history collection, and this can be of critical importance in checking the historical background of a monster sighting. It's also very likely to take part in the Interlibrary Loan system, which allows you access to books from libraries across the country if your own library doesn't have what you're looking for. Talk to a librarian about both of these.

Other sources of monster books worth trying are local museums and historical societies, which sometimes have libraries of their own; universities and colleges; and used bookstores. Historical societies may restrict library use to members, but the dues are rarely high and the monster-hunting benefits can be substantial. Universities and colleges rarely give checkout privileges to anyone but students, faculty, and staff, but the monster-hunting resources are often very substantial, and no one will ask questions if you settle down at a convenient table with a stack of books and start taking notes.

Used bookstores are another matter. If there are gods who rule the art of monster hunting, used bookstores are where they most often manifest their power. You can visit a certain used bookstore a thousand times and come up with nothing. On the thousand and first visit, you come across the only surviving copy of a battered, dog-eared, mimeographed pamphlet, privately published before you were born by a monster hunter neither you nor anyone else alive has ever heard of. As you pull the pamphlet off the shelf, wondering what on earth it is, it falls open to page 28, where you find a footnote that happens to contain the piece of information you desperately needed to know to understand the most baffling feature of a case. Used bookstores are like that.

### Historical Societies

If your town, city, or area has a historical society, find out about the resources it offers, and consider joining. Most monsters have a historical dimension, and the more access you have to historical information, the better off you are. Many historical societies have members who have been doing historical research on their own for years without benefit of government grants or research assistants. In many cases, these amateur historians know the local information resources inside and out, and can pass on tips and connections of immense value.

Most historical societies are short on people and do their best to get the word out to people who might be interested. Start by asking at the public library or simply looking in the phone book under "Historical Societies," "Museums," or "Community Associations." When they ask you about your interests, tell them that you want to research local folklore concerning ghosts and the like, and you'll probably find yourself with more resources and contacts than you know what to do with.

## Public Records

City, county, state, and federal offices all have different kinds of information to offer. Exactly what you can find, and where you can find it, varies so widely from jurisdiction to jurisdiction that you'll need to consult local resources (such as the public library—do you begin to see a pattern here?) for the details. Generally speaking, though, the two most important things you'll find in public records are information on the history of a building or a piece of real estate, on the one hand, and anything having to do with a criminal case or other legal matter on the other.

With regard to real estate, your city or county government will usually be able to give you a complete history of the ownership of any real estate within its borders, and there are likely to be blueprints or construction drawings for any building or remodeling project that required a permit. This can be of great importance when researching a haunted house or any other site where strange things have been reported.

In most jurisdictions, all records of criminal and civil cases are normally open to the public, although here again there may be local variations about what you can and can't see. Any given area will be under the jurisdiction of several different courts, each of which handles different kinds of cases. If a long-unsolved crime, a disappearance, or some other legal matter is tangled up in a monster investigation, you may be able to find important clues by locating the relevant legal records.

## The Internet

This is the new frontier in monster research, as in nearly anything else connected with information flow, and there are already monster websites, monster e-mail lists, and monster Usenet newsgroups enough to satisfy all but the most dedicated netheads. None of them will be listed here, since the net changes so fast that most of the listings will be obsolete by the time this book finishes its journey into print. Your best bet is to hit a good search engine on a regular basis and keep a file of the results.

Internet-based research is faster and a good deal easier than any of the other kinds discussed here. The downside is that the percentage of nonsense you'll get is much higher as well. In nearly every other information medium, someone besides the author has the job of looking over the text and weeding out the most obvious forms of stupidity. Even though these people fail now and again—sometimes spectacularly—their efforts still make a difference. The alternative can be seen in full flower on the Internet, and it isn't always very pretty. Plan on double- or even triple-checking any online information against non-net resources.

### Your Own Notes and Records

Gathering information is the first step of the research process, not the whole of it. You'll also need to take notes on what you find, and keep the notes organized in some way that will allow you to find what you want when you need it. If you devote any significant amount of time to monster research, you'll need to deal with an ever-larger collection of information on the subject—a liability if you don't deal with it effectively, a vital tool if you do.

A good set of files is worth an enormous amount to the monster hunter. Since the monsters of any given area tend to fall into the same patterns and categories, you're likely to end up with most of the information you need right at your fingertips, saving you hours of time and making your investigations more effective. Detailed files also allow you to track the activities of local monsters across space and time, to look for connections between different types of monster-related activity, and so on.

Several rules are worth keeping in mind when you're dealing with your files. The first rule is *always write down the source*. If it's a book, you need the author, title, publi-

cation data, and page where the information appears; for a magazine or newspaper article, the author, article title, name of the periodical where it appeared, date of publication, and page numbers; for information from any other written source, enough information that you or anyone else could find it again without having to search. Interviews should be marked with the name of the person interviewed and the date and time of the interview; notes on your own investigations should be labeled with date, time, and place. Make it an iron-clad rule always to note down the source of every piece of information, and you'll save yourself hours of wasted effort.

The second rule to keep in mind is *file everything so you can find it*. A file box, of the sort you can get at any office-supply store, and a package of manila file folders will get you started—though you'll end up with multiple filing cabinets if you keep hunting monsters for any length of time. How you arrange information among file folders is your choice, though you'll want to wait until you have things to file before you start writing category titles on the folders! As a general rule, it's probably better to have too many folders than too few, although this can be taken to extremes. Label each of your folders, in ink, and sort them alphabetically.

The third rule is *when in doubt, photocopy*. Under current fair-use guidelines, you can make one photocopy of nearly any document for personal, noncommercial research purposes. Short passages in books, articles in newspapers and magazines, and similar source materials will be much more useful to you in the long run if you make your own copy, rather than simply noting down the information that looks important right now.

This assumes you'll be keeping your records on paper, rather than in some electronic form. This is usually wise. Though they've gained a good deal in reliability over the last decade, electronic media still don't have the durability of old-fashioned paper records, and you're going to have wasted an enormous amount of effort if all your monster records get turned into magnetic hamburger by a hard-drive crash. If you must keep everything on your computer, back it up regularly!

## Essential Skills: Handling Publicity

As you pursue your monster-hunting career, many of the difficulties you'll face have nothing to do with monsters and everything to do with the reactions of other people. As already mentioned, the systematic and scrupulous habits of honesty, courtesy, thoughtfulness, and tact will do more to prevent such difficulties than anything else. Even so, you can count on getting a wide range of negative reactions from people. It's one of the risks of the trade.

Considerations like these lead many monster hunters to carry on their investigations quietly, without any publicity at all. There's much to be said for this approach. If you do decide to seek out cases more publicly, be aware that you'll attract at least ten skeptics, hoaxers, and lunatics for every one honest person who has actually had an encounter with a monstrous being. Plan on using a post office box, an answering service, and/or a web-based e-mail address for contacts, and get an unlisted phone number; the last thing you want is a barrage of half-coherent phone calls at 3 A.M. or, worse, the caller showing up at your front door half an hour later.

This assumes that you choose to go looking for publicity. Now and again, however, it happens that publicity comes looking for you, if the mainstream media get wind of a case or your activities as a researcher. If this happens, you may suddenly have to deal with reporters, local talk-show staff, and other media figures. If the situation gets enough media exposure, you may also run up against people from one of the debunking organizations. All this attention can be a heady mix, especially for inexperienced monster hunters, and it's important to have a clear sense of what's involved if you hope to handle the situation effectively.

How should you deal with the media if they come looking for a story? Most of the time, your best strategy is not to deal with them at all. It's important to remember that, whatever you heard in high-school journalism classes, the mass media are not in the business of reporting facts. They are in the business of selling advertising. Few journalists like to admit it publicly, but most things get printed or broadcast because they will keep advertisers happy and audiences staring at the ads, and every other consideration takes a back seat.

What this means is that as a monster researcher, you can't *ever* count on fairness or objectivity from the mainstream media, and in many cases you can't even expect accuracy or basic honesty. If the reporter who interviews you thinks he or she can get a better story by making you look like a moron, that's how the story will be written. If the editor thinks this—even if the reporter doesn't—that's how the story will appear. If your words have to be quoted out of context or subjected to various kinds of spin doctoring to make that work, that's what will happen—and God help you if you don't have your own tape recording of the interview, so that what you actually said isn't a matter of your word against the interviewer's.

This may sound excessively cynical, but it's based on decades of hard experience. If you're hunting monsters, the mass media are not your friends. The best you'll get from them, even if they decide to give you sympathetic coverage, is fifteen minutes of

fame before the next fad moves in—and the worst can be pretty nightmarish. On the other hand, if you refuse requests for interviews, tell the media nothing, and simply go about your work, they'll rarely hang around for long.

The same rule holds for debunkers as well. CSICOP, the Committee for Scientific Investigation of Claims of the Paranormal, and a variety of smaller organizations of the same kind have been active for several decades now in the monster-hunting scene, as well as other areas where unexplained phenomena crop up. These groups and their supporters claim to be carrying out rational, scientific investigation of such subjects; many other people (not all of them believers in the reality of the paranormal) argue that their actual agenda is the defense of a particular worldview—the worldview of hardcore scientific materialism—by any means necessary.

The fog of controversy around these debunking organizations is thick enough that it's hard to sort out the competing claims. Certainly, though, books on the paranormal published by CSICOP members often fall very short in the objectivity department. A good example is *Missing Pieces* by Robert A. Baker and Joe Nickell (Buffalo: Prometheus Press, 1992), a guide for investigators that was heavily praised in the debunking press. The authors, both of them CSICOP members, start with the assumption that all puzzling phenomena *must* have causes that are already known to modern science, and they interrupt their discussions of investigative technique to spend page after page denouncing people who accept the possibility of the paranormal. They also quote approvingly arch-debunker Philip Klass' notorious essay "Ten Ufological Principles," which argues that investigators should ignore the testimony of trained professional eyewitnesses if it doesn't square with the investigator's notions about what "really" happened. All in all, it's not a very promising picture.

Individuals differ, and it's always possible that the debunker who shows up to investigate a case you're researching will turn out to be polite, fair, and open-minded. Still, to judge by the experiences of other monster researchers, odds are that you'll get something very different. Furthermore, it's rarely worth your time to find out. Your best strategy is to ignore them completely and go about your own researches.

All this may sound as though there's never a good reason to tell anyone else what you're doing. Fortunately, this isn't true. Word of mouth, always the best form of advertising, is also the best form of publicity for a monster hunter. There are also magazines and newsletters that cover monster-related phenomena, and if you're willing to take the time to learn how to write clearly and effectively—another skill poorly taught in American schools, but one that can readily be learned—you may want to turn your notes from investigations into articles, so that other monster hunters can benefit from your discoveries.

## Essential Skills: Search

If you're lucky (or unlucky, depending on your perspective), sooner or later your monster investigations may involve something more direct than interviewing witnesses in someone's living room or looking up details in libraries and county records buildings. The transition into the more active mode of monster hunting may be as prosaic as an offer by an old family friend to show you the bedroom where he was hagged twenty years earlier, or as dramatic as a sudden, panicked phone call asking for help in the middle of a full-blown poltergeist outbreak. Either way, there are certain skills you need to have in hand before you head out into the field with your monster kit in one hand and a hastily written address in the other.

One of the most important of these skills is a basic knowledge of how to carry out an effective search of an area. Just as a crime scene search can make or break a criminal case, depending on how well it's carried out, the accuracy and completeness of your search of the place of a monster sighting can make the difference between a failed investigation and a successful one. At the same time, searching for evidence of a monster's presence is often a good deal more difficult than most crime scene searches. Criminals have physical bodies, but most monsters don't; some monsters leave clear physical traces, but the great majority leave either vague and inconclusive ones or none at all.

Your search of the scene of a monster sighting, or any other monster-related place, has two apparently contradictory goals. The first goal is to find any evidence that supports the idea that a monster has been present; the second is to find any evidence that argues that a monster has not been present, and that the apparent sighting was the result of natural causes, a hoax, or psychological issues on the part of the witness or witnesses. It's crucial to keep both of these in mind at all times; as mentioned before, a mind open to all possibilities is the single most important piece of equipment in the kit of any monster investigator.

Each search is different, but certain points are always worth keeping in mind:

## Preparation

Your search needs to be carried out within an awareness of the wider context of local history and folklore, local geography, information about monsters in general, and the specific details of the event you're investigating. If you have the time to do so, find out as much as possible about the place *before* you go there. If other unusual events have occurred in the area, of course, you need to be aware of that, but your research should extend a good deal further than that. A house or building built over an abandoned mine shaft, a sinkhole, or an active fault can do a fine imitation of a poltergeist as a result of complex settling and shifting patterns. The same thing can happen in the aftermath of fire, flood, or other natural disasters; if these have occurred in the area you'll be searching, you need to know about them.

On the other hand, old graveyards, temples and sacred spaces from earlier (and more magically aware) cultures, standing stones, burial mounds, and certain natural geographical features such as steeply pointed peaks are often places where supernatural forces come into sharp focus and give rise to monstrous phenomena. Look for nearby place names that suggest the presence of something uncanny; Fortean researcher Loren Coleman has shown that places in North America containing the word "Devil's" (as in Devil's Swamp, Devil's Cave, and so on) are often associated with strange phenomena. The same is true of other spooky place-name elements, such as "Superstition," "Witch," and "Ghost."

In North America and Australasia, you should certainly find out as much as you can about the traditions and myths of the local tribes; in areas where the current inhabitants have been around longer, look into the meanings of local place names and check into local history as far back as it can be traced.

If you get that sudden panicked call mentioned above, of course, you won't have the option of spending a few evenings mulling over the details of local geography and legendry before you arrive on the scene. In such cases, you'll have to do the research afterwards, and odds are you'll find yourself groaning over the questions you could have asked if you had only known that they were important. Except in emergencies, then, *always* do your research first, so you know what you're looking for.

### Arriving Onsite

When you get to the place you intend to search, your first task—after making sure that everyone present is safe, that there are no monsters strolling about at the moment, and that you actually have permission to enter the area—is to make sure that any evidence in the area will stay undisturbed until you get to it. This can be a lot easier said than done, of course; the more people are there with you, the more likely one or more of them will be to wander through the area and leave large muddy footprints all over the clues that you need to find.

Since you're not a police officer and have no particular right to insist that people do what you tell them, there are real limits to how much control you have over situations like this. Certainly, though, it's often a good idea to try to explain to anyone else there why you need the site where the monster appeared left undisturbed, and if there are children present you should do your best to have someone take them somewhere else as soon as possible.

If the people onsite understand your concerns and are willing to cooperate, ask them to take up positions around the specific area to try to keep anyone else from straying into the area; this can also have the useful effect of keeping witnesses separate from one another, so they do not have the opportunity to talk about what they've seen and contaminate one another's testimony. Once the boundaries of the area are more or less secure, you can proceed in a systematic manner.

If you don't get that kind of cooperation, move fast, send anyone who tries to accompany you on whatever time-consuming errand you can think of, and do your best to get as much information as you can from the area before blundering passersby obscure or destroy the clues you need. It helps to work with other investigators, so that one can distract the other people present while the rest carry out the search.

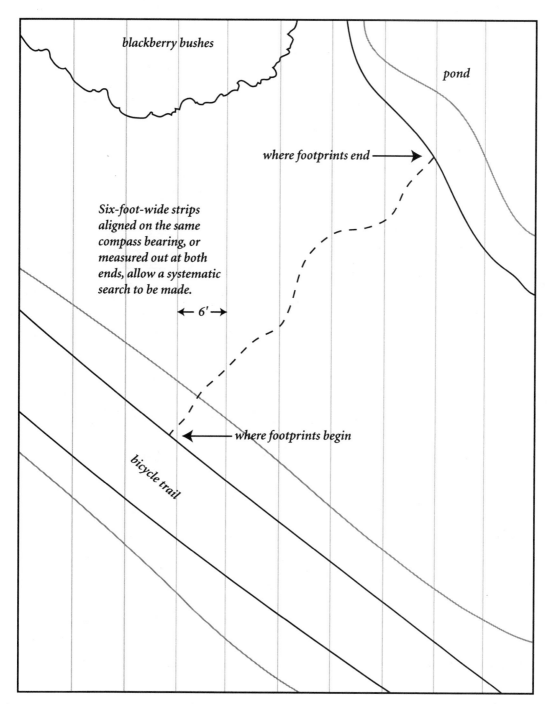

blackberry bushes

pond

where footprints end

*Six-foot-wide strips aligned on the same compass bearing, or measured out at both ends, allow a systematic search to be made.*

← 6' →

where footprints begin

bicycle trail

*Searching an Area for Monster Traces*

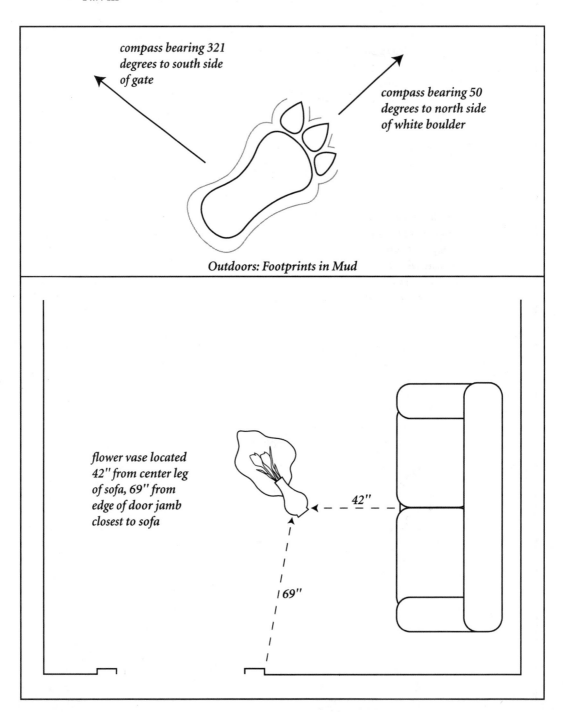

*compass bearing 321 degrees to south side of gate*

*compass bearing 50 degrees to north side of white boulder*

**Outdoors: Footprints in Mud**

*flower vase located 42" from center leg of sofa, 69" from edge of door jamb closest to sofa*

42"

69"

**Indoors: Traces of a Poltergeist**

## Searching the Space

The most important thing to do, if circumstances allow you to do it, is to go through the entire area in a systematic manner, noting down everything you perceive. If you have the time to be systematic, divide the area up into manageable units and search each one in turn. In a house or other building, for instance, take each room in turn, and search it from end to end before you go into the next one. In an outdoor setting, use your compass and any convenient landmarks to divide up the area into strips six feet wide and as long as the area requires, then go down each strip in turn, noting anything you find.

When you do find something, don't move it or touch it until you've taken a photo, made a drawing, and written down its location relative to at least two fixed objects. Inside, you can use the tape measure—"the blood on the carpet was 34 inches from the left front leg of the couch and 62 inches from the right front corner of the file cabinet"—while outdoors, you're more likely to need to use the compass—"from the footprint, the south side of the gray boulder was at a bearing of 155 degrees and the closest corner of the blue house was at a bearing of 315 degrees." Either way, this allows you to triangulate, so that the location can be determined exactly by anyone else who visits the site.

Any photo you take should have something of known size next to whatever you're photographing to provide scale. Any photo or drawing should have the date, place, time, and a number written on it, and the notes you take in your notebook should list the numbers in relation to specific locations and clues.

Remember to pay attention to things you can't see. Sounds, smells, and less easily definable perceptions are all sources of information, and should go into your notebook in detail.

## Tracks and Marks

As mentioned in Part I, etheric substance is on the edge of the physical, and can leave physical traces when it's at maximum condensation; for example, the etheric teeth of a werewolf can rip human flesh, and the feet or body of an etheric entity can leave a trail on the ground. Tracks and marks thus are a common source of evidence in monster cases but they can also be a fertile source of confusion as well. If you expect to deal with tracks often, you need to learn how to read them, and this is much like learning to read a foreign language. There are a handful of good books on the subject, but no book by itself will teach you what you need to know. What trackers call "dirt time"—time actually spent out in the field, following tracks in their natural context—is the essential key, and a good teacher is nearly as important.

If you don't have the time, inclination, or resources to learn tracking, be aware of that limitation and don't try to read messages you don't know how to interpret! If you encounter tracks, photographs and detailed drawings are a must; you should take photos that show more than one track at the same time, to show the gait of whatever made them, as well as close-ups of individual tracks. Measure the distance between tracks with a tape measure as well, and locate them precisely on your sketch map. Plaster casts of good examples are also useful.

Most of the above is also relevant in the case of other kinds of marks. These represent solid physical traces of whatever you are investigating; in the case of a monster, they may be the only solid physical traces you'll ever get, while in the case of a hoax, they may lead you straight to the perpetrators. Pay careful attention, take copious notes, but don't try to push your knowledge beyond your abilities and training.

## Building Issues

Indoor environments offer many opportunities for the hoaxer, and can also produce a fine imitation of a monster on the loose even when there is nothing out of the ordinary involved. In terms of potential hoaxing, look for concealed entrances and exits, unexplained hooks or eye bolts on the ceiling or in the walls, and any sign of human presence or movement in places where the

witnesses saw the "monster." In terms of potential misinterpretations of ordinary events, look for warped or weathered window frames, leaks or burst pipes in the plumbing, badly done remodeling or repair jobs, and any sign of water damage, which can cause a host of bizarre effects.

On the other side of the equation, indoor environments offer many opportunities for gathering information on authentic monsters as well. If objects have been moved, check the distribution of dust; few people keep their furniture so well dusted that some trace of an object's presence won't remain behind. If a ghost was seen to walk through a wall, look for signs that a door may have been there in the past.

## Animal Behavior

This can be one of the best sources of evidence either for or against the presence of a real monster. Different kinds of animals—rats, mice, skunks, opossums, raccoons, rabbits, squirrels, and feral cats and dogs, among others—can get into the walls, attics, basements, ventilation ducts, and crawl spaces of a building, producing various noises and disruptions that can be mistaken for monster activity. All of these leave telltale traces, and the perceptive monster hunter will quickly learn to tell when it's time to call a pest control company rather than a psychic or a priest.

On the other hand, animals react strongly to monstrous beings, and one of the best ways to check for real monsters is to take a dog through an area where a monster has supposedly been seen. If Rover barks frantically at (or backs away in fear from) something you can't see, or simply bolts in stark panic, you may well have an actual monster on your hands.

## Unusual Phenomena

Keep your eyes (and other senses) open for strange phenomena, but remember that these are often produced by perfectly natural causes or by deliberate deception. Anything out of the ordinary should be carefully investigated while it is happening, if at all possible, and the exact spot noted down; afterwards, the area should be searched a second time, looking for potential causes or evidence of fakery.

## Hot or Cold Spots

In many sites haunted by ghosts, or by some other types of monsters, one of the most obvious signs of a preternatural presence is an area that seems abnormally hot or cold. If you find one or more of these, measure the actual temperature with your thermometer, and then do the same in two or three areas that don't show the same sort of temperature effect. If at all possible, repeat the measurements at a different day and time. Always search around such an area for natural causes, such as furnace or air conditioning vents, loose floorboards, cracks in walls, and so on; it's also useful to light a candle and set it in the area to see, from the movement of the flame, if there's an unnoticed draft.

## Final Steps

You should *always* thank the people who allowed you onto their property or helped you in the course of the investigation. Get their names and contact information if they are willing to give it, and give them yours. Before you leave, again, make sure that everyone present is safe and accounted for, and that there are no signs of renewed monster activity.

# Essential Skills: Surveillance

Another fundamental skill you may need to put to use in a monster investigation is surveillance. If a location has been visited multiple times by a monster, and the visits seem to follow a predictable pattern—on the night of the full moon, on the anniversary of a long-ago murder, on windless summer days, or what have you—it may well be worth the time and inconvenience to stake out the area and keep watch.

On the other hand, there are few more boring tasks in the monster hunter's repertoire. Police officers and private investigators have been known to make very rude remarks about stakeouts on TV crime shows, in which a few minutes of waiting invariably leads to some sensational discovery. In reality, a detective assigned to surveillance duty knows that he or she can expect to spend hours at a time staring at a closed door and shuttered windows from across the street, waiting for a few minutes or seconds of activity that may or may not happen.

The monster hunter on surveillance faces the same sort of experience. Given that monsters are elusive and unpredictable at the best of times, you can expect most monster stakeouts to draw a complete blank. At the same time, if the surveillance isn't carried out competently, or if you let your attention and awareness waver for as little as a moment, a potentially successful stakeout can be wasted. Harsh? Granted, but then no one said that hunting monsters is easy.

If you've ever been birdwatching, you actually know most of what you need to know to carry out a successful surveillance. Wild birds, like monsters, show themselves only to those who are willing to master stillness, attentiveness, and perceptiveness. These are the three crucial abilities you need to develop:

- the ability to remain absolutely motionless for long periods of time;

- the ability to keep your mind focused on the task at hand, instead of letting it run off on tangents that may distract you;

- the ability to pay attention to what is going on all around you—not just right in front of you—and to notice the cues given by all your different senses.

Most people have trouble with at least one of these, but like all things, such skills develop with practice. Perhaps the easiest way to develop them is to go to a park, a vacant lot, a patch of woods, or some similar place, sit down on the ground, and stay there without moving for ten minutes or so. Try to keep your mind empty of its usual chatter; instead, pay attention to everything going on around you. What animals or birds do you see? What sounds come to you, and from what directions? From where does the wind blow? What scents does it bring with it? When you can do this easily for ten minutes, increase the time to a half hour.

Another useful exercise is "Kim's game," from Rudyard Kipling's novel *Kim*. This needs two partners, paper and pens, a clock with a second hand, and a large, relatively flat box with a lid or some other covering (such as a towel or blanket). While partner A is somewhere else, partner B assembles a collection of twenty or so small objects that are completely unrelated to one another, arranges them in the box, and covers them with the lid. A is called into the room when this is done; B then raises the lid, and A has thirty seconds exactly to look at them. At the end of the time, the lid goes down, and A then writes down everything he or she remembers seeing in the box. When A is finished, the lid comes off again, and the list is checked against the actual contents. The partners then switch roles.

Most people do embarrassingly poorly when they first try this—five to seven items out of twenty is not unusual—but the more you practice, the more your powers of awareness will expand. When you can get twenty out of twenty items, you will be ready for almost anything a monster surveillance can throw at you.

Given the right preparation, surveillance itself is a simple process. Your first task is to define the area you will be watching, indoor or outdoor, and then choose a place from which to watch it. Your watching station should have a clear view of as much as possible of the area, but it should provide at least some concealment, both from monsters and from passersby. Of course, it should also be safe and legal for you to spend several hours there. If it's on private property, get written permission from the owner in advance; if it's on public property, make sure to find out which agency (local, county, state, or federal) administers the property, pay a visit to the local office, and make sure you are in compliance with whatever laws and regulations apply.

If at all possible, spend some time walking through the area in advance of your surveillance, and try to get a sense of the possibilities for concealment. Outdoors, a dip or rise you barely notice can be enough to shield an area from view; indoors, furniture and details of construction can do the same thing. Find any information you can about the exact locations and movements of the monster or monsters you hope to sight, and try to relate this to the realities of the ground in front of you. You should also look for tracks and other marks that are already there, so you don't mistake them for traces left by a monster.

If you will be carrying out the surveillance outdoors at night, remember that darkness will change the appearance of the area completely. If there are lights of any sort—streetlights, outdoor lights of houses, windows that may be lit, streets down which cars with headlights may drive—keep this in mind, and make sure your choice of location won't leave you blinded or silhouetted by a strong light. If there are no lights at all, be aware that you may be able to see precisely nothing, even if a whole army of monsters rambles past fifty feet from where you will be keeping watch. Check the phase of the moon and the expected weather conditions to get some sense of the potential for visibility.

Weather, in general, is a crucial factor in any outdoor surveillance. Always assume that the weather may turn bad, and bring rain gear and an extra sweater as needed. Decide in advance what you will do if weather conditions make the stakeout useless—for example, if fog rolls in and drops visibility to a few feet, or if freezing rain brings a serious risk of hypothermia.

A vacuum bottle of hot coffee or tea can be a godsend on a nightlong stakeout, but this has its drawbacks as well. Your bladder capacity, as much as anything else, will determine just how long you can keep your attention continuously focused on the area under surveillance. Men have certain advantages here; it's not too hard to keep a wide-mouthed bottle with a watertight lid handy for emergencies, and for the really dedicated, home health care suppliers sell "Texas catheters"—essentially, condoms with the end clipped off and a rubber hose attached—with urine bags that can be conveniently strapped to one leg. Women have fewer options, although it's possible to find specially shaped funnels designed for long-distance car trips, which can be used with any convenient bottle.

The aftermath of a surveillance is in many ways as important as the surveillance itself, and more often neglected. Whether or not you have encountered anything unusual, make notes on the surveillance immediately, and if you can search the area, you should certainly do so. If you've been up all night watching, it may be difficult to keep your wits about you, but do your best.

## Essential Skills: Encounter

Most people go through their entire lives without ever encountering a monstrous being, and even those who devote their lives to the search for such entities may never actually face one in person. On the other hand, the more time and energy you put into tracking monsters, learning their ways and habits, and waiting silently in places where they tend to appear, the more likely you are to suddenly find yourself face to face with the reality of the impossible. If this ever happens, you need to know what to do.

At best, you will probably have no more than a few minutes to get as much information as you can before the monster becomes aware of your presence and makes itself scarce. At worst, you may have no more than a handful of seconds to save your life, or the lives of those with you. Either way, there may be little margin for error.

Much will depend on the nature of the monster, the circumstances of the encounter, and the conditions of time and space. The following guidelines may be of use:

### If the monster does not seem to have noticed you

In this case, the "naturalist" side of your monster-hunting background comes to the fore. You are in exactly the same position as the biologist who sights a rare animal in the wilderness. Your tools are the same as well: absolute stillness and silence, careful attention to the entity and the circumstances, and detailed notes. If you can take photographs without giving your presence away, do so. Never attempt to approach the entity, or even to change your position in the hope of getting a better view; most monsters, like most wild animals, are far more perceptive than you are, and the faintest sound or stirring may end the encounter at once.

### If the monster has apparently noticed you and does not appear hostile

In this case, stand your ground, move slowly if at all, and don't do anything that might be taken as a potential threat. Judge your actions on the basis of your best guess as to the entity's nature. Consider speaking to the entity—many types of monsters can understand human speech, if folklore is any guide. If you do speak to it, be polite, honest, and respectful. Watch for evidence of hostile intentions on the monster's part, but try not to jump to conclusions. If the entity makes a request of you, it's normally both courteous and wise to do as it asks, as long as this doesn't involve actions that would put you under its power or leave you vulnerable to attack.

### If the entity has noticed you and behaves in a hostile or predatory manner

This is a worst-case scenario, and you need to make use of whatever protective gear or magical weaponry you have, as efficiently as possible. This is potentially a deadly serious situation, and if you fumble it badly enough you or those with you could end up injured, possessed, or dead. You will need to move fast, hit hard, and use whatever strengths and skills you have available.

If you are hunting an entity that is even potentially dangerous, basic protective amulets of the sort described in the section on Natural Magic (pp. 217–227) should be worn at all times. Iron or steel blades are another source of strength that should be kept at hand, as few monsters can face cold steel. If you have made and consecrated the Trident of Paracelsus, as described in Part IV, it should be with you whenever you are on the hunt, and in your hand at the first sign of hostile action. Any other natural or ritual magic you can use effectively should be put to use as appropriate.

At several other places in this section, the point has been made that the best preparations in the world are worth nothing if you don't know how to use them. This point bears repeating here more than anywhere else. Dealing effectively with an attack by a monstrous being requires focus, swift action, and a mastery of the methods you intend to use. The best way to see to it that you can manage these things is to practice the techniques in question, over and over again, until you can do them from memory under any conceivable circumstances.

To use magic adequately in a crisis, in other words, it's necessary to become at least a little bit of a magician. Whether you choose to go beyond that "little bit" is up to you, but certainly a set of basic techniques (including an effective banishing ritual) should be learned, memorized, practiced, and mastered if you will be pursuing monsters onto their own ground.

*Part IV*

# MAGICAL
# SELF-DEFENSE

# NATURAL MAGIC

The traditions and theory of magic, as we've seen, offer perspectives that can be useful for making sense of a range of monstrous creatures. If you happen to be in the middle of a haunting, a case of demonic obsession, or some other disruptive form of monster-related experience, though, theoretical perspectives may not be the first thing on your mind! Fortunately, magic also has more practical help to offer.

In nearly all of the world's cultures, magical methods are the first and most important line of defense against the more destructive kinds of monster activity. There's a good reason for this. Monsters, as shown elsewhere in this book, are creatures of the subtle dimensions of existence, those realms—etheric, astral, and mental, in the language of magical philosophy—that lie between the physical realm of sensory experiences and the spiritual realm of transcendent reality. This is the same territory in which magic operates, and in which it has its direct effects.

There has been a good deal of confusion about this point, and it has been amplified by the same kind of distortions that we've already traced in monster lore. Magic is not a substitute for technology; while it can have physical effects in some situations, these are indirect, and usually subtle. Physical phenomena need to be handled with physical tools; if you need to walk through a solid wall, in other words, you need a bulldozer, not an incantation.

By the same token, though, physical tools and techniques generally have very little effect on the subtler levels (unless they involve one of the interfaces between the physical level and the other, subtler levels—a point we'll return to shortly). To deal with etheric and astral phenomena, you need etheric and astral tools. These are precisely what magic provides.

In the following pages, we'll be covering some of the basic magical techniques that can be of use to people who are either dealing with monstrous beings directly, or who intend to investigate monsters and want to do so with some degree of safety. These techniques are no more than a small sample of the full armamentarium of magical methods. Partly this is a matter of space, but it's also important to note that many of the more potent magical methods require a great deal of systematic training and practice to use.

Like any other art, magic has its basic, intermediate, and advanced techniques, and beginners who try to copy the methods of an adept usually end up creating a mess and nothing more. Those who wish to pursue the study of magic beyond the techniques covered here can find the necessary information in books on the subject, including several by the present author.

## The Magical Universe

In order to understand and use this material with any degree of effectiveness, it's necessary to have some sense of the way that magicians understand the universe. This understanding is sharply different from the habits of thought that are normal in our present society—a point that has caused a good deal of the confusion surrounding the whole issue of magic nowadays.

The heart of the magical view of reality is a vision of the universe as a vast dance of interpenetrating patterns of force, which flow outward from a common source—the transcendent unity of the spiritual level—and cascade down the levels of being to coalesce into material forms on the physical level. These patterns can be understood in many different ways, and at least three formulations are common in magical theory. The one most useful to us here, though, represents them as currents of energy that surround and penetrate everything that is.

Each of the levels of being corresponds to a different set of these energies. Those of the spiritual and mental levels are not particularly relevant to the needs of the student of monster lore, although they have a great deal of importance in other branches of magical work.

Those of the astral level are a good deal more relevant. These energies move constantly through a series of cycles and tides, affecting different parts of the world at different intensities on a moment-by-moment basis. The tides of astral energy move in step with the relationships of the sun, moon, planets, and stars to the Earth, a point that is both the magical basis for astrology and the reason why the term "astral"—from the Greek *astron*, "star"—was chosen for this level in the first place.

The relation of these astral tides to monster lore is complex. Some relatively recent research, and a good deal of older lore, suggests that the appearance and activities of at least some monsters correlates closely to particular astrological factors. A great deal of further work needs to be done in this area before anyone can say for sure what the connections might be, but they represent one of the more intriguing frontiers of monster research.

The influence of the etheric level and its tides on monstrous phenomena is more certain. The substance of the etheric level has been described as a subtle fluid that permeates and flows through all things. Like matter in some ways, like energy in others, ether can be concentrated or dispersed by a number of means, and it can also take and hold patterns. These patterns form the templates on which the particles of physical matter collect to form the objects we perceive with our five ordinary senses; they also make up the organizing principle behind biological life, and define the physical bodies of all living beings.

Like the astral (or, for that matter, the physical) oceans, the ocean of ether surrounding us has its tides and currents, its patterns of movement and cycles of energy, and these play an important role in nearly all kinds of magical practice. Various complex systems have been used to track these tides in various magical traditions, but the major influences on the ether's ebb and flow are a much simpler matter, and follow patterns that are fairly well known even in our present culture.

The most important of these derives from the phases of the moon. The moon dominates the etheric tides as it does the physical ones of the Earth's oceans, and the cycle of lunar phases thus has a potent influence on all magical work directed at or through the etheric level. Etheric energies are at their strongest at the full moon and their weakest at the new; when the moon is waxing—growing from new to full—those energies support increase and upward motion, while the waning moon—shrinking from full to new—marks a time of decrease and downward motion.

This plays an important part in magical practice, for the perceptive magician quickly learns what types of workings succeed best under different lunar conditions. The full and new moon, and the three days immediately before each of these points, are the most important stages of the cycle; the former is commonly associated with the appearance of many monstrous beings— particularly, but not only, werewolves— while the latter, which is called the dark or eld of the moon, was once greatly feared, as it is the most effective time for evil magic.

These lunar cycles are paralleled by another set of patterns based on the daily and yearly positions of the sun. As the primary source of every kind of energy in the solar system, the sun floods the Earth with a constant stream of ether, and this stream can effectively drown out other patterns in the etheric ocean; this is why, for example, ghosts and other etheric phenomena are rarely seen while the sun is above the horizon. Similarly, objects charged with etheric patterns will gradually lose their charge if exposed to unfiltered sunlight.

## Natural Magic

The presence of astral and etheric forces in the very substance of the world we inhabit opens up a wide range of possibilities to the magician. Energies on these levels interact with the matter and energy of the physical level, but different kinds of matter interact in different ways. Some materials hold astral and etheric charges well, others poorly, while still others will erase such charges,

and still other substances affect the subtle levels in more specialized ways.

These effects are the basis for what magicians call *natural magic*. Natural magic relies not on the inner powers of the magician but on the subtle relationships between physical substances and nonphysical energies. Natural magic and ritual magic are thus two different ways of accomplishing magical work, and although they are not incompatible—in fact, properly used, they reinforce each other—they follow different laws and use different approaches.

The use of crystals and metals as etheric condensers is one very common application of natural magic. An etheric condenser is like a battery, which can be charged with ether and then used as a source of power for etheric workings. Pure mineral crystals do this better than anything else. Pure metals also hold charges well; each metal corresponds, in magical lore, with one of the seven traditional planets, and will efficiently hold charges that are harmonious with that planet's nature.

Still water, similarly, will hold etheric charges very effectively. Moving water, on the other hand, is an etheric eraser. A charged object immersed in running water will quickly be stripped of its charge; the purer and colder the water is, the stronger the effect. This is the basis for the tradition that ghosts and evil magic cannot cross running water.

The use of holy water, which is water that has had consecrated salt dissolved in it, is a further application of the same principle. Holy water is typically flicked from the fingers, and the fine spray of droplets this produces has a double effect. First, it sends moving water through any etheric patterns present in the area; second, as the smallest droplets evaporate in midflight, they produce tiny salt crystals that, like any other crystal, will soak up whatever ether happens to be present. The combination makes holy water one of the more effective tools for magically cleansing a space, and a method for preparing and consecrating it will be given below.

A subtler effect with similar uses involves evaporated acids. A shallow bowl half full of vinegar left out in a room will cause the ether present in the air to gradually lose any patterns it may contain. Stronger acids do the same thing more forcefully, although they should be diluted with water to prevent accidents. This is a good way to interfere with a haunting or any other disruptive monster activity, as etheric entities can't accomplish much in such an atmosphere and risk dissolution if they remain there for more than a short time.

Similarly, when dealing with etheric entities of any kind, it's often useful to wash your entire body daily with cold water—the colder the better—mixed with a little vinegar. This is good for your skin and circulation as well as for your etheric body, and it will help keep larvae and other low-grade etheric entities from parasitizing you. Some magicians make this a daily habit, and there's much to recommend it.

Another far more extensive field of natural magic involves volatile aromatics from plant sources. Most often used in amulets or incense, these substances have a vast range of effects. The space available here does not permit anything like an adequate discussion of this side of natural magic, but two examples may be worth mentioning, as they have direct applications in monster-related magic.

The first is frankincense, an aromatic resin traditionally associated with the sun. This incense has a powerful purifying and harmonizing effect, and it can be used in any situation where healing, blessing, and protection are needed.

The second is asafoetida. This vile-smelling herb, associated with Saturn, is perhaps the most effective means of banishing known in natural magic. Used as incense, it strips etheric charges from whatever its smoke touches, and will drive away spirits when other methods fail; a small airtight container of asafoetida is a wise thing to have on hand when performing high-risk monster investigations. It smells unbelievably foul when burnt—like a mixture of sulfur and rotting onion—and for this reason alone, it's best used only in emergencies.

One final element of natural magic worth using in monster-related work derives from the special etheric effects of certain metals. Of these, the best known is iron. It's a commonplace of folklore that sharp iron will dispel hostile magic and drive off or destroy certain kinds of spirits, and this is quite accurate: a knife, a nail, a sword, or any other sharp iron object, thrust into a concentration of etheric energy, will cause something not unlike an etheric short-circuit, dispersing the ether and obliterating whatever patterns may have been present in it. This effect is the basis for the Trident of Paracelsus, one of the basic tools of the monster hunter's trade, which is described in detail at the end of this chapter.

Silver has similar effects, although in a more limited range of phenomena. The use of silver as a way to chase off or kill werewolves is a matter of common knowledge even today. Creatures of the densest levels of the etheric, or those who have artificially condensed an etheric body of transformation, may be able to resist the effects of iron—although folklore gives wildly variable testimony on this point. Silver's extremely high conductivity and its special etheric resonances, though, make it a potent tool for disrupting dense etheric lat-

tices. A silver-tipped walking stick (as described in Werewolves, pp. 71–81) or some similar device may be worth keeping close to hand in the event that an entity of this sort is likely to be present.

## The Magical Emergency Kit

Just as the basic tools of the monster hunter's trade can easily be assembled in advance and kept in one place so that nothing is forgotten in the hurry of preparing for an investigation, some basic natural magic equipment and supplies might usefully be gathered and packed in a bag for emergencies. This sort of "magical emergency kit" has uses that go far beyond the needs of monster investigation, but it's particularly useful to have handy when monstrous beings are around.

To some extent, the contents of your magical emergency kit will depend on the tradition of magic you practice, if any, and on the skill and experience you've developed in whatever magical techniques you've learned. Much will also depend on your own strengths and weaknesses. Still, the following items should probably find a place in your kit.

### A Steel-Bladed Athame, Ritual Dagger, or Trident

As mentioned above, the subtle-energy effects of iron and steel are a useful tool for protection against hostile or disruptive entities. If you have studied a specific tradition of magic, whatever tool your tradition uses for these purposes should be part of your kit. If it's been ritually consecrated—and it should be, if at all possible—keep it wrapped in silk or linen to protect it from unwanted energies. The hilt should be insulated so that you won't get the etheric equivalent of a shock when you use it; if an insulated hilt can't be arranged, a cotton or leather glove is a workable alternative.

### A Portable Censer, Charcoal, Waterproof/Windproof Matches, and a Folding Fan

Incense is one of the more useful tools in any magical emergency. Having these items at hand will ensure that you can use incense in nearly any situation. The fan is used to direct the incense smoke where it's needed.

### Blessing Incense

These will vary somewhat, depending on your preferences, but frankincense is nearly always a good bet. Rosemary, sage, and vervain are also common choices. All incenses should be kept in airtight containers.

### Banishing Incense

Again, your choices here should be guided by your background and preferences. Cedarwood, mugwort, and myrrh are generally good options.

### Red Oil

This is an ancient bit of natural magic well worth bringing back into common use. Take a cup or more of St. John's Wort flowers, as fresh as possible, and put them in a clear glass jar; pour in olive oil, while stirring, until the oil just covers the flowers. Put in a place where the jar will receive direct sunlight for at least a few hours each day, and let stand for two to four months. If the flowers are fresh, the oil will turn blood red. Strain, and store the oil in a cool, dark place. A drop of red oil rubbed onto the forehead will banish disruptive energies and help restore peace even in the most trying of times; a drop on the back of the neck will help prevent obsession by demons or spirits.

### Salt

Many magical traditions use this to purify and banish. Good-quality kosher salt or sea salt is best.

### A Small Bowl or Cup, and a Sealed Container of Incense Ash

These, together with salt and clean water, can be used to consecrate holy water for use in blessings and purifications. Any sort of incense ash will do, although frankincense ash seems to be particularly useful.

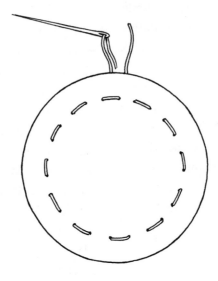

*Amulet 1*

### Holy Water

To make holy water, pour water into a cup or bowl and add a pinch each of salt and ash. Then hold both your hands over the water and speak an appropriate blessing, concentrating on your intention. Holy water can be sprinkled around the edge of a circle to purify it of unwanted energies. If there is any left over at the end of a working, it should be poured out on the earth.

### Protective Talismans or Amulets

Different schools of magic have different versions of these common tools, ranging from little bags of herbs and graveyard dust to pasteboard disks covered with geometrical diagrams and Hebrew letters. Whatever the details, though, something of the sort is well worth having in your kit; it should be wrapped in silk or linen to keep its charge at full intensity. The following two amulets will provide good basic protection from many monstrous beings.

AMULET 1. Take a circle of red flannel two to three inches in diameter. With red thread and an over-and-under stitch, as shown in the diagram, make a seam halfway between the outside edge and the center, running all the way around the circle of cloth, and leaving both ends of the thread free on the underside of the cloth. In the center, put a teaspoon or so of pure salt, and a bright nail—a small brad or paneling nail will do—that you have previously bent into an angle using two pairs of pliers. Pull both ends of the thread to draw the circle of cloth into a bag, tie tightly, wrap the ends of the thread in opposite directions around the neck of the bag, and tie again. This works well hung by a red cord around your neck, so that it rests in the area of your heart.

AMULET 2. Take another circle of red flannel and prepare it with thread as before, but fill it with a mixture of St. John's Wort, vervain, and angelica root. If you have access to a rowan or mountain ash tree, a single dried berry can also be added with good effect.

Whatever you put in your magical emergency kit, of course, the same rule applies as with all the other tools of the monster hunter's trade: if you don't know how to use it, it isn't going to do you any good when you need it. If you have an incense burner and self-starting charcoal, practice lighting the charcoal and burning incense under less-than-perfect conditions before you pack it with you on a monster hunt. If you plan on being able to make holy water, familiarize yourself with the process in advance so that you'll be able to do it in a hurry when something paranormal is breathing down your neck.

## The Trident of Paracelsus

This was once a central tool of Western magicians, and instructions for making and consecrating it can still be found in some older sources. Unlike the more common magical working tools used in most traditions nowadays, it doesn't require a great deal of experience in ritual technique to prepare and use, and this makes it particularly useful for the monster investigator with a limited magical background.

The blade of the trident is made of sheet iron or steel—12 to 16 gauge usually works well—cut out with a hacksaw in the pattern shown below; the dimensions can vary, but a length of around one foot and a width around six to eight inches works well. The hilt is a piece of one-inch diameter wooden dowel, one to two feet long, with a slit cut in one end to receive the blade. Both the blade and the hilt should be sanded smooth, and the hilt should be painted with a good enamel paint for the sake of etheric insulation. Hilt and blade can be joined with a strong all-purpose glue, or a pilot hole can be punched in the end of the blade that joins the hilt, and a metal screw used to make the connection secure. The three points of the trident should be sharpened with a file, and kept sharp for use; the blade should be lightly treated with a preservative oil or wax to prevent rust.

*The Trident of Paracelsus*

If you have the necessary magical background, appropriate sigils and words of power can be etched or engraved on the blade, and any convenient form of consecration ritual used to charge the trident. A simpler approach, though, will be found to produce a perfectly effective trident. The following basic consecration ritual is to be used as soon as the trident is finished and ready for use.

### Basic Consecration Ritual

1. Just before midnight, cover a small table with a white cloth to serve as an altar. Place two white candles in candlesticks on the altar, light them, and set the trident between them with the points facing away from you. Light some incense—frankincense is best, and cone, stick, or loose incense may be used as you wish. You should also have a flat box large enough to hold the trident, and a piece of silk or linen to wrap it so that no part is exposed.

2. At midnight exactly, with absolute concentration on each word, repeat the following blessing three times:

"Infinite and eternal Light,
bless this magical weapon and
its wielder, and preserve them
from all the shadows of evil,
so that they may serve Thee
by banishing the evil
and protecting the good."

(Depending on your own religious beliefs, you may wish to use the name and titles of a deity in place of the phrase "Infinite and eternal Light," and end the blessing with "Amen" or "So mote it be.")

3. Take the trident by its hilt and hold it before you for a moment, points upward. Then wrap it in its wrappings and put it away in its box. This concludes the ceremony.

Once the trident is made and consecrated, it should not be taken from its box except to be used. In particular, it's a very poor idea to go around showing it to other people at random; the more time it spends outside its protective wrappings, the more likely you are to disperse the energies of the consecration. The trident is a tool, not a toy, and should be treated as such.

In use, the trident is wielded like a sword. The three points form the business end, and they may be used either to thrust or to slash. The trident may also simply be used to bar a monster's way; few monstrous beings will risk confronting cold iron backed with a magical consecration. Some entities may try to bluff or trick their way past the trident, of course, and this should be kept in mind when using it.

Those who need more information about natural magic, or want to learn more about this branch of the magical art, can find the details in my book *Natural Magic: Potions and Powers from the Magical Garden* (St. Paul: Llewellyn, 2000).

# RITUAL MAGIC

With ritual magic we move into a radically different form of working. Natural magic can be used for protection by anyone who understands its formulae, or simply knows whatever recipes happen to be current in a given culture. Ritual magic is another matter. Where natural magic draws on the subtle energies that move through the natural world, ritual magic relies on the powers hidden away within each individual human being. Those powers, if they are to be summoned and controlled reliably, must be developed by training and systematic practice. Simply knowing a formula or a ceremony of ritual magic, in other words, isn't enough; it's also necessary to have developed the inner skills of will, imagination, awareness, and subtle energy that turn a formula or a ceremony from a lifeless structure into a vehicle for living power.

The rituals included in this section, then, cannot be used like recipes from a cookbook. If you intend to put them to work in the field, you need to have practiced them literally hundreds of times beforehand and mastered their intricacies. If you want to use ritual magic like a real magician, in effect, you need to become a real magician, or something close to one.

The following basic rituals should be learned and practiced as tools for magical protection well before they are likely to be needed. As soon as possible in the learning process, they should be committed to memory, and then practiced several times a week at minimum until you can do them effectively even when flustered, frightened, or half asleep. Even then, one practice a week is a good idea, so that the rituals stay fresh in your memory and imagination.

All the following rituals, it may be worth noting, are from one particular tradition of ceremonial magic, the Golden Dawn tradition, which is the system of magic I primarily teach. If you already have some training in a different system of ritual magic, on the other hand, you may need to replace the rituals given here with equivalent ceremonies from your own tradition.

Those who need more information about these techniques of ritual magic, or who are interested in learning more advanced techniques of magical working, can find the details in my book *Circles of Power* (St. Paul: Llewellyn, 1997).

## The Cabalistic Cross

This first ritual is not really an independent ceremony, but rather an opening and closing gesture that is used in nearly all Golden Dawn ceremonial workings. It should be practiced and memorized on its own, as a first step in your ritual training, since you'll be using it in every other ceremony covered here.

This ritual has a certain similarity to the Christian practice of making the sign of the cross over the body, and there are probably historical connections, but the Cabalistic Cross is not simply a gesture of blessing. It is designed to awaken four energy centers in the aura, and to focus the awareness on the subtle connections between the magician and the cosmos.

The words printed IN CAPITALS are intended to be *vibrated* rather than simply spoken. In magical terminology, vibration refers to a particular way of intoning or chanting words of power that arouses magical energies. To learn how to do it, chant a vowel tone—a simple "aah" is best—while changing the way your mouth and throat shape the sound. You are trying to find a tone that sets up a buzzing or tingling sound somewhere in your body. The effect may be very faint at first, but practice will improve and strengthen it. Given more practice, you can learn to make the vibrating effect move from place to place in your body, and even to project it outside yourself.

The vibrated words in the Cabalistic Cross, which are in Hebrew (the traditional language of Western high magic), repeat an ancient prayer that was also borrowed long ago by the Christian church. *Ateh* means "unto thee," *Malkuth* "the kingdom," *ve-Geburah* "and the power," and *ve-Geburah*, "and the glory." *Le-Olam* means both "through the world" and "through the age"—like most ancient terms for the cosmos, the Hebrew word *olam* includes both space and time—while *Amen*, which has been reduced to a kind of spoken punctuation at the end of modern prayers, was once recognized as an important word of power.

The Cabalistic Cross is performed as follows:

1. Stand straight, feet together, arms at sides, facing east. Pause, clear your mind, and then visualize yourself expanding upward and outward, through the air and through space, until your body is so large that your feet rest on the Earth as though on a ball a foot across. Raise your right hand above your forehead; draw it down, palm toward your face, visualizing a beam of light descending from far above your head. Touch your fingers to your forehead, and visualize the descending light forming a sphere of light, the same size as the Earth beneath your feet, just above the crown of your head. Vibrate the word ATEH (pronounced "ah-teh").

2. Draw your hand down to touch your solar plexus, just below the lower point of the breastbone, and visualize a shaft of light descending from the sphere above your head to the visualized Earth beneath your feet. Vibrate MALKUTH (pronounced "mahl-kooth").

3. Bring your hand back to the center of your chest, and then over to the right shoulder; visualize a beam of light extending from the vertical shaft to a point just past your shoulder, where it forms a sphere of brilliant red light, the same size as the others. Vibrate VE-GEBURAH (pronounced "veh geh-boo-rah").

4. Bring your hand straight across from your right shoulder to your left shoulder; visualize a beam of light extending from the vertical shaft to a point just past your left shoulder, where it forms a sphere of brilliant blue light the same size as the others. (At this point, you have visualized a cross of light within your body, with each of its ends forming a sphere.) Vibrate VE-GEDULAH (pronounced "veh geh-dyoo-lah").

5. Join the hands in front of the center of the chest, fingers together and pointed upward, palms together and flat. Visualize the Earth and the three spheres of energy joined by the cross of light. Vibrate LE-OLAM, AMEN (pronounced "leh o-lahm, ah-men"). This completes the rite.

## The Lesser Ritual of the Pentagram

The essential protective ritual in the Golden Dawn magical tradition is the Lesser Ritual of the Pentagram. This uses the symbolism and energy of the pentagram or five-pointed star, one of the major figures of sacred geometry. In this ritual, the pentagrams are traced in a particular way, to establish balance not only within the magician but also within an area of physical space, which is traced out by a circle. That area is guarded with pentagrams, with four words of power that are four of the traditional Names of God, and also with the images of the four archangels who govern the four directions and the four magical elements. The Cabalistic Cross begins and ends the ceremony. The result is to cleanse the area in which the ritual is performed, banishing magical energies and spirits of all kinds.

It should be noted that each of the ten ways of tracing a pentagram has a different magical effect. The one given here is a general banishing pentagram, suitable for clearing an area from the effects of magical workings or preternatural beings. Some of the other ways will invoke rather than banish, so be careful to trace the pentagram the right way!

The Lesser Ritual of the Pentagram is performed as follows:

1. Stand in the center of your practice space, facing east. Clear your mind, and then perform the Cabalistic Cross.

2. Step to the eastern edge of the space. With the first two fingers of your right hand, and the arm itself held straight, trace a pentagram some three feet across in the air before you, in the way shown in the illustration. The pentagram should be made as even and exact as possible. As you trace it, visualize the line drawn by your fingers shining with brilliant blue-white light, so that you finish the process visualizing the pentagram before you as being traced in lines of incandescence.

*Banishing Pentagram*

When you have finished tracing the pentagram, point to the center of the pentagram and vibrate the Name YHVH (pronounced "yeh-ho-wah").

3. Holding your arm extended, trace a line around a quarter circle to the southern edge of the space, visualizing that line in the same brilliant blue-white light. Trace the same pentagram in the south, with the same visualization; point to the center, and vibrate the Name ADNI (pronounced "ah-dough-nye").

4. Trace the line around a quarter circle to the western edge of the space and repeat the process, this time vibrating the Name AHIH (pronounced "eh-heh-yeh"). Then trace the line around a quarter circle to the north and repeat, this time vibrating the Name AGLA (pronounced "ah-geh-lah").

5. Trace the line back around to the east, completing the circle. You are now standing inside a ring drawn in visualized light, with a pentagram shining in each of the four quarters. Return to the center and face east, as you were at the opening, but raise your arms to the sides like the arms of a cross, palms forward. Say aloud:

"Before me, Raphael
(pronounced "ra-fa-ell");
behind me, Gabriel ("gah-bree-ell");
to my right hand, Michael
("mee-ka-ell"); to my left hand,
Auriel ("oh-ree-ell").
For about me flame
the pentagrams,
and upon me shines
the six-rayed star!"

While naming the archangels, visualize them as conventional winged angelic figures standing outside the circle, larger than human height and blazing with light. Raphael wears yellow and violet, and carries a sword; Gabriel wears blue and orange, and carries a goblet; Michael wears red and green, and carries a staff; Auriel wears every shade of earth and green growth, and carries a disk bearing a pentagram. When the pentagrams are mentioned, visualize them as clearly as possible. When the six-rayed star is named, visualize a hexagram (a conventional Star of David made of two interlaced triangles) on the front of your body, about two feet across, the upward-pointing triangle red, the downward-pointing triangle blue.

6. Repeat the Cabalistic Cross. This completes the ritual.

## The Ritual of the Rose Cross

The Golden Dawn tradition provides another effective ritual of protection that can be used against hostile entities. This is the Ritual of the Rose Cross. Where the Lesser Ritual of the Pentagram drives beings and spirits away by main force, the Ritual of the Rose Cross brings energies of healing and blessing into focus. The Ritual of the Rose Cross also veils the aura of anyone present in the space where it is performed, making it difficult or impossible for monstrous beings to perceive or act on them.

The Pentagram and Rose Cross rituals can be combined for a mode of protection that will send nearly anything about its business. Simply do the Lesser Ritual of the Pentagram, exactly as given, and then do the Ritual of the Rose Cross immediately afterward in the same space. In the event of psychic attack or nocturnal haunting, this combination is a good thing to do in the bedroom each night before going to sleep; if at all possible, the bed should be pulled out from the wall so that the rituals can be done around it, and it should be left in the center of the lines of woven force until sunrise.

To do this ritual, you'll need to know how to perform four Signs, which are special patterns of body movement used in Golden Dawn magic. The four Signs used in this ritual are the Signs of Isis, Apophis, Osiris Slain, and Osiris Risen. To perform the Sign of Isis, raise your right arm straight up from the shoulder, extend your left arm out to the side and down at a slight angle, and bow your head. The Sign of Apophis is made by raising your arms up to form a *V* shape, and throwing back your head; the Sign of Osiris Slain is made by extending your arms out to the side, palms forward, as though forming a cross, and bowing your head; the Sign of Osiris Risen is made by crossing your arms on your chest, right over left, so that the fingertips of each hand are touching the opposite shoulder, and bowing your head. These Signs also spell out the letters L, V, and X, which make the Latin word LVX, *lux*, "light"—a detail that plays a part in the ceremony.

The Ritual of the Rose Cross also requires a stick of incense; frankincense, or some other purifying and protective scent, is best. It is performed as follows:

1. Standing in the middle of your practice space, facing east and holding the lit stick of incense in your right hand, perform the Cabalistic Cross, tracing the lines of the Cross with the tip of the incense.

2. Go to the southeast corner of your space. There, trace the symbol of the Rose Cross in the air before you with the incense, as shown in the illustra-

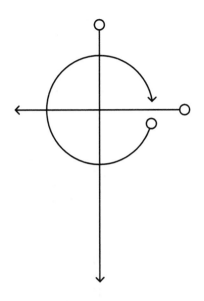

*The Rose Cross*

there, and do the same to the northeast corner, repeating the process there also.

4. Trace the line back around to the southeast, completing the circle. Then draw a line with the incense up and over your head, diagonally across toward the northwest corner of the space. At the center of the room stop, trace the symbol of the Rose Cross directly above you, point to its center and vibrate the Name. Then continue to the northwest corner. From there, trace the line down and across the floor, diagonally across to the southeast corner again; stop in the middle of the room, draw the symbol of the Rose Cross just above the floor, point to its center and vibrate the Name. Then finish tracing the line back to the southeast.

tion. The symbol should be about three feet high, with the upper end of the cross at the level of the top of your head, and it should be visualized in white light. Point the lit end of the incense at the center of the cross, and vibrate the Name YHShVH (pronounced "yeh-heh-shu-ah").

3. Trace and visualize a line around to the southwest corner of the space, and repeat the same process, tracing the symbol and vibrating the same Name. Then trace the line around to the northwest corner, repeating the process

5. Retrace the line from the symbol in the southeast corner to the one in the southwest corner, and then trace another line up over your head, across to the symbol in the center of the ceiling, across and down to the northeast corner, down and across to the symbol in the center of the floor, and back across and up to the southwest corner again. Then retrace the line back around to the southeast. (The result of all this tracing is shown in the illustration.) There, draw the symbol of the

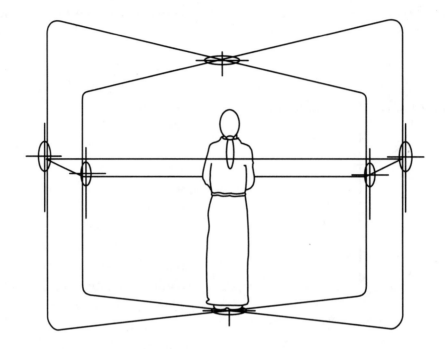

*The Rose Cross Ritual*

Rose Cross again, over the first one but somewhat larger; while tracing the lower half of the circle, vibrate YHShVH; while tracing the upper half of the circle, vibrate YHVShH (pronounced "yeh-ho-wah-shah").

6. Return to the center. Stand, facing east, and say the Analysis of INRI aloud:

"I, N, R, I. Yod, Nun, Resh, Yod.
Virgo, Isis, mighty mother.
Scorpio, Apophis, the destroyer.
Sol, Osiris, slain and risen. Isis,
   Apophis, Osiris. I, A, O."

Vibrate, as forcefully as possible: "IAO!" (pronounced "Eee-Aaa-Oh")

7. Make the Sign of Osiris Slain. Say: "The Sign of Osiris Slain!"

Make the Sign of Isis and say: "The Sign of the Mourning of Isis!"

Make the Sign of Apophis, and say: "The Sign of Apophis and Typhon!"

Make the Sign of Osiris Risen by standing with head bowed and crossing your arms across your chest, hands palms-down on opposite shoulders, and say: "The Sign of Osiris Risen!"

Then repeat the Signs of Isis, Apophis, and Osiris, saying: "L, V, X."

Lower your arms to your sides, and say: "Lux—Light—the Light of the Cross."

Raising your arms up above your head, as though reaching out, say: "Let the Divine Light descend!"

8. At this point visualize a shaft of brilliant white light, wide enough to encompass the entire space within the lines you have traced, descending from far above and shining on you. Hold the image as intensely as you can for as long as you wish, and then release the image and perform the Cabalistic Cross. This completes the ritual.

## The Middle Pillar Exercise

This last magical ritual is not a protective ceremony, but it forms an essential foundation of magical training in the Golden Dawn tradition. The Middle Pillar exercise is designed to awaken, charge, and balance five major energy centers along the midline of your body. These centers have much the same role in Golden Dawn magic that the chakras have in yoga and related Eastern spiritual disciplines. The difference between chakras and Middle Pillar centers has been a source of some confusion, but unnecessarily; the human body contains 360 energy centers, each with its own effects on the subtle energies, and different spiritual and magical systems use different centers because they use different kinds of meditation and ritual, and require different patterns of subtle-energy work.

The five centers of the Middle Pillar are as follows:

### Kether

Just above the top of the head, associated with the color white and the spiritual level.

### Daath

At the center of the throat, associated with the color light gray and the mental level.

### Tiphareth

At the center of the chest, associated with the color gold and the astral level.

### Yesod

At the genitals, associated with the color violet and the etheric level.

### Malkuth

Between the soles of the feet, associated with the colors dark green or black and the material level.

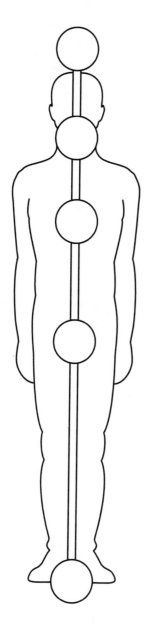

*The Centers of the Middle Pillar*

In the Middle Pillar exercise, all five of these centers are awakened by focused will and imagination, and the energies are then circulated through the body. The result is to charge, balance, and focus the energy centers; to bring health and balance to all the different levels of the self; and to heighten the ability to perform effective ritual magic. As a result, this exercise is one of the best possible preparations for dealing with the realm of monstrous beings, and it should be done once a day during any period when you are investigating a monster or in some other way dealing with the Unseen. (Serious students of Golden Dawn magic do the Middle Pillar exercise every day, as a rule, and this may not be a bad habit to take up if you expect to deal with monsters on a regular basis.)

The Middle Pillar exercise is performed as follows:

1. Perform the complete Lesser Ritual of the Pentagram, exactly as given above.

2. Standing in the center of the space, facing east, with legs together and arms at sides, turn your attention to a point infinitely far above your head. Visualize the point shining with light, like a star. Next, drawing in a breath, visualize a stream of light descending from that point to the area just above your head, where it forms a sphere of intense white light about eight inches across.

The bottom of the sphere is just above the crown of your head. Concentrate on the sphere while you breathe in; on the outbreath, vibrate the Name AHIH (pronounced "eh-heh-yeh"). Repeat this process three more times, focusing on Kether on the inbreath, vibrating the Name on the outbreath. Try to make the vibration resonate within the sphere of light itself.

3. With the next inbreath, bring the stream of light down to the middle of your throat, and there form another sphere of light of the same size, this one a soft gray color. Concentrate on it while you breathe in slowly and deeply; on the outbreath, vibrate the Name YHVH ALHIM (pronounced "yeh-ho-wah ell-o-heem"). Again, repeat this three more times, and try to make the vibration resonate in the sphere itself.

4. In the same way, establish the golden sphere of Tiphareth at the level of the heart, and vibrate the Name YHVH ALVH VDAaTh ("yeh-ho-wah ell-o-ah vah da-ath") four times; the violet sphere of Yesod at the genitals, and vibrate the Name ShDI AL ChI ("shah-die ell chye") four times; and the sphere of Malkuth at the soles of the feet, which may be black or dark green, and vibrate the Name ADNI HARTz ("ah-dough-nye ha ah-retz") four times.

5. Pause, and then direct your attention upward again toward the Kether center above your head. Draw in a breath, and visualize a shaft of brilliant light descending with the inbreath to the Tiphareth center at your heart; visualize the Tiphareth center shining more brightly as you breathe out. Repeat this process four times; on the last outbreath, the Tiphareth center should blaze like the sun.

6. Draw in a breath slowly, feeling the air pass through your nostrils and down your windpipe. Visualize it as passing into the Tiphareth center at your heart, and from there out to your left side, down the left flank and leg, to the Malkuth center at the feet. Hold the breath there for the same amount of time you took to breathe in, then breathe out at the same pace, visualizing the breath passing up the right leg and flank, into the Tiphareth center, and then up and out the windpipe and nostrils; then, hold the outbreath for the same amount of time. (It's helpful to use the Fourfold Breath during these four phases to get the rhythm. Draw in a breath through the nose, mentally counting to four slowly; hold the breath for the same count; breathe out, also through the nose, to the same count; hold the breath out for the same count, and repeat. The breath should

be held with the muscles of the chest and diaphragm, not the throat; a sharp tap on the chest should be able to drive out air. The rhythm should be as slow as you can manage comfortably without gasping.) Make the visualization of the moving breath as concrete as possible, so that you feel the path of the breath down and up again as though it were a physical movement. Repeat this whole process four times.

7. Pause, and then perform the Cabalistic Cross. This completes the exercise.

# A GLOSSARY OF
# MONSTER LORE

AMULET: a substance or collection of substances with magical effects; a basic tool of natural magic, amulets are commonly used as protective devices against monstrous beings in many cultures

ANGEL: a spiritual entity of wholly positive nature; in the traditional lore, a messenger or emissary of the Divine

ANIMISM: in anthropological jargon, the belief or perception that life and intelligence are present in some part of the universe, which is classified as "dead matter" by current scientific thought

ARCHANGEL: a type of angel, the eighth of nine angelic orders in Christian angel lore, but a class superior to the ten angelic orders in Cabalistic tradition

ARCHFAY: one of the major types of fay, commonly experienced by humans in the form of tall and regal humanlike beings, often with blond hair; their actual nature is uncertain due to the effects of glamour; probably equivalent to UFO Nordics

ASTRAL BODY: the level of the human subtle body corresponding to ordinary personality and consciousness; the vehicle for astral projection

ASTRAL PROJECTION: the process by which the conscious self of a living person leaves the physical body and travels in another, subtle body that can penetrate solid matter

AUPHANIM: in Cabalistic angel lore, the second of ten orders of angels

BENI ELOHIM: in many versions of Cabalistic angel lore, the eighth of ten orders of angels; *see also* Tarshishim

BERSERKER: in Norse tradition, a human shapeshifter who takes the form of a bear

BHM: acronym for "Big Hairy Monster"; in current anomaly research, a standard term for sasquatchlike entities, including some who may be solitary fays

BIGFOOT: alternate name for sasquatch

BODY OF TRANSFORMATION: etheric structure created by shapeshifters as an artificial etheric body

CABALA: a tradition of mystical spirituality, originating in Judaism and currently found in Jewish, Christian, and magical variants, which is central to most Western occultism

CHALKYDRI: a type of angel in traditional lore, associated with the sun; they are reported to have twelve wings, crocodiles' heads, and serpent's bodies

CHANGELING: in faery lore, a sickly and voracious nonhuman substitute left in place of a child abducted by fays

CHASHMALIM: in Cabalistic angel lore, the fourth of ten orders of angels

CHERUBIM: an order of angels variously assigned in different systems of angel lore; ninth of the ten orders of angels in Cabalistic lore, but second of the nine orders in Christian angelology

COMMUNAL FAY: a type of fay, experienced by human beings in the form of humanoid entities smaller than normal human size; their actual form is uncertain due to the effects of glamour; probably equivalent to UFO grays

CONTINUING APPARITION: the ghostly image of a person that appears to the living over an extended period, frequently appearing to more than one person; a type of ghost

CRISIS APPARITION: the ghostly image of a person that appears to friends, relatives, or others when that person is undergoing a major crisis such as an accident, a severe illness, or death; in many cases, a type of ghost

CRYPTOZOOLOGY: the study of biological entities whose existence has not yet been accepted by the scientific mainstream

CULTURAL SOURCE HYPOTHESIS: the theory that sightings of monstrous beings are the result of cultural sources such as legends, which are then projected onto ambiguous phenomena by believers

DAB: in Hmong tradition, a monster or hostile spirit; pronounced "da"

DAB TSOG: in Hmong tradition, a type of dab who sits on the chest of sleepers and suffocates them; effectively equivalent to the Old Hag; pronounced "da cho"

DAIMON: in ancient Greek lore, one of a class of beings intermediate between humanity and the gods

DEMON: a spirit whose actions and apparent intentions toward human beings are malicious, hurtful, and destructive; in Cabalistic lore, an entity surviving from a universe prior to our own

DIVINATION: a branch of occultism that seeks to predict future events, or to gain otherwise inaccessible information about the past or present, by means of subtle factors acting in the present moment

DOMINATIONS: in Christian angel lore, the fourth of nine orders of angels

DRAGON: a monstrous being characterized by serpentine form and aquatic habitat, found in monster lore from around the world

ELEMENTAL: in magical lore, a being that inhabits one of the four magical elements; the four types of elementals are generally called gnomes, sylphs, undines, and salamanders

243

ELEMENTARY: in magical lore, a being composed of two or three elements; probably equivalent to fays

ELEMENTS: fire, water, air, and earth; the four basic building blocks of the magical universe, united and shaped by the "fifth element" of spirit

ENTITY HAUNTING: a continuing apparition in which evidence suggests that a conscious being, rather than a "recording" of past events, is involved

ETHER: a subtle substance that, in magical theory, forms the framework for material objects, and which is closely linked with life; most monster-related phenomena have a very important etheric component

ETHERIC BODY: the level of the human subtle body closest to the material, and most often affected directly by monstrous beings and factors

ETHERIC REVENANT: a dead human being who has avoided the Second Death by stabilizing his or her etheric body through any of several different means

EXPERIMENTAL APPARITION: the ghostly image of a living person who consciously sets out to appear to another person some distance away; often associated with astral projection

EXORCISM: a religious or magical ritual process by which a possessing or obsessing entity is driven away from its victim; exorcism is a difficult and demanding art and cannot be practiced safely by amateurs

FAY: any of a class of entity found in worldwide monster lore, usually experienced by human beings in a variety of humanoid shapes but capable of deluding and misleading humans to an almost unlimited degree by means of glamour

FAERY-LED: *see* pixy-led

FIRST DEATH: in magical lore, the process by which the subtle body leaves the physical body at the end of an incarnation; corresponds to biological death as understood by medical science

FOLKLORE: the unofficial knowledge held in common by most members of a given culture; the folklore of most cultures is a rich source of information about monsters

GHOST: the image of a dead person or animal seen by the living; in magical lore, ghosts are individuals between the First and Second Deaths

GLAMOUR: the power of illusion possessed by fays, capable of misleading and deluding human beings to an almost unlimited extent

GNOME: an elemental of earth

GOETIA: the branch of ritual magic concerned with the evocation of demons

GRAYS: the most common type of UFO inhabitant reported by modern witnesses; despite the assumption that such entities must be from other planets, grays show important similarities to communal fays

GREMLIN: an implike, mischievous creature believed to infest aircraft; apparently related to the house fay

HAGGING: term (drawn from Newfoundland folklore) for a very common form of attack by a vampire, magical sending, hostile ghost, or demon; the victim of a hagging awakens but is unable to move or cry out, becomes aware of a presence in the area, and experiences feelings of suffocation and of extreme fear; according to folklore, hagging may be associated with illness or death, and medical researchers have connected it to the SUNDS epidemic among Hmong refugees in Thailand and America

HAUNTING: a continuing apparition

HOUSE FAY: one of a class of fays that established friendly relations with human beings, performing housework and protecting the house in exchange for gifts of food and drink; the type seems to be extinct at present

INTELLECTUS: according to traditional angel lore, the mode of perception possessed by angels, by which they are aware of everything in the universe at once

INTELLIGENCE: in Western magical lore, one of a class of spirits inhabiting the mental level, centers of consciousness embodied in what human beings experience as patterns of thought

ISHIM: in Cabalistic angel lore, the tenth of the ten orders of angels

KA: Egyptian term for etheric body

KERUBIM: alternative spelling of Cherubim

KHU: "Luminous one," Egyptian term for an etheric revenant

KLABAUTERMANN: in German and Baltic lore, a shipboard fay who helps to maintain the ship and harasses or punishes lazy sailors; the maritime equivalent of a house fay

LAKE SERPENT: the freshwater equivalent of a sea serpent; the Loch Ness Monster of Scotland is the most famous lake serpent

LARVA: a type of spirit, a primitive, nearly mindless etheric scavenger

LOWER ASTRAL: the denser and more concrete aspect of the astral level of reality

LYCANTHROPE (from Greek *lykos*, "wolf," and *anthropos*, "human"): another term for werewolf

MAGIC: the art and science of causing changes in consciousness in accordance with will, usually divided into natural magic and ritual magic; worldwide, magic is the most common human method for dealing with monstrous beings

MALEKIM: in Cabalistic angel lore, the sixth of ten orders of angels

MENTAL BODY: the lower of the two immortal aspects of the human subtle body, corresponding to the essential structure of the self

MERMAID: a monstrous entity perceived, by human beings, as a composite of human and fish or dolphin; probably the aquatic equivalent of a fay

MONSTER (from Latin *monstrum*, "that which is shown forth or revealed"): an entity that is not included in the worldview of current scientific thought, but is described in folklore and regularly experienced by human beings as a real phenomenon

NAHUAL: a shapeshifter, in the traditions of Tlaxcala and other parts of Mexico

NATURAL MAGIC: the branch of magic dealing with the subtle powers of physical substances

NORDICS: a type of UFO inhabitant frequently reported by modern witnesses, although less often than grays; despite the assumption that such entities must be from other planets, Nordics show important similarities to archfays

OBSESSION: process by which a demon or other hostile entity inserts destructive thought processes into the mind of a human being

OCCULTISM (from Latin *occultus*, "hidden"): term used for various traditions, teachings, and philosophies surviving from earlier times that are rejected by current scientific thought; includes magic, alchemy, astrology, divination, and various other branches of lore

OLD HAG: in Newfoundland tradition, the entity responsible for hagging attacks

PIXY-LED: *see* faery-led

PHYSICAL BODY: the densest aspect of the human organism, formed of ordinary matter; in magical thought, the physical expression of the higher levels of the self

POLTERGEIST: a monster-related phenomenon in which an unseen force moves objects around a particular place; attributed to ghosts or other monstrous beings by some researchers, and to uncontrolled human psychokinetic powers by others

POSSESSION: the process by which a demon or other hostile entity takes over the mind and body of a human victim

POST-MORTEM APPARITION: the image of a dead person seen some time after the person's death; a type of ghost

POWERS: in Christian angel lore, the sixth of nine orders of angel

PRINCIPALITIES: in Christian angel lore, the fifth of nine orders of angels

PSYCHIC VAMPIRES: living human beings who have acquired the vampiric habit of feeding off the etheric energy of others

PURPOSEFUL GHOST: a type of ghost that makes contact with the living in order to accomplish some task left undone at death

QLIPPOTH: in Cabalistic theory, malignant entities surviving from a universe prior to our own; according to the Cabala, this is the origin of demons

REPLAY HAUNTING: a type of haunting in which no actual entity is present, but the images of past events replay themselves over and over to the psychically sensitive

RITUAL MAGIC: the branch of magic dealing with the subtle effects of symbol and ritual

SALAMANDER: an elemental of fire

SASQUATCH: a large, hairy apelike creature not yet known to science, but frequently seen in the mountains of western North America; probably a living animal descended from known fossil types, related to gorillas and other primates, rather than a monstrous being of the BHM type; also known as Bigfoot

SEA SERPENT: one of several different large marine creatures not yet known to science, but frequently seen in some areas of the ocean; some types are probably living animals of two or three different kinds, related to seals, whales, or other seagoing mammals, while others may be monstrous beings such as dragons; freshwater species are known as lake serpents

SECOND DEATH: the process by which the human soul frees itself from its etheric body; usually occurs several days to several weeks after physical death

SELKIE: a seal-human shapeshifter in Scottish and Irish tradition, with some links to faery lore

SERAPHIM: in Christian angel lore, the first of nine orders of angels

SHAPESHIFTER: a being who has learned to construct an etheric shell of some other form than its own, and either physically or astrally travels about in it

SKINWALKER: Southwestern Native American term for a shapeshifter belonging to a tradition of evil magic; a partial translation of Navajo *yenaaldlooshi* (literally, "[one who goes] by means of trotting like a canine")

SOLITARY FAY: a type of fay normally encountered alone, and often in wilderness areas; possibly involved in modern sightings of hairy humanoids of the BHM type

SPIRIT: traditional term for an intelligent, disembodied entity, also used for the "fifth element" or transcendent factor that unites and shapes the four magical elements

SUBTLE BODY: that part of the human individual lying between the material body and the immortal spirit; according to magical lore, the subtle body is composed of several different levels or aspects

SUNDS: Sudden Unexplained Nocturnal Death Syndrome, a fatal epidemic disease of unknown cause affecting Hmong and other Southeast Asian refugees; according to Hmong tradition, caused by dab tsog in response to failure to perform traditional religious duties

SYLPH: an elemental of air

TALISMAN: a magical device charged and consecrated by ritual methods for a specific purpose; a standard tool of ritual magic, talismans are sometimes used for protection against monstrous beings

TARSHISHIM: in some traditions of Cabalistic angel lore, the seventh of ten orders of angels; *see also* Beni Elohim

THRONES: in Christian angel lore, the third of nine orders of angels

TRANSITIONAL GHOST: a ghost who appears to the living while still in the process of the First Death; a type of crisis apparition

TRAP QUESTION: a deliberately misleading question used when interviewing a witness to purported monster activity, as a way to help detect dishonesty

TRIDENT OF PARACELSUS: a three-pronged iron trident with an insulated handle; traditionally used in magic as a means of defense against hostile spirits

TSOG TSUAM: Hmong term for an attack by dab tsog; effectively equivalent to hagging; pronounced "cho chua"

UNDINE: an elemental of water

UPPER ASTRAL: the subtler and less concrete aspect of the astral level of reality

VAMPIRE: an etheric revenant that survives by feeding on the life energy of the living

WEREWOLF: a human shapeshifter who takes on the form of a wolf

# AN ANNOTATED
# BIBLIOGRAPHY
# OF MONSTER LORE

Adler, Shelley R., *The Role of the Nightmare in Hmong Sudden Unexpected Nocturnal Death Syndrome: A Folkloristic Study of Belief and Health* (Ph.D. diss., UCLA, 1991).

———, "Terror in Transition: Hmong Folk Belief in America," in *Walker* (1995).
Adler's work with the interface between Hmong folklore and SUNDS is central to any study of the inner dimensions of the epidemic, although she studiously avoids those dimensions herself.

Baker, Robert A., and Joe Nickell, *Missing Pieces: How to Investigate Ghosts, UFOs, Psychics, and Other Mysteries* (Buffalo: Prometheus, 1992).
Written by two members of CSICOP, this book starts from the assumption that the whole paranormal realm is bunk, and spends dozens of pages at a time denouncing the phenomena it claims to be studying impartially, as well as the people who fail to hew to the authors' rationalist party line. Still, between rants, it contains some useful practical information on investigating the unexplained.

Barber, Paul, *Vampires, Burial, and Death* (New Haven: Yale University Press, 1988).
A detailed study of the way that processes of decomposition have influenced vampire legends. Not for the weak of stomach.

Barber, Richard, and Ann Riches, *A Dictionary of Fabulous Beasts* (New York: Walker, 1971).

A useful guide to the legendary creatures of the world, with a good bibliography for further research.

Baring-Gould, Sabine, *The Book of Were-Wolves* (London: Senate, 1997).

————, *Curious Myths of the Middle Ages* (London: Jupiter, 1977).

The Reverend Sabine Baring-Gould was one of those astonishingly learned Victorian clergymen whose studies make life so much easier for the modern student of the weird. The first of these books is a very good survey of werewolf and shapeshifter lore from around the world; the second contains a variety of strange branches of medieval legend, some with significant connections to monster lore.

Becker, Carl B., *Paranormal Experience and Survival of Death* (Albany: SUNY Press, 1993).

A solid survey of the empirical evidence for life after death, this book also deals intelligently with the way that beliefs and assumptions among scientists prevent discussion of this and other issues involving the supernatural.

Bennett, Ernest, *Apparitions and Haunted Houses* (London: Faber and Faber, 1939).

A solid study of the evidence for ghosts and haunting-related phenomena, focusing largely on English cases.

Benwell, Gwen, and Arthur Waugh, *Sea Enchantress: The Tale of the Mermaid and her Kin* (New York: Citadel, 1965).

The best general guide to mermaid lore, concentrating on the British Isles, with a refreshing willingness to consider the possibility of the reality of a "mythical" being.

Berger, Arthur S., *Aristocracy of the Dead* (London: McFarland, 1987).

A clear and rather startling look at what a hundred years of psychical research have taught us about life after death. Berger argues that, despite the cliché that everyone is equal in death, there is good reason to think that different people enter very different states after physical death.

Berger, Peter L., *A Rumor of Angels: Modern Society and the Rediscovery of the Supernatural* (Garden City, New York: Doubleday, 1969).

Berger's earlier sociological study of religion, *The Sacred Canopy,* is often quoted by those trying to define the spiritual out of existence by classifying it as a wholly cultural construct. This book, which sets out to undercut that project and does a good job of pointing out the flaws in rationalist approaches to the subject, is rarely mentioned but well worth reading.

Bernheimer, Richard, *Wild Men in the Middle Ages* (New York: Octagon, 1970).

Medieval European folklore was crowded with accounts of what we would now call sasquatches or yetis—humanlike but taller than our species, covered with thick fur, incapable of human speech, and most often found in wilderness regions far from human settlement. While the author of this study apparently never considered the possibility that these legends might be based on actual living creatures, he has collected and synthesized a great deal of useful information on the subject, and in the process has shown how such cryptozoological lore can contaminate and be contaminated by the lore of gods, demons, and faeries, in cultural contexts where hard and fast boundaries were hard to find.

Bett, Henry, *English Legends* (London: Batsford, 1950).

A pleasant collection of folklore, much of it concerning monsters, illustrated with excellent woodcuts.

Blackman, W. Haden, *The Field Guide to North American Hauntings* (New York: Three Rivers, 1998).

With detailed descriptions of sixty-one haunted sites in North America, less extensive information about more than a hundred others, and a guide for beginning ghost hunters, this is a very good introduction to the wakeful dead.

Bodine, Echo, *Relax, It's Only a Ghost* (Boston: Element, 2000).

Bodine is a psychic and healer with plenty of experience with ghosts as well as a savvy sense of media presence, and this book (based on her own ghostly encounters) is a good general guide to the realm of the wakeful dead.

Bogatyrev, Petr, *Vampires in the Carpathians: Magical Acts, Rites, and Beliefs in Subcarpathian Rus'* (New York: East European Monographs, 1998).

An excellent study of monster folklore in a little-known part of Eastern Europe, placing the vampire in its social and magical context.

Bord, Janet, Fairies: *Real Encounters with Little People* (New York: Dell, 1997).

An excellent study of faery lore by a capable Fortean researcher, this book covers modern-day encounters, physical traces of fays, the UFO connection, and a good deal more.

Bord, Janet, and Colin Bord, *Alien Animals* (London: Granada, 1980).

A good general study of "mystery animals" on the fringes of parapsychology, including dragons, phantom panthers, black dogs, and more. The Bords operate the Fortean Picture Library, and many of the better exhibits from their collections appear in this book.

Borges, Jorge Luis, *The Book of Imaginary Beings,* tr. Norman Thomas di Giovanni (New York: Avon, 1969).

The greatest work of literature yet to come out of the realm of monster lore, this collection of short pieces by the Argentine master of magical realism belongs on any monster researcher's reading list.

Brandon, Jim, *The Rebirth of Pan: Hidden Faces of the American Earth Spirit* (Dunlap, Ill.: Firebird, 1983).

———, *Weird America* (New York: Dutton, 1978).

Two useful books on very strange things. *Weird America* is a state-by-state guide to places associated with bizarre phenomena of different kinds; Brandon casts his net wide, but monsters are among the things caught up in it. *The Rebirth of Pan* is more concerned with interpretation, proposing that many anomalies are the result of the living energies of the Earth itself.

Briggs, Katharine M., *An Encyclopedia of Fairies* (New York: Pantheon, 1976.)

———, *The Anatomy of Puck* (London: Routledge and Kegan Paul, 1959).

———, *The Vanishing People* (London: Batsford, 1978).

Katharine Briggs is probably this century's most distinguished and capable scholar of faery lore, with numerous books and articles on the subject to her credit, of which these three are representative. *An Encyclopedia of Fairies* is the best general guide to faery lore available; *The Anatomy of Puck* is a study of English lore about spirits of all kinds at the time of William Shakespeare and his immediate successors, on the eve of the Scientific Revolution; *The Vanishing People* is a general survey of faery folklore from the British Isles. All three are full of detailed information from primary sources, and are good starting places for any research into fays and their habits.

Bringsvaerd, Tor Age, *Phantoms and Faeries from Norwegian Folklore*, tr. Pat Shaw Iversen (Oslo: Johan Grundt Tanum Forlag, n.d.).
A good general survey of monster lore from Norway, illustrated with unnerving woodcuts.

Buss, Reinhard J., *The Klabautermann of the Northern Seas* (Berkeley: Univ. of California Press, 1973).
Buss' book is the one good work in English on this particular denizen of the faery realm.

Carrington, Richard, *Mermaids and Mastodons: A Book of Natural and Unnatural History* (New York: Rinehart, 1957).
A shallow survey of the interface between monster lore and zoology, written from a stance of solid (and too often unthinking) scientific orthodoxy.

Clark, Jerome, *Encyclopedia of Strange and Unexplained Physical Phenomena* (Detroit: Gale, 1993).
———, *Unexplained!* (Farmington Hills, Mich.: Gale, 1999).
These are earlier and later editions of the same work, a good illustrated survey of the more concrete types of unexplained phenomena. Clark, a veteran UFO researcher and former editor of *Fate* magazine, tends to be dismissive of magical perspectives on the oddities he has compiled, but this book remains an extremely useful source for the monster researcher.

Clark, Jerome, and Loren Coleman, *Creatures of the Outer Edge* (New York: Warner, 1978).
A detailed catalogue of reports of paranormal creatures, this book is a useful introduction to modern monsters.

Cohen, Daniel, *A Modern Look at Monsters* (New York: Dodd, Mead & Co., 1970).

———, *Encyclopedia of Monsters* (Waltham Abbey, Essex: Fraser Stewart, 1992).

Daniel Cohen's books on monsters, many of them intended for the children's book market, have provided a first introduction to monster lore for many young readers. These two are representative.

Coleman, Loren, *Curious Encounters* (Boston: Faber & Faber, 1985).

———, *Mysterious America* (Boston: Faber & Faber, 1983).

Two good travelogues for the student of the bizarre, covering a variety of weird creatures and phenomena in North America.

Colombo, John Robert, *Mysterious Canada* (Toronto: Doubleday, 1988).

A survey of strange phenomena from Canadian sources.

Copper, Basil, *The Vampire in Legend, Fact, and Art* (London: Robert Hale, 1973).

———, *The Werewolf in Legend, Fact and Art* (New York: St. Martin's Press, 1977).

Two basic surveys of the lore concerning these monsters.

Crowley, Aleister, *Magick in Theory and Practice* (New York: Dover, 1976).

The most famous book by one of the twentieth century's most infamous mages, this work provides some details of magical lore concerning monsters.

Cryptozoological Society of London, The, *A Natural History of the Unnatural World* (New York: St. Martin's Press, 1999).

A clever work of fiction that draws heavily on actual resources, this is great entertainment but should not be treated as a reliable source!

D'Assier, Adolphe, *Posthumous Humanity: A Study of Phantoms* (San Diego: Wizards Bookshelf, 1981).

Originally published in 1887, this is a solid introduction to ghost lore based on historical examples and the author's own experiences.

Davidson, Gustav, *A Dictionary of Angels* (New York: Macmillan, 1967).

The standard reference work on this subject. A comprehensive guide to the angel lore of Judaism, Christianity, and Islam, with some information on Eastern traditions, this is the best starting point for any useful investigation of angels.

Davidson, Hilda R. Ellis, and W. M. S. Russell, eds., *The Folklore of Ghosts* (Cambridge: D. S. Brewer, 1981).

An excellent anthology with articles ranging over the entire history of ghost lore, from ancient Babylon and Egypt to the present day. Very useful to the ghost hunter.

Davis, Caroline Franks, *The Evidential Force of Religious Experience* (Oxford: Clarendon, 1989).

This book, written by a philosopher for philosophers, can be dense going for the lay reader, but it contains solid arguments for the suggestion that experiences can't reasonably be dismissed out of hand simply because they deal with nonphysical phenomena.

Davis, Jefferson, *Ghosts and Strange Critters of Washington and Oregon* (Vancouver, Wash.: Norseman Ventures, 1999).

For students of monster lore in the upper left corner of the US, this uneven but readable book on our local "strange critters" is well worth having.

Deem, James M., *How to Find a Ghost* (Boston: Houghton Mifflin, 1988).

Despite the fact that this book is written for older children (with delightful illustrations by True Kelley), it may be the best introduction to ghost hunting in English. Highly recommended.

DeLoach, Charles, *Giants: A Reference Guide from History, the Bible, and Recorded Legend* (London: Scarecrow, 1995).

An encyclopedia of giant lore that starts out by accepting the possibility that larger-than-usual humanoids once existed and goes on to collect evidence for that claim. DeLoach accepts the narratives of the Bible as accurate history, and relies on other sources that are at least open to question, but some of the more modern material he collects rests on stronger foundations.

Den Boeft, J., *Calcidius on Demons* (Leiden: Brill, 1977).

A scholarly translation of the treatise on demonology by Calcidius, an important figure in the Neoplatonic philosophical movement of Roman times. Some background in philosophy required.

Denning, Hazel M., *True Hauntings* (St. Paul: Llewellyn, 1998).

An intelligent book by a longtime ghost researcher and psychic, full of case histories of interactions with ghosts.

Dodds, E. R., *The Greeks and the Irrational* (Berkeley: UCLA Press, 1964).

A classic study of the ancient Greek attitude to gods, spirits and other supernatural powers.

Eberhart, George M., *A Geo-Bibliography of Anomalies* (Westport, Conn.: Greenwood, 1980).

————, *Monsters: A Guide to Information on Unaccounted-for Creatures, Including Bigfoot, Many Water Monsters, and Other Irregular Animals* (New York: Garland, 1983).

These are among the standard reference works for any monster hunter, with book-size bibliographies packed full of useful references. *The Geo-Bibliography* lists American and Canadian references to strange phenomena of all types by geographical area—great not only for finding out what monsters infest your hometown, but for tracing geographical and spatial trends in monsterdom. *Monsters*, organized by type, is principally of interest to the cryptozoologist but overlaps on this book's territory on a regular basis.

Evans-Wentz, W. Y., *The Fairy-Faith in Celtic Countries* (New York: University Books, 1966).

An essential book for anyone interested in the faery realm, this study (by a noted scholar who later translated the Tibetan Book of the Dead) starts with one of the best collections of Celtic faery lore in any language, and goes on to argue for the reality of faeries on the basis of solid evidence.

Fodor, Nandor, *The Haunted Mind* (New York: Helix, 1959).

A study of supernatural and preternatural phenomena by an unusually open-minded psychoanalyst.

Fortune, Dion, *Applied Magic* (Wellingborough: Aquarian, 1987).

————, *Aspects of Occultism* (Wellingborough: Aquarian, 1987).

————, *Psychic Self-Defence: A Study in Occult Pathology and Criminality* (Wellingborough: Aquarian, 1988).

————, *The Secrets of Dr. Taverner* (St. Paul: Llewellyn, 1962).

Dion Fortune was one of the major figures in the development of modern ritual magic, and her many books cover most branches of magical lore. The first two titles listed here are collections of essays, and contain several pieces dealing with elementals, spirits, and similar topics. *Psychic Self-Defence* covers monsters as well as sorcery, and provides a good deal of practical guidance; *The Secrets of Dr. Taverner*, a collection of short stories, presents many of the same concepts (and some of the same incidents) as *Psychic Self-Defence* in lightly fictionalized form.

Freed, Ruth S., and Stanley A. Freed, *Ghosts: Life and Death in North India* (New York: American Museum of Natural History, 1993).

An extraordinarily detailed account of ghost lore, customs, traditions, and magic from a culture where the presence of the wakeful dead is a matter of common knowledge and experience, this may be the most comprehensive book on ghosts ever written.

Gallup, George, Jr., with William Proctor, *Adventures in Immortality* (New York: McGraw-Hill, 1982).

The results of a Gallup poll on American attitudes toward life after death, containing some information about the frequency of near-death experiences.

Garner, Betty Sanders, *Canada's Monsters* (Hamilton, Ontario: Potlatch, 1976).

Mostly cryptozoological in focus, this book remains one of the few studies of monster lore from the second largest nation on the planet.

Goldberg, Bruce, *Protected by the Light: The Complete Book of Psychic Self-Defense* (St. Paul: Llewellyn, 1998).

Very much a mixed bag. This book contains a great deal of extremely useful and practical material on subtle-energy work and dealing with psychic and magical attacks, but it also contains a good many historical and factual inaccuracies, and its approach may not appeal much to those outside the New Age movement.

Gooch, Stan, *Creatures from Inner Space* (London: Rider, 1984).

An uneven but interesting study of various preternatural phenomena, with particular attention to incubi and succubi. Gooch suggests that the whole range of preternatural phenomena are actually produced by human psychic abilities, although his arguments for this are less than wholly convincing.

Goodman, Felicitas D., *How About Demons? Possession and Exorcism in the Modern World* (Bloomington, Ind.: Indiana University Press, 1988).

A well-researched survey of possession phenomena by a researcher famous for her work on trance states, *How About Demons?* presents a substantial amount of cross-cultural data on the experience of possession.

Gordon, David George, *Field Guide to the Sasquatch* (Seattle: Sasquatch Books, 1992).

A short but useful guide to what is known about this elusive primate.

Gould, Charles, *Mythical Monsters* (London: W. H. Allen, 1886).

A classic of dragon lore, this book argues for the existence of various dragonlike creatures in ancient times as biological realities.

Grasse, Ray, *The Waking Dream: Unlocking the Symbolic Language of our Lives* (Wheaton, Ill.: Quest, 1996).

An interesting study of meaningful coincidence and the subtle interfaces between consciousness and the world. Grasse argues forcefully that the events of ordinary life, like those of dreams, form meaningful symbolic patterns not because we put meaning into them, but because the meaning is already there in the universe we experience.

Greeley, Andrew M., *The Sociology of the Paranormal: A Reconnaissance* (Beverly Hills: Sage, 1975).

Results and interpretations of a survey of American experience of preternatural and supernatural beings, somewhat statistics-heavy.

Green, Andrew, *Ghost Hunting: A Practical Guide* (London: Garnstone, 1973).

A good practical introduction to ghost investigation, written from a British viewpoint but useable anywhere.

Greer, John Michael, *Circles of Power: Ritual Magic in the Western Tradition* (St. Paul: Llewellyn, 1997).

———, *Natural Magic* (St. Paul: Llewellyn, 2000).

———, *Paths of Wisdom: The Magical Cabala in the Western Tradition* (St. Paul: Llewellyn, 1996).

These three books form a general introduction to the modern Western magical tradition, and can serve as a resource for those interested or puzzled by the magical material in the present book.

Griffin, David Ray, *Parapsychology, Philosophy, and Spirituality: A Postmodern Exploration* (Albany: SUNY, 1997).

Griffin is one of the major modern exponents of the thoughts of Alfred North Whitehead, whose "process philosophy" avoids most of the worst drawbacks of modern scientific thought. This book applies Whiteheadian ideas to a variety of preternatural events with a great deal of subtlety and skill. Heavy going for the philosophical layperson, but worth the struggle.

Griffin, Dorsey, ed., *Silkie! Seal-folk Tales, Ballads and Songs* (Netarts, Ore.: Griffin, 1985).

A collection of traditional lore about the silkies or seal-people of Scotland and Ireland.

Guiley, Rosemary Ellen, *Atlas of the Mysterious in North America* (New York: Facts on File, 1995).

———, *The Complete Vampire Companion* (New York: Macmillan, 1994).

———, *The Encyclopedia of Ghosts and Spirits* (New York: Facts on File, 1992).

A more than competent collector of lore and a ghost and anomaly hunter in her own right, Guiley has produced several good reference books on monster-related subjects, of which these three are of special interest.

Harpur, Patrick, *Daimonic Reality: A Field Guide to the Otherworld* (New York: Viking, 1994).

This extraordinary book should be on the required reading list for any student of monstrous beings or mysterious phenomena. Starting from the torrent of unexplained events that have perplexed observers and irritated scientists in the last few decades, Harpur explores the interconnections between these seemingly disparate phenomena, shows how they undercut the currently accepted scientific models of reality, and demonstrates how older ways of understanding the world (notably the ancient philosophies underlying the magical tradition) make perfect sense of these otherwise baffling phenomena.

Hauck, Dennis William, *Haunted Places: The National Directory* (New York: Penguin, 1996).

This book belongs on the shelf next to Eberhart's *Geo-Bibliography of Anomalies* as a sourcebook for locating places associated with monstrous beings.

Heuvelmans, Bernard, *On the Track of Unknown Animals* (London: Kegan Paul, 1995).

For all practical purposes, this book created the science of crptozoology when it first appeared in 1955, and it remains the best book on the subject. Useful for those interested in the less spooky side of monster lore.

Hitching, Francis, *The Mysterious World: An Atlas of the Unexplained* (New York: Holt, Rinehart and Winston, 1978).

A general survey of mysterious phenomena, provided with plenty of maps and illustrations; a short section on dragons covers much of the legendary territory.

Holiday, F. W., *The Dragon and the Disk: An Investigation into the Totally Fantastic* (New York: Norton, 1973).

———, *Creatures from the Inner Sphere* (New York: Popular Library, 1973).

———, *The Goblin Universe* (St. Paul: Llewellyn, 1986).

Holiday's researches of the Loch Ness monster and related phenomena convinced him that "lake monsters" were actually evil supernatural beings, held in check by powers of good in the form of flying saucers. This forms the subject of *The Dragon and the Disc* (which was also published under the title *Creatures from the Inner Sphere*), while *The Goblin Universe* takes on the entire subject of anomalies, arguing that neither physical nor psychological explanations make sense of the evidence. Both books suffer in places from sloppy research and questionable logic, but present some curious data well worth taking into account.

Holtan, Neal, et al., *Final Report of the SUNDS Planning Project* (St. Paul: St. Paul–Ramsey Medical Center, 1984).

Largely technical, this report is a useful resource for those exploring the preternatural side of the SUNDS epidemic.

Holzer, Hans, *Ghosts* (New York: Black Dog & Leventhal, 1997)
Holzer has spent a lifetime researching ghosts and related topics, and has published dozens of books on the subject. This massive 758-page tome may be the single largest work on ghosts, and is probably your best source if you want to get a sense of the range and variety of ghost phenomena.

Hufford, David, "Beings Without Bodies: An Experience-centered Theory of the Belief in Spirits," in *Walker* (1995).
———, *The Terror That Comes in the Night* (Philadelphia: U. Pennsylvania P., 1982). David Hufford's "experience-centered" approach to the supernatural and preternatural realms represents one of the first major breaks in the wall of denial around these subjects, and an approach fundamental to any intelligent study of monsters. The article and book cited here provide a solid introduction to his ideas, and the book should certainly belong on the required reading list for would-be monster investigators.

Huxley, Francis, *The Dragon: Nature of Spirit, Spirit of Nature* (New York: Thames and Hudson, 1979).
A lavishly illustrated introduction to dragon lore.

Huyghe, Patrick, *The Field Guide to Extraterrestrials* (New York: Avon, 1996).
An intelligent and illustrated summary of the dizzying array of entities reported by UFO contactees, abductees, and witnesses.

Ingersoll, Ernest, *Dragons and Dragon Lore* (New York: Payson & Clarke, 1928).
An old but still worthwhile study of dragon traditions.

Irwin, H. J., *An Introduction to Parapsychology,* third ed. (Jefferson, N.C.: McFarland, 1999).
Perhaps the best general introduction to scientific parapsychology, this textbook covers the entire field in some detail, with an abundance of facts and figures.

Jamal, Michele, *Deerdancer: The Shapeshifter Archetype in Story and in Trance* (New York: Arkana, 1995).
A collection of shapeshifter legends from various cultures, woven together around a framework of Jungian theory.

Johnson, F. Roy, *SUPERnaturals Among Carolina Folk and Their Neighbors* (Murfreesboro, N.C.: Johnson Pub. Co., 1974).

A delightful collection of traditional monster lore from the Carolina backwoods, much of it gathered directly from living oral tradition, and most of it focusing on ghosts and the Devil.

Keel, John A., *The Complete Guide to Mysterious Beings* (New York: Doubleday, 1994).

————, *The Mothman Prophecies* (New York: Signet, 1976).

————, *Strange Creatures from Time and Space* (New York: Fawcett, 1970).

Longtime UFO researcher Keel was probing the paranormal and preternatural side of the phenomenon when most people in the UFO research community were still committed to the "hardware hypothesis" of extraterrestrials in nuts-and-bolts spacecraft. His books are controversial, speculative, and sometimes pretty bizarre, but well worth reading. *The Complete Guide to Mysterious Beings* is a revision and reprint of *Strange Creatures from Time and Space*; *The Mothman Prophecies* is an account of one of the weirder and more complex cases Keel has faced.

Keightley, Thomas, *The World Guide to Gnomes, Fairies, Elves, and other Little People* (New York: Avenel, 1978).

Originally published as *The Fairy Mythology* over a century ago, this wide-ranging collection centers on European lore but does its best to cover faery entities from around the world. Essential for those seeking a good overview of faery phenomena.

Kirk, Robert, *The Secret Commonwealth of Elves, Fauns and Fairies* ed. S. Sanderson (repr. Cambridge: Folklore Society, n.d.).

The author of this classic study of Scottish faery lore, originally published in 1690, was said to have been kidnapped by the fays shortly after the book's appearance. Page for page, it contains more information about Faery and its inhabitants than any other source.

Konstantinos, *Vampires: The Occult Truth* (St. Paul: Llewellyn, 1998).

A readable introductory book on vampirism written from an occult perspective, with limited value to the scholar but a good deal of useful, practical advice.

Lambert, R. S., *Exploring the Supernatural: The Weird in Canadian Folklore* (Toronto: McClelland & Stewart, 1955).

Well worth reading even for those who have no interest in Canadian monsters, this book provides a good general survey of supernatural folklore in an ethnically complex society.

Lavater, Lewes, *Of Ghostes and Spirites Walking by Nyght* (1572; repr. Oxford: University Press, 1929).

A major work of Reformation-era scholarship on ghosts, Lavater's book (reprinted here in its original Elizabethan English translation) defends the Protestant side in the great ghost debate of the sixteenth century, but also provides a great deal of information on ghost lore of the time.

Leavy, Barbara Fass, *In Search of the Swan Maiden* (New York: New York University Press, 1994).

A work of feminist literary criticism that assumes the completely imaginary character of the legends it studies, this is still the only significant work to date on animal–shapeshifter legends of the swan maiden type.

Lethbridge, T. C., *Ghost and Ghoul* (London: Routledge and Kegan Paul, 1961).

A largely anecdotal study of certain monster-related phenomena, important in the history of modern monster studies.

Lévi, Eliphas, *Transcendental Magic* (York Beach, Maine: Weiser, 1972).

A pioneering figure in modern magic, Alphonse Louis Constant (under the pen name Eliphas Lévi) wrote several works on magic that have shaped the field ever since. In this, his most important work, Lévi includes an important discussion on shapeshifting and several other passages of significance to the student of monster lore.

Lewis, C. S., *Miracles* (repr. New York: Touchstone, 1996).

Written from a Christian (but by no means fundamentalist) perspective, this work by the well-known Anglican scholar and fantasy author challenges the logical basis for scientific materialism in the course of arguing for the possibility of supernatural events.

Lysaght, Patricia, *The Banshee* (Boulder, Colo.: Roberts Rinehart, 1986).

The banshee (Gaelic *bean sidhe*, "faery woman") is a spectral messenger of death who is heard weeping or screaming before someone dies. There are Irish families with their own banshees, and other such entities that seem to work on a more free-lance basis. This excellent study draws on actual experiences of the banshee as well as folklore accounts, and should not be missed by those interested in faery traditions.

Mack, Carol, and Dinah Mack, *A Field Guide to Demons, Fairies, Fallen Angels, and Other Subversive Spirits* (New York: Arcade, 1998).

A cross-cultural collection of dangerous spirits, with methods of banishing drawn from folklore when these are known. Not really a field guide, but worth a place on a monster researcher's reading list.

Mackal, Roy P., *Searching for Hidden Animals* (Garden City, N.Y.: Doubleday, 1980).

A readable introductory work on cryptozoology, principally focusing on unknown animals left out of Heuvelmans' massive surveys.

Masters, Anthony, *The Natural History of the Vampire* (New York: Putnam, 1972).

An uneven and somewhat journalistic study of vampire legends, lore, and literature, this book quotes some otherwise hard to find source material.

Mathers, S. L. MacGregor, "The Qlippoth of the Qabalah," in R. A. Gilbert, ed., *The Sorcerer and His Apprentice* (Wellingborough: Aquarian, 1983).

Mathers, one of the founders of the Hermetic Order of the Golden Dawn—the premier English magical order at the turn of the last century, and the fount of much of today's occult revival—was a capable if eccentric scholar of the occult. This essay of his is one of the few English-language works on Cabalistic demonology.

McClenon, James, *Deviant Science: The Case of Parapsychology* (Philadelphia: U. of Pennsylvania Press, 1984).

——, *Wondrous Events: Foundations of Religious Belief* (Philadelphia: U. Pennsylvania Press, 1994).

McClenon, a sociologist, is one of the major figures currently applying David Hufford's "experience-centered" approach to supernatural events. *Deviant Science*, a sociological study of the way that parapsychology has been stigmatized by the broader scientific community, provides an uncomfortably clear look at the political processes by which the official version of reality is generated, while *Wondrous Events* explores the origins of religious belief from an experience-centered standpoint.

McCloy, James F., and Ray Miller Jr., *The Jersey Devil* (Wallingford, Pa.: Middle Atlantic, 1976).

A fine book on one of America's home-grown horrors, capably researched and illustrated with maps, photos, and old drawings.

McLean, Adam, ed., *A Treatise on Angel Magic* (Grand Rapids, Mich.: Phanes, 1990).

An anonymous seventeenth-century handbook of ritual magic, preserved in the form of a single manuscript in the British Library, and edited and annotated by a well-known Scottish alchemical researcher, this text provides a clear look at the interface between magical practice and a variety of supernatural beings in the early years of the Scientific Revolution.

Meurger, Michel, and Claude Gagnon, *Lake Monster Traditions: A Cross-Cultural Analysis* (London: Fortean Tomes, 1988).

A very mixed bag, this book combines a praiseworthy degree of thoroughness in folklore research with a rigid adherence to the cultural source hypothesis, backed up by various kinds of postmodernist smoke and mirrors.

Michael of Greece, Prince, *Living with Ghosts* (New York: W. W. Horton, 1995).

Eleven accounts of haunted castles in Europe. It's hard to get more romantic than that, and the book is well-written into the bargain. Worth reading for those of Gothic sensibilities and Old World ghost hunters generally.

Michell, John, *The Earth Spirit: Its Ways, Shrines and Mysteries* (New York: Crossroad, 1975).

———, *The New View Over Atlantis* (London: Thames & Hudson, 1983).

———, *The View Over Atlantis* (New York: Ballantine, 1969).

*The View Over Atlantis*, with its Roger Dean cover and sweeping claims, introduced an entire generation to ley lines, stone circles, and Earth mysteries; a wild, visionary work based more on poetic inspiration than on strictly factual history, it is well worth reading but should not be used as a source for historical details without confirmation elsewhere. Michell's later *The Earth Spirit* and *The New View Over Atlantis* are more careful, and should be on the reading list for any monster researcher interested in the interface between subtle Earth energies and monstrous phenomena.

Michell, John, and Robert J. M. Rickard, *Living Wonders: Mysteries and Curiosities of the Animal World* (London: Thames and Hudson, 1982).

————, *Phenomena: A Book of Wonders* (New York: Pantheon, 1977).

These two books, teaming Earth-mysteries researcher John Michell with *Fortean Times* editor Robert Rickard, provide a good general survey of the bizarre events and entities with which we share the world.

Mitchell, W. J. T., *The Last Dinosaur Book: The Life and Times of a Cultural Icon* (Chicago: U. Chicago P., 1998).

The dinosaur covers much the same cultural and psychological territory as the dragon once did, a point usefully (and skillfully) made in this study of the many roles of the dinosaur in modern American culture. Some useful discussions of dragon legendry are included as well.

Montgomery, John Warwick, ed., *Demon Possession: A Medical, Historical, Anthropological, and Theological Symposium* (Minneapolis: Bethany Fellowship, 1976).

The essays in this book are written from the standpoint of conservative Protestant Christianity, but contain some useful information on the possession phenomenon.

Murray, Earl, *Ghosts of the Old West* (Chicago: Contemporary, 1988).

The American West had more than its share of tragedies during the frontier era, and tragic events are a classic source of ghosts. This collection provides a good overview, although it lacks a bibliography or any other way of tracing sources.

Newman, Paul, *The Hill of the Dragon: An Enquiry into the Nature of Dragon Legends* (Totowa, N.J.: Rowman and Littlefield, 1979).

Far and away the best book to date on dragon lore, this considers the whole range of dragon phenomena from a refreshingly open-minded perspective.

Nigg, Joseph, ed., *The Book of Fabulous Beasts* (New York: Oxford University Press, 1999).

An anthology of writings about monsters from ancient, medieval, Renaissance, and modern sources, focused mostly (as the title suggests) on monstrous animals.

Nutini, Hugo G., and John M. Roberts, *Bloodsucking Witchcraft: An Epistemological Study of Anthropomorphic Supernaturalism in Rural Tlaxcala* (Tucson: University of Arizona Press, 1993).

A detailed anthropological study of one Mexican region's traditions of magic, sorcery, and shapeshifting, focusing on the *tlahuelpuchi* or bloodsucking sorcerer of the Nahuatl people. An excellent resource, especially for those with no experience of the complexity of Native American lore.

O' Donnell, Elliott, *Elliott O' Donnell's Casebook of Ghosts* (New York: Taplinger, 1969).

O' Donnell was one of the great ghost hunters of the first half of the twentieth century, and for many years wrote a syndicated newspaper column on his adventures in the spectral realm. This volume is a collection of some sixty years of ghostly experiences and should not be missed. No bibliography, unfortunately.

Otten, Charlotte F., ed., *A Lycanthropy Reader: Werewolves in Western Culture* (Syracuse: Syracuse University Press, 1986).

A very mixed bag, this anthology contains articles from a range of perspectives—all of them well within scientific orthodoxy. Some useful material is included, however.

Omand, Donald, *Experiences of a Present Day Exorcist* (London: William Kimber, 1970).

A remarkable book by a remarkable figure, this book is one of the better discussions of demonic obsession, possession, and exorcism in print, by an Anglican priest with decades of experience as an exorcist.

Perkowski, Jan L., *The Darkling: A Treatise on Slavic Vampirism* (Columbus, Ohio: Slavica, 1989).

———, ed., *Vampires of the Slavs* (Cambridge, Mass.: Slavica, 1976).

Both these highly intelligent and well-documented books are crucial sources for the student of authentic vampire lore, providing a glimpse at the realities behind the current flood of media imagery.

Pyle, Robert Michael, *Where Bigfoot Walks: Crossing the Dark Divide* (New York: Houghton Mifflin, 1995).

This book by a talented nature writer provides an absorbing look at an unknown animal, the people who pursue it, the subculture that has grown up around it, and the wilderness landscape where it dwells.

Ramsland, Katherine, *Piercing the Darkness: Undercover with Vampires in America Today* (New York: HarperCollins, 1998).

Journalistic and rather breathless, this is still a good glimpse at the current vampire-wannabe subculture.

Regardie, Israel, *The Golden Dawn* (St. Paul: Llewellyn, 1971).

Regardie's classic collection of the rituals and instructional papers of the Hermetic Order of the Golden Dawn, the most important of the magical orders in the occult revival of the late nineteenth century, has had a powerful influence on magical thought and practice since its original publication in four volumes in 1937–1940. Golden Dawn instructional papers quoted in this book may be found in this collection.

Rieti, Barbara, *Strange Terrain: The Fairy World in Newfoundland* (St. John's: ISER, 1991).

One of the few really solid studies of faery lore from any New World region, this book is somewhat hindered by a topheavy apparatus of theory but contains much useful information.

Rogo, D. Scott, *An Experience of Phantoms* (New York: Taplinger, 1974).

———, *The Haunted Universe* (New York: Signet, 1977).

Scott Rogo, up to the time of his still-unsolved murder, was one of the more innovative researchers into the realms where parapsychology and monster studies intersect, and these two books offer a good introduction to his approach. *An Experience of Phantoms* is a popular introduction to ghosts and ghost lore from a parapsychological standpoint; *The Haunted Universe* uses a similar standpoint as a basis for approaching the whole range of unexplained phenomena.

Rogo, D. Scott, and Jerome Clark, *Earth's Secret Inhabitants* (New York: Grossett and Dunlap, 1979).

A survey of modern monsters by two veteran researchers, focusing on the weirder forms of recent monster activity.

Roper Organization, *Unusual Personal Experiences: an analysis of the data from three national surveys conducted by the Roper Organization* (Las Vegas: Bigelow, 1992).

The results of a 1991 poll of preternatural experience among Americans, largely focusing on the "UFO abduction" phenomenon.

Rose, Carol, *Spirits, Fairies, Goblins and Gnomes: An Encyclopedia of the Little People* (Santa Barbara: ABC–CLIO, 1996).

An uneven but sometimes useful encyclopedic guide to faery lore.

Sanderson, Ivan T., *Investigating the Unexplained* (Englewood Cliffs, N.J.: Prentice-Hall, 1972).

A wide-ranging collection of mysteries, including chapters on the Loch Ness monster and an Alaskan sea serpent.

Sedgwick, Paulita, *Mythological Creatures: A Pictorial Dictionary* (New York: Holt, Rinehart and Winston, 1974).

A lightweight but engaging survey of monstrous beings, enlivened by charming illustrations.

Senn, Harry A., *Were-Wolf and Vampire in Romania* (New York: Columbia University Press, 1982).

If you want to know about Transylvanian vampires, why not go ask the people who live in Transylvania? This was Senn's approach, and the result is this valuable collection of authentic vampire and werewolf folklore, required reading for anyone interested in these monster traditions.

Settanni, Harry, *The Philosophical Foundations of Paranormal Phenomena* (Lanham, Md.: University Press, 1992).

A slim but interesting study of the philosophical implications of psychic phenomena.

Shuker, Dr. Karl P. N., *From Flying Toads to Snakes with Wings* (St. Paul: Llewellyn, 1997).

An engaging miscellany of cryptozoological lore, mostly concentrating on the less-publicized, unknown animals and including some creatures that are probably not biological in nature.

Smith, G. Elliot, *The Evolution of the Dragon* (Manchester: Longmans, Green, 1919).

A classic study of dragon lore, largely based on old (and now discarded) notions about mythology.

South, Malcolm, ed., *Mythical and Fabulous Creatures: A Source Book and Research Guide* (New York: Greenwood, 1987).

A collection of essays with substantial bibliographies, somewhat overweighted toward the creatures of Greek and Roman myth.

Spalding, Thomas Alfred, *Elizabethan Demonology* (London: Chatto and Windus, 1880).

This survey of demon lore from the period of English history right before the Scientific Revolution was written for the benefit of literary historians and Shakespeare fans, but contains material on demons that is hard to find elsewhere.

Spence, Lewis, *The Fairy Tradition in Britain* (repr. Kila, Mont.: Kessinger, n.d.).

Another classic work of faery lore, full of detailed information on faery legends from all parts of Britain. Spence's discussions of faery society and culture are particularly useful.

Stewart, R. J., *Robert Kirk: Walker Between Worlds* (Longmead, Dorset: Element, 1990).

———, "The Tomb of a King," pp. 261–266, in *The UnderWorld Initiation* (Wellingborough: Aquarian, 1985).

One of the significant figures in the development of modern magical theory, R. J. Stewart has written several books on the interface between magic and the monstrous and magical entities of Celtic tradition. *Robert Kirk* is a study of Kirk's *The Secret Commonwealth* with extensive commentary; "The Tomb of a King" discusses traditions of mound burial from the point of view of modern magical practice.

Summers, Montague, *The Vampire In Europe* (New Hyde Park, N.Y.: University Books, 1966).

———, *The Werewolf* (New Hyde Park, N.Y.: University Books, 1966).

Montague Summers, an eccentric of the classic English type who used to parade about Depression-era London dressed in sixteenth-century clerical garb, was perhaps the last person in the Western world to believe devoutly and completely in medieval Catholic doctrines concerning witches, werewolves, ghosts, and vampires. His works are short on critical thought but very long on carefully researched and well-documented information from the Middle Ages, Renaissance, and early-modern periods.

Sweeney, James B., *A Pictorial History of Sea Monsters* (New York: Crown, 1972).

Shallow and spectacularly inaccurate, this book can be found in far too many libraries and should be avoided as a source.

Taillepied, Noel, *A Treatise of Ghosts*, tr. Montague Summers (London: Fortune Press, n.d.).

Taillepied, a French Franciscan friar of the seventeenth century, produced this detailed study of the ghost lore of his time as part of his counterattack against Protestantism and atheism, arguing that the existence of ghosts proved the survival of the soul after death. Despite some lengthy doctrinal discussions, it's well worth reading as a source for ghost lore.

Thompson, David, *The People of the Sea: A Journey in Search of the Seal Legend* (London: Barrie and Rockliff, 1965).

An extraordinary and beautiful book, *The People of the Sea* is an account of the folklore of the selkie, the shapeshifting seal folk of the Scottish isles, worked into a narrative by the author. Well worth reading.

Thompson, Keith, *Angels and Aliens: UFOs and the Mythic Imagination* (Reading, Mass.: Addison-Wesley, 1991).

One of the best studies of the deeper aspects of the UFO phenomenon, this book breaks entirely with the "hardware hypothesis" to look at UFOs both as a truly unexplained phenomenon and as the focus for a dizzying array of evolving mythologies. Well worth careful study.

Tyrrell, G. N. M., *Apparitions* (London: Duckworth, 1953).

The standard work on the subject, this book sums up decades of work under the auspices of the Society for Psychical Research.

Underwood, Peter, *Peter Underwood's Guide to Ghosts and Haunted Places* (London: Piatkus, 1996).

Underwood is one of Britain's most prominent ghost hunters and the author of dozens of good books on the subject. This volume is a good starting place for any excursion into ghost lore.

Walker, Barbara, ed., *Out of the Ordinary: Folklore and the Supernatural* (Logan, Utah: Utah State University Press, 1995).

A very useful anthology, with several articles based on an experience-centered approach—that is, one in which the reality of preternatural experience is accepted.

Walker, D. P., *Unclean Spirits: Possession and exorcism in France and England in the late sixteenth and early seventeenth centuries* (London: Scolar, 1981).

A historical study of possession cases in early modern Europe, valuable as a look at traditions on the eve of the Scientific Revolution.

Whitlock, Ralph, *Here Be Dragons* (London: Allen & Unwin, 1983).

A detailed geographical study of British dragon legends and traditional lore, essential reading for anyone who hopes to track dragons on their home turf.

Wilson, Colin, and Damon Wilson, *The Mammoth Encyclopedia of the Unexplained* (New York: Carroll and Graf, 2000).

This 662-page paperback lives up to its title (although it contains nothing about mammoths—you'll have to read Heuvelmans for that). Covering just about everything unexplained from Atlantis and the Comte de St. Germain to UFOs and the death of Glenn Miller, it deals with a range of monsters.

Wyman, Walker, *Mythical Creatures of the United States and Canada* (River Falls, Wis.: U. Wisconsin–River Falls Press, 1978).

A survey of the creatures from North American tall tales and liars' contests (the hairy-legged Stuka parrot, which divebombs passersby with its eggs, being only one of the more memorable); very little of serious interest, but a lot of fun to read.

Zhao, Qiguang, *A Study of Dragonology, East and West* (Ph.D. diss., University of Massachusetts, 1988).

A good cross-cultural study of dragon lore from East Asian and European cultures.

# INDEX

# REACH FOR THE MOON

*Llewellyn publishes hundreds of books on your favorite subjects!*
*To get these exciting books, including the ones on the following pages,*
*check your local bookstore or order them directly from Llewellyn.*

## Order by Phone

- Call toll-free within the U.S. and Canada, 1-877-NEW WRLD
- In Minnesota, call (651) 291-1970
- We accept VISA, MasterCard, and American Express

## Order by Mail

- Send the full price of your order (MN residents add 7% sales tax) in U.S. funds, plus postage & handling to:

  **Llewellyn Worldwide**
  **P.O. Box 64383, Dept. 0-7387-0050-9**
  **St. Paul, MN 55164–0383, U.S.A.**

## Postage & Handling

- Standard (U.S., Mexico, & Canada)

  If your order is:
  $20.00 or under, add $5.00
  $20.01–$100.00, add $6.00
  Over $100, shipping is free

(Continental U.S. orders ship UPS. AK, HI, PR, & P.O. Boxes ship USPS 1st class. Mex. & Can. ship PMB.)

- Second Day Air (Continental U.S. only): $10.00 for one book + $1.00 per each additional book
- Express (AK, HI, & PR only) [Not available for P.O. Box delivery. For street address delivery only.]: $15.00 for one book + $1.00 per each additional book
- International Surface Mail: Add $1.00 per item
- International Airmail: Books—Add the retail price of each item; Non-book items—Add $5.00 per item

*Please allow 4–6 weeks for delivery on all orders.*
*Postage and handling rates subject to change.*

## Discounts

We offer a 20% discount to group leaders or agents. You must order a minimum of 5 copies of the same book to get our special quantity price.

## Free Catalog

Get a free copy of our color catalog, *New Worlds of Mind and Spirit*. Subscribe for just $10.00 in the United States and Canada ($30.00 overseas, airmail). Call 1-877-NEW WRLD today!

**Visit our website at www.llewellyn.com for more information.**

## Magickal Mystical Creatures
### *Invite Their Powers in to Your Life*

### D.J. CONWAY

Unicorns . . . centaurs . . . bogies and brownies. Here is a "Who's Who" of mystical creatures, an introduction to them, their history, and how they can be co-magicians in magickal workings. Ride Pegasus on a soul journey to the Moon. Call upon the Phoenix for strength and renewing energy when facing trials in life. In ancient times, magicians knew the esoteric meanings of these beings and called upon them for aid. This ability remains within us today, latent in our superconscious minds, waiting for us to reestablish communication with our astral helpers. Short chapters on candle burning, ritual, and amulets and talismans help you more easily and safely work with these creatures.

1-56718-149-x
272 pp., 6 x 9, 80 illus. $14.95

# Grave's End
## *A True Ghost Story*

### Elaine Mercado

Foreword by Hans Holzer

A first-person account of a haunted house in Brooklyn and the family that lived there . . . When Elaine Mercado and her first husband bought their home in Brooklyn, N.Y., in 1982, they had no idea that they and their two young daughters were embarking on a 13-year nightmare.

Within a few days of moving in, Elaine began to have the sensation of being watched. Soon her oldest daughter Karin felt it too, and they began hearing scratching noises and noticing weird smells. After they remodeled the basement into Karin's bedroom, the strange happenings increased, especially after Karin and her friends explored the crawl space under the house. Before long, they were seeing shadowy figures scurry along the baseboards and small balls of light bounce along the ceilings. In the attic they sometimes saw a very small woman dressed as a bride, and on the stairs they would see a young man. Then the "suffocating dreams" started. Yet her husband refused to sell the house.

This book is the true story of how one family tried to adjust to living in a haunted house. It also tells how, with the help of parapsychologist Dr. Hans Holzer and medium Marisa Anderson, they discovered the identity of the ghosts and were able to assist them to the "light."

0-7387-0003-7

6 x 9, 192 pp.                                                                                                $12.95

## Paths of Wisdom
### *Principles and Practice of the Magical Cabala in the Western Tradition*

### John Michael Greer

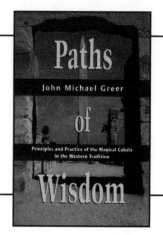

Unlock the hidden potentials of your self and the universe—of macrocosm and microcosm—with the key of the Cabala. *Paths of Wisdom* gives you complete instruction to perform Cabalistic magic. This general introduction to the magical Cabala in the Golden Dawn tradition will be used by the complete beginner, as well as by the more experienced magician or Cabalist. But *Paths of Wisdom* also contains practical material on the advanced levels of Cabalistic work, based on a perspective inherent in most of the Golden Dawn–derived approaches to magic. Originating as a secret mystical school within Judaism, Cabala was transmitted to the great magicians of the Renaissance and became the engine behind the body of Western magical methods. From Cornelius Agrippa to the adepts of the Golden Dawn, the magicians of the West have used the Cabala as the foundation of their work. Central to this tradition is an understanding of magic that sees esoteric practice as a spiritual Path, and an approach to practical work stressing visualization and the use of symbolic correspondences. Through meditation, Pathworking, magical rituals, and mystical contemplation you'll incorporate the insight of the Cabala into your daily life.

1-56718-315-8
416 pp., 6 x 9, illus.

$20.00

### To order, call 1-800-THE MOON
**Prices subject to change without notice**

# Natural Magic
## *Potions & Powers from the Magical Garden*

### John Michael Greer

Natural magic is the ancient and powerful art of using material substances—herbs, stones, incenses, oils, and much more—to tap into the hidden magical powers of nature, transforming your surroundings and yourself.

Not just a cookbook of spells, *Natural Magic* provides an introduction to the philosophy and ways of thought underlying the system, gives detailed information on 176 different herbs, trees, stones, metals, oils, incenses, and other magical substances, and provides dozens of different ways to put them to use in magical workings. With this book and a visit to your local herb store, rock shop, or even your backyard garden, you're ready to enter the world of natural magic!

1-56718-295-X
312 pp., 7½ x 9⅛, illus.                                  $16.95

## Inside a Magical Lodge
### *Group Ritual in the Western Tradition*

### John Michael Greer

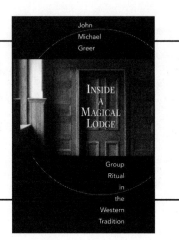

For centuries, magical lodges have been one of the most important and least understood parts of the Western esoteric traditions. The traditional secrecy of lodge organizations has made it next to impossible for modern students of magic to learn what magical lodges do, and how their powerful and effective traditions of ritual, symbolism, and organization can be put to work.

This is the first book to reveal the foundations of lodge work on all levels—from the framework of group structure that allows lodges to efficiently handle the practical needs of a working magical group, through the subtle approaches to symbolism and ritual developed within lodge circles, to the potent magical methods that lodges use in their initiations and other ceremonial workings.

It is a must-read for members of existing lodges, for students of magical traditions such as the Golden Dawn, for practitioners of other kinds of group magical work, and for all those who have wondered about the hidden world behind lodge doors.

1-56718-314-X
360 pp., 6 x 9                                                                          $17.95

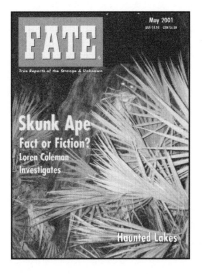

FATE **Magazine** has been bringing true reports of the Strange, the Unexplained, and the Unknown to the world for over 50 years. Mysteries and Monsters abound in each fact-packed monthly issue. Real stories from real people. Experience the Mystery. Experience FATE.

"FATE is America's leading authority at the edge. Sitting down to a copy of FATE is one of my favorite great adventures."

—Whitley Strieber

"**FATE** has become the monthly bible for those fascinated by this remarkable world of interminable possibilities that we all share, but don't always understand."

—Brad Steiger, author of *Shadow World*